Praise for Mike Miller and *A Community Organizer's Tale*

What representatives of America's major organizing networks say:

"Mike Miller has captured the wisdom and experience of people who built a powerful organization that improved the quality of life for their families. He reminds us how organizing makes democracy work."

—John Baumann, S.J., Executive Director, PICO National Network

"Anyone interested in knowing what community organizing is would do well to read this book. Mike Miller is a well-known and respected organizer. He spans the experience from the civil rights movement to today. With today's interest in and focus on community organizing, *A Community Organizer's Tale* is timely and important."

—Arnie Graf, National Executive Team Member, Industrial Areas Foundation (IAF)

"Community organizing played a major role in the political formation of President Barack Obama. He was trained in the Saul Alinsky model of community organizing. Very few people understand what it is. Mike Miller is both a practitioner and a theoretician of the art and science of community organizing. He became one of the foremost experts in the Saul Alinsky model. For anyone concerned about democracy in America and wanting a clear, accurate, and eminently readable description of community organizing, this book would be ideal."

—Gregory Galluzzo, Executive Director, Gamaliel Foundation

"This last election showed the country what a community organizer can do. For those who want to understand what it is really like, how to do it, and learn from a master, read this book. It is the real thing. Miller brings clarity, insight, and large lessons from the specifics of his experience organizing in the Mission District in San Francisco. This is a classic case study with relevance to the battles we still face today."

—Heather Booth, President, the Midwest Academy

"*A Community Organizer's Tale* is an excellent 'insider's' history of an important transition organization by a skilled and seasoned veteran. Mike Miller and MCO were at the cross-roads of civil rights, the war on poverty, and the emerging engagement with community. He loads the book full of insights into organizing and the people who make it happen, while refusing to sand down the rough spots. This is a must-read book—for organizers and anyone who wants to understand how to build community in difficult times."

—Wade Rathke, Chief Organizer, ACORN International

"*A Community Organizer's Tale* takes us on an intimate journey through the world of community organizing. Miller puts the icing on the cake with his argument against so-called 'community control,' which, he says, means 'control the community.' A community organization is meant to be in the crowd with the people shouting, 'The emperor has no clothes!'—not parading down the street, playing the role of emperor."

—Shel Trapp, former coordinator for the National Training and Information Center, and author of *Dynamics of Organizing: Building Power by Developing the Human Spirit*

The names of organizations and job titles on these pages are meant to help identify the people who have commented on *A Community Organizer's Tale*, and not to imply that those organizations have endorsed the book.

"*A Community Organizer's Tale* is a great story, offering important lessons for all of us who want a more just society. The book describes what to do and what not to do to create collective power. It also illustrates problems, such as 'macho male' organizing culture, that feminism highlighted with its emphasis on organizational dynamics, cooperative leadership models, and the importance of including women at all levels of decision-making."

—Jo Freeman, author of *At Berkeley in the Sixties: The Education of an Activist* and *The Politics of Women's Liberation*

"*A Community Organizer's Tale* is a great case study for a workshop or course on community organizing, and should be of interest to anyone who cares about social and economic justice in our nation's cities. It combines rich historical description with insightful organizer's analysis of the dynamics of movement building."

—Michael Eisenscher, National Coordinator, US Labor Against the War

"As the executive director of an association of over 250 foundations and philanthropies from all across the United States, I know how valuable this book will be. Many of our members provide grants to community organizing and I know many of them would find the book both interesting and educational. No other book on community organizing effectively tells the exciting story of a community organizing process and also explains the political forces at play both in and on the community organization."

—Spence Limbocker, former Executive Director of the Neighborhood Funders Group and former Associate Director of the Catholic Campaign for Human Development

"A compelling narrative that is a sympathetic, but tough-minded, analytical assessment based on deep experience with community organizing."

—Joe Sneed, Professor Emeritus, Liberal Arts and International Studies, Colorado School of Mines

"As Mike Miller correctly reports, foundations are now accountable to no one. *A Community Organizer's Tale* suggests ways to change that."

—Bill Somerville, President and Founder, Philanthropic Ventures Foundation

"This book will have strong appeal for a broad range of people in both academia and community practice. It will make an excellent second text for both undergraduate and graduate courses in fields such as social work, sociology, urban studies, and political science."

—Lee H. Staples, M.S.W., Ph.D., Clinical Professor, Boston University School of Social Work, and author of *Roots to Power: A Manual for Grassroots Organizing*

"Mike Miller's tale conveys the daily hard work, personal stories, and organizational tensions that mobilized and united voices in neighborhoods and communities in the 1960s and 1970s. Students of American social history need to learn the wide range of community organizing endeavors during this dynamic period of social expression and change—a perspective that is important in today's climate where the historic values of community organizing are breathing new air and being refreshed."

—Janet E. Furness, Associate Professor of Social Work, Union University

"The Mission Coalition Organization was important during its heyday of thirty-five to forty years ago. Many [San Francisco] Archdiocese-related organizations were members....As a newly ordained priest, I remember the excitement and sense of hope that the coalition engendered in the community. That hope empowered many of us to continue to struggle for affordable housing and quality of life issues."

> —Most Reverend William J. Justice, Auxiliary Bishop of San Francisco, the Archdiocese of San Francisco, from his greetings to the 40th anniversary celebration of MCO

"Full of anecdotes and lore about organizing, Miller is one of the key theorists of the community organizing movement....His writings in the early 1970s were widely reproduced and read by a new generation of young organizers who came from Sixties protest efforts."

> —from *Community Is Possible: Repairing America's Roots*, by Harry Boyte

"The largest urban popular mobilization in San Francisco's recent history...the MCO probably involved up to 12,000 people...showing a remarkable capacity to combine grassroots organization with institutional social reform....[Mike Miller was] an experienced community organizer, trained by Saul Alinsky himself."

> —from *The City and the Grassroots: A Cross-Cultural Theory of Urban Social Movements*, by Manuel Castells

"Although the [San Francisco] Redevelopment Agency was able to buy up and knock down many blocks of the Western Addition, it was not able to do so in 1968 in...the Mission District, long the home to the new immigrants who do the janitorial and other service work for those in the central business district. Instead, the Redevelopment Agency drew back in the face of organized opposition from the Mission Coalition Organization."

> —from "Why San Francisco Is Different: Progressive Activists and Neighborhoods Have Had a Big Impact," by G. William Domhoff

"MCO came to encompass more than one hundred churches and block clubs and homeowner, tenant, senior citizen, youth, community social agency, small merchant, and other groups. Their tactics embraced militant marches and demonstrations—rent strikes, sit-ins, and other disruptive actions—mixed with lobbying based on careful research."

> —from *City for Sale: The Transformation of San Francisco*, by Chester Hartman

■ Three Republicans and the president: what politicians think about community organizing

"[Barack Obama] was a community organizer. What in God's name is a community organizer? I don't even know if that's a job."
— former New York Governor George Pataki at the 2008 Republican Party Convention

"He worked as a community organizer. What? Maybe this is the first problem on the resumé." — former New York Mayor Rudy Giuliani at the 2008 Republican Party Convention

"I guess a small-town mayor is sort of like a community organizer, except that you have actual responsibilities."
— Vice-presidential Nominee Sarah Palin at the 2008 Republican Party Convention

"In theory, community organizing provides a way to merge various strategies for neighborhood empowerment. Organizing begins with the premise that (1) the problems facing inner-city communities do not result from a lack of effective solutions, but from a lack of power to implement these solutions; (2) that the only way for communities to build long-term power is by organizing people and money around a common vision; and (3) that a viable organization can only be achieved if a broadly based indigenous leadership—and not one or two charismatic leaders—can knit together the diverse interests of their local institutions."
— former community organizer Barack Obama in "Why Organize? Problems and Promise in the Inner City," *Illinois Issues*, August/September 1988

A COMMUNITY

ORGANIZER'S TALE

A COMMUNITY

ORGANIZER'S TALE

People and Power in San Francisco

Mike Miller

Heyday Books, Berkeley, California

Library of Congress Cataloging-in-Publication Data

Miller, Mike, 1937-
    A community organizer's tale : people and power in San Francisco / Mike Miller.
        p. cm.
    Includes index.
    ISBN 978-1-59714-118-5 (pbk. : alk. paper)
    1. Community organization--California--San Francisco. 2. Political participation--California--San Francisco. 3. Mission Coalition Organization (San Francisco, Calif.) I. Title.
    HN80.S4M55 2009
    307.3'4160979461—dc22   2009018105

Cover Art: MCO pickets Crown Theater,
    photo by Spence Limbocker
Cover Design: Lorraine Rath
Interior Design and Typesetting:
    Leigh McLellan Design
Printed by Thomson-Shore, Dexter, MI

Orders, inquiries, and correspondence should be addressed to:

Heyday Books
P. O. Box 9145, Berkeley, CA 94709
(510) 549-3564, Fax (510) 549-1889
www.heydaybooks.com

10 9 8 7 6 5 4 3 2 1

green press INITIATIVE

Heyday Books is committed to preserving ancient forests and natural resources. We elected to print this title on 30% post consumer recycled paper, processed chlorine free. As a result, for this printing, we have saved:

15 Trees (40' tall and 6-8" diameter)
5,346 Gallons of Wastewater
10 million BTU's of Total Energy
623 Pounds of Solid Waste
1,182 Pounds of Greenhouse Gases

Heyday Books made this paper choice because our printer, Thomson-Shore, Inc., is a member of Green Press Initiative, a nonprofit program dedicated to supporting authors, publishers, and suppliers in their efforts to reduce their use of fiber obtained from endangered forests.

For more information, visit www.greenpressinitiative.org

Environmental impact estimates were made using the Environmental Defense Paper Calculator. For more information visit: www.papercalculator.org

The whole history of the progress of human liberty shows that all concessions yet made to her august claims have been born of earnest struggle. The conflict has been exciting, agitating, all-absorbing, and for the time being, putting all other tumults to silence. It must do this or it does nothing. If there is no struggle there is no progress. Those who profess to favor freedom, and yet depreciate agitation, are men who want crops without plowing up the ground, they want rain without thunder and lightning. They want the ocean without the awful roar of its mighty waters.

This struggle may be a moral one, or it may be a physical one, and it may be both moral and physical, but it must be a struggle. Power concedes nothing without a demand. It never did and it never will. Find out just what any people will submit to and you have found out the exact measure of injustice and wrong which will be imposed upon them, and these will continue until they are resisted with either words or blows, or with both. The limits of tyrants are prescribed by the endurance of those whom they oppress...Men may not get all they pay for in this world; but they must certainly pay for what they get. If we ever get free from the oppressions and wrongs heaped upon us, we must pay for their removal. We must do this by labor, by suffering, by sacrifice, and, if needs be, by our lives and the lives of others.

> —*Frederick Douglass, from the 1857 pamphlet "Two Speeches, By Frederick Douglass: One on West India Emancipation... and the Other on the Dred Scott Decision"*

Contents

My Road to the

Mission District

I began my activist life in the early days of the student movement at UC Berkeley, organizing a liberal-radical slate of students to run for student government there. It was the tail end of the McCarthy era. We doubled the electorate and averaged 35 percent of the vote. That encouraged us to form a permanent organization; we called it "SLATE," but it wasn't an acronym until a few years later when university administration harassment led us, in a moment of humor, to turn "SLATE" into the "Student League Accused of Trying to Exist." I got a grad school fellowship at Columbia and at the end of my first year accidentally fell into a job organizing public housing tenants on New York's Lower East Side. It was perfect for me, so I thought. I'd grown up in a public housing project. But after six months I was fired for being too militant and called "a little Alinsky." "Who's he?" I asked. I learned that Saul Alinsky was the dean of American community organizing, had taken on the New York City social work establishment, and was anathema in that world—the world from which I was fired.

In late 1959, with the Alinsky tag attached to my name, I couldn't find similar work in New York City. So it was back to California, now to work as the statewide coordinator of a campaign against capital punishment—a job that ran out of money in six months. I was back in graduate school, and again involved in SLATE. The organization held an annual summer conference on issues. At the time, the AFL-CIO's Agricultural Workers Organizing Committee (AWOC) was trying to organize farmworkers in California. It was before Cesar Chavez put farmworkers on the map. Hank Anderson, AWOC's research director, came to the SLATE conference to talk with us about how student support could help the organizing. I noticed after lunch that he was leaving the campgrounds. "Where you going, Hank?" I asked. "To meet a guy named Saul Alinsky. He knows a lot about Mexicans and Mexican-Americans in California," he replied (as it turned out, Alinsky's knowledge of California's Mexican immigrant and Mexican-American population was mostly indirect: his on-the-scene organizer in the Southwest was Fred Ross Sr., who was the organizer of the Community Service

Organization, a major political voice for urban Mexican-Americans in California). "Mind if I tag along?" I asked. "I'd like to meet him." Hank didn't mind, so the two of us showed up at Alinsky's summer home in Carmel.

In what I later learned was a characteristically blunt manner, Alinsky immediately pointed at me and asked Hank, "What's this guy doing here?" Hank was put off-balance by the question, so I chimed in: "I was fired for being 'a little Alinsky' and wanted to meet the big one." That tickled his large ego. For the next hour he regaled us with stories of his New York City battles with Hudson Guild Settlement House and urban renewal—occasionally saying to Hank, "Don't worry; we're going to talk about the Mexicans." That's how I met the best-known community organizer in the United States.

A couple of years later, Alinsky offered me a job in Chicago, the city that had made him famous. I was by then deeply involved in the civil rights movement as a field secretary for the Student Nonviolent Coordinating Committee, but we maintained a relationship. He would fly into San Francisco on his way to Carmel, where his wife lived year-round because of her multiple sclerosis. I'd meet him at the airport, and we'd talk while he waited for his commute flight to Monterey, or I would sometimes drive him to Carmel. I had a several-year tutorial with him that took place in the San Francisco airport, my car, and his home in Carmel. Sometimes I'd be joined by Ross, who instructed me in his particular ways of thinking about organizing, which differed in nuanced but important ways from Alinsky's.

The next step in my journey was with the Deep South civil rights movement—both a 1963 stint in the Delta of Mississippi and a number of years in the San Francisco Bay Area doing fund-raising, education, and political pressure on behalf of the Student Nonviolent Coordinating Committee (SNCC), or "The Movement," as we called it in those days. SNCC's approach to social change included organizing as well, and SNCC had some talented organizers from whom I learned more. In particular, people like Bob Moses, Stokely Carmichael, and Rev. Charles Sherrod were applying organizing principles to their work with southern Black communities. I also began to read as much as I could about organizing, particularly from labor history.

During this time, I learned about urban renewal—called then "Negro removal" because of its devastating impact across the country on low-income Black neighborhoods; Puerto Rican, Mexican-American, Anglo, and other working-class and poor urban neighborhoods were also targeted for bulldozers that tore down affordable housing and destroyed small stores, familiar institutions, restaurants and bars, and other sites of local social capital, and replaced them with convention centers, sports arenas, shopping centers or malls, and high-cost apartment buildings and townhouses. In conversations with both Alinsky and Ross, I heard about urban renewal battles in cities across the country.

I got involved in fighting urban renewal in San Francisco. SNCC support work went well in the Bay Area, so national headquarters waived the usual rule that "field secretaries" in the north were only to work on southern support. I was able to divide my time between support work for the South and participation in several losing San Francisco battles against urban renewal. I also became codirector of the first national farmworker boycott.

In late 1966 I got my big break in the world of community organizing. Alinsky asked me to direct his failing project in Kansas City. With little hesitation, I was ready to go. For several reasons, the work in Kansas City was going badly. First off, the initial momentum for the project had been interrupted by the sudden withdrawal of one of the funders. Also, at a time when "Black Power" was an increasingly influential slogan, the boundary area within which the organizing was to take place excluded the more working- and middle-class sections of the Black community while including low-income white and Latino areas. The organizer who was finally dispatched by Alinsky to Kansas City when the funding was assured decided to leave the project after a year—he was black and I was white. Alinsky told me before I left, "Kansas City is going to be your school." Perhaps a graduate student could have saved the Council for United Action (CUA). I couldn't. While we accomplished some good things, I knew that a permanent, powerful organization would not be left behind—and that was the acid test to define success.

Before my departure to Kansas City I got involved in San Francisco's Mission District, a polyglot, primarily Latino neighborhood in the heart of the city that was slated by the city's Redevelopment Agency for urban renewal.

▓ The Offer to Work in the Mission

It was late spring, 1968. I was in my office in Kansas City, Missouri, when a call came from my hometown, San Francisco. Any call from San Francisco was guaranteed to lift my spirits. My life in Kansas City was, to say the least, not going well. My marriage was on the rocks; I had few friends there; and as depressing as the personal side, my work was not going well. Little did I know what I was about to be asked.

"Mike," the low-key voice of Ben Martinez said, "we'd like you to be the lead organizer for our community organization in the Mission District." He was joined on the call by Rev. Dave Knotts. I was wrong. Not all calls from San Francisco were going to lift my spirits.

By the end of my first Kansas City year, I was being greeted every morning by a pounding headache. The doctor I saw told me my job was its source. I had six months to go, and I wasn't going to quit. With assurance that I was soon leaving Kansas City, the doctor gave me Darvon—"a narcotic analgesic used to treat mild to moderate pain." I had pretty much concluded that I couldn't handle the stress of community organizing, though I had no idea in the world what I was going to do next. That was my frame of mind when Martinez's call from San Francisco came. I wasn't ready to jump from the frying pan into the fire.

"I'll be back in town in a month, Ben, let me tell you then." That wasn't good enough for him; he wanted an answer on the phone. We reached a compromise: I would work for two months helping the newly forming organization hold its founding convention. That satisfied him. The details would be worked out when I got home.

Upon my return, I insisted that there be a meeting of community leaders to hire me. And in that meeting I had one condition for my employment: the organization that would be developed would be "multi-issue" in character. That is, it would respond to whatever were the concerns of its members, not just one issue—such as the newly developing Federal Model Cities program that was targeted for the Mission District. The two months turned into almost three years. The work went well. I was the principal organizer for what became San Francisco's indisputably most powerful grassroots group. Along with me there emerged a diverse, committed, and talented core of people who put their hearts, bodies, and minds to work on building what a founding convention named the Mission Coalition Organization (MCO). This is the story of that organization's rise and fall, and the lessons to be learned from it.

▓ Writing This Book

The field notes for this text were written in 1971, when the MCO experience was sharply in my mind. They've been supplemented by the extensive files I have from 1965 to 1972. I have made use of those field notes and files and added interpretative material, recent interviews with people who were at the center of MCO at the peak of its influence and power, and a brief look at more recent developments in the Mission. I've woven analysis based on my now-forty additional years of experience into the narrative. Toward the end, I have added my thoughts on the gentrification process that is now going on in the Greater Mission—an area in which I now live and have lived most of my life.

I've used the language of the days in which this story took place. "Mass organization," for example, has disappeared for the most part from current organizer talk and been replaced by "broadly-based organization." I want to give some of the flavor of the period as well as the content.

This is a very personal history. For reasons which will become obvious as it is read, such stories are difficult to tell without violating personal and confidential relationships. In telling this story, I seek to present each of the actors in the drama in the best light. If, for example, it was my opinion in a given situation that an individual was taking a position on a question to further his own personal fortune, I have not tried to discredit the point of view by ascribing personal motivation. My own experience leads me to conclude that opportunism finds its way into all camps; it is an organizational given. In this story, I have tried to present different points of view, strategies, groups, and individuals as if they sincerely believed the positions they held.

Let me also say a word about my own bias. As a community organizer I had ideas about how the most effective organization would operate, what it would look like, what its vision, strategy, and tactics would be. Most important, I thought that such an organization should be an "adversary organization," serving as the voice of its constituency in relation to various "outside forces," primarily big business and government. My "model" was a tough, independent, democratic, mass participation organization that fights for the interests and values of the people it represents. Since the majority of the people represented by MCO were of low-to-moderate income and minority backgrounds, it was they who I thought the organization should represent. And, because of my own analysis of the War on Poverty, Model Cities, and a number of other federally funded "citizen participation" programs or "components," it was my view that the organization should remain independent of them. These government-sponsored citizen-participation efforts did not offer communities a vehicle to build power. At best, they involved people in program implementation. That could create better programs, but it couldn't deal with more fundamental questions. The latter required independence of action.

It takes more than federal patronage disguised as citizen participation to deal with the problems of poverty and alienation found—more widely than ever, now—in the ghettos and barrios of the nation. The vast inequalities in the distribution of wealth and power must be challenged. And, there must be a revitalization of small-d democratic institutions in all phases of our political, social, and economic life.

In 1972 I became the founding executive director of ORGANIZE! Training Center (OTC), which has been my base of operation ever since. I have forty years of organizing experience behind me, working with community, religious, and labor organizations, including almost five years on the staff of SNCC, mostly as its representative in the San Francisco Bay Area working with Friends of SNCC, and as lead organizer for Saul Alinsky's Kansas City (MO) community organizing project. MCO remains one of my organizing high points. I've consulted with and led workshops for numerous public and private sector union locals, as well as state and national groups of organized labor; for Catholic, mainline Protestant, Evangelical, and Pentecostal groups and organizations; and for women's, senior, racial and ethnic, welfare rights, and other groups. I've written and reflected on my organizing experience in a variety of publications and have taught community organizing, political science, or urban studies at UC Berkeley, Stanford, San Francisco State, Hayward State, Lone Mountain College, and Notre Dame University. From 2001 to 2004, I was editor of the thirty-year-old quarterly *Social Policy*. At age seventy-two, I thought it was time to tell one of my organizing stories in greater detail.

Acknowledgments

This book is dedicated to the leaders, members, and staff of MCO, whose tale this is; Naomi Lauter, my non–blood sister, who made much of what I've done in the world possible; and Herb Mills, my most important mentor and non–blood brother.

Many, many people deserve thanks for making this book possible. My dedication is to two of them, but I'd like to say just a bit more about each here. I met Naomi Lauter in 1962 when I was the representative of the Student Nonviolent Coordinating Committee (SNCC) in the San Francisco Bay Area. Already a highly regarded leader in liberal and Jewish community affairs in San Francisco, she became chair of the San Francisco Friends of SNCC and stayed with SNCC long after most liberals had abandoned it. When I started ORGANIZE! Training Center (OTC) in 1972, she was an incorporator and for many years she was its board chair. She opened more doors into the world of people who could financially support the work I believe in than I can count.

Herb Mills is a dear friend; his knowledge of both political theory and the practicality of politics is tremendous. When we first met, he was a graduate student and teaching assistant at Cal. He was central to making the Berkeley student movement a school for the student movement across the country. He later walked away from a promising career as a political scientist and became a Bay Area longshoreman, then a leader in the longshoremen's union. Over the years, I've learned a lot from him. I think of Naomi and Herb as my non–blood sister and brother.

I first wrote this "tale" in mid-1971, when I could see MCO's people power eroding under the impact of Model Cities money. I went back to it in an off-again, on-again fashion for almost thirty-five years and got deeply into a rewrite in 2005. Along the way, a number of people read different drafts and gave me the benefit of their comments. I'm sure I'm going to miss someone, but here are readers I'd like to thank for their questions, comments, suggestions, and encouragement: Charles Bolton, Henry di Suvero, Tom Edminster, Michael Eisenscher, Max Elbaum, Jo Freeman, Herman Gallegos, Nathan Glazer, Susan Griffin, Robert D. Haas, Chester Hartman, Adam Hochschild, Spence Limbocker, Patricia Lynden, David Mann, Elizabeth "Betita" Martinez, Michael McCone, S. M. Miller, Herb Mills, Marion Nestle,

Tom Ramsay, Al Richmond, Beth Roy, Rollie Smith, Joe Sneed, and Lee Staples. And as the standard line goes, I'm responsible for the final product.

Sharon Johnson spent a morning poring over City and County Board of Supervisors records to tie down the details of the board's votes against urban renewal in the Mission. Clerk of the Board Angela Calvillo assigned her staff member Madeline Licavoli to help and let me know that "the work you did years ago in the Mission was wonderful…"

Money for writing doesn't come easily. The OTC board of directors did not hesitate in making writing part of my executive director job description. Thanks to current Board Chair Tom Sinclair and members Ken Hecht, Clarence Johnson, and Mary Louise Lovett, and past members Alvin Baum, Maria Bernal, Joan Bordman, Warren Breed, Rev. Warner Brown, Rafael Espinosa, Victor Garlin, Jim Goodwin, Dr. Zuretti Goosby, Hon. Thelton Henderson, Angeline Johnson, Walter Johnson, Naomi Lauter, Kathy Lowe, Curtis McClain, Herb Mills, Jim Mosher, Bill Russell Shapiro, Maria Vargas, Robin Wechsler, Dr. Raymond Weisberg, and Rev. Wesley Woo for that vote of confidence. The Evelyn and Walter Haas, Jr. Fund provided a writing grant of $5,000 in the mid-1990s which gave me a needed break to get seriously into rewriting the book. There were some "angels" along the way as well who made substantial contributions to OTC's core budget, including Warren Breed, Mary Jane Brinton, Tony Fazio, Ken Hecht, Polly Howells and Eric Werthman, Bud Kaufer, Nancy Kittle, Prentice and Paul Sack, Bill Russell Shapiro, Tom Sinclair, and Frank Soracco.

With a publisher in hand, I asked some friends who I thought could stretch their wallets to give $500 and up to make the difference between the money the nonprofit publisher Heyday Books committed and what was needed to go to press. A number responded, including Michael McCone, S. M. Miller, Peter Wiley, Luisa Ezquerro, Joe Schwartz, Tom Sinclair and Kathy Fisher, Nancy McWilliams, and these members of Jim Ballard's family: Marcy Ballard, Teena Ballard Keiser and Rich Keiser, and Mark Ballard and Dora Ballard. You'll read about Jim in the book.

Others contributed as well, including The San Francisco Foundation, Ida and Dion DuBois, Tony Fazio and Marie Jobling, Dick Flacks, Ken Hecht, Thelton Henderson, Naomi Lauter, Alan Madian, David and Penny Mann, Julianne Morris and Barry Shapiro, Beth Roy, Janet Saglio and Ken Galdston, Lillian Rubin, Joe Sneed, Carolyn and Stan Wiener, and Howard Zinn. From the Evelyn and Walter Haas, Jr. Fund came another $2,000; from Community Action Fund came $2,500.

Mark di Suvero donated one of his limited edition lithographs, but I had no idea in the world how to sell it. Friend and collector Robert Lauter, the already mentioned Frank Soracco, and Nancy Escher of Escher Associates, Appraiser of Fine Art and Rare Books, are helping me sell Mark's work—no commission involved! Let me know if you're interested—it might still be available.

OTC's partner in the post-publication Education Project is Acción Latina, a Mission-based nonprofit, whose executive director is Eva Martinez. I'll join them and my publisher in the post-publication Education Project that is built around this book. Acción Latina will be archiving and documenting the history of MCO, and recording interviews with veterans of the period. The Education Project, which will include my national speaking tour, supplementary discussion guides to the book, and Acción Latina's documentation, archives, and interviewing project, already received contributions from Herman Gallegos and the Philanthropic Ventures Project. (We're still looking for funds for the Education Project—feel free to contribute!)

Heyday Books publisher Malcolm Margolin went against his better judgment to take on this project. He initially wrote his board chair, Michael McCone (both a figure in the book and a supporter of its writing and publication): "I looked over [the book] with genuine admiration…Mike Miller didn't just muddle through some events in a daze; he thought about them deeply, from a theoretical as well as practical perspective, and he presents them in a way that is thought-provoking and instructive…I've agonized as to what to do with this as a publisher…I wrestled with it, and in the end lost the match. I can't see how this is something Heyday could publish successfully…" I was already depressed by a series of rejection letters, and this one was even more depressing because here was a publisher who really liked the book but didn't think he could make it work. One, two, or three conversations took place between McCone, Herman Gallegos (an important figure in the book), and Margolin. Next thing I knew, Malcolm and I were having lunch together. He reconsidered and not only agreed to be my publisher but took on the further task of building an education project around the book's release. Thanks, Malcolm!

Peter Franck, another good friend, gave me the benefit of some pro bono legal advice that led to a contract that both publisher and author feel good about.

Heyday's editor assigned to this project is Gayle Wattawa. She's young enough to be my granddaughter! Further, her academic majors were English literature and mathematics. "God help me," I muttered to myself when we first met. She turned out to be terrific. Her ability to grasp concepts and get into the story made the two major rewrites a pleasure. Her generous and warm laugh was an uplift every time we met. Her wisdom and clarity helped immensely in making the book more readable, its case more intelligible and, I hope, persuasive. The fine-tuning was done by an equally fine editor, Jeannine Gendar, who caught dozens of little things that would have been distractions at best or muddled the story at worst, had it not been for her eagle eye. With the text finally edited, I was passed on to the production (Diane Lee), design (Lorraine Rath and Leigh McLellan), events (Lillian Fleer), publicity (Wendy Rockett), and book sales (Julian Segal) staff at Heyday Books. I am grateful for their skillful efforts and look forward to our continuing work together.

I should mention three traditions which have nourished my core values, the values that keep me going when the going gets rough and the picture of where we are as a country looks bleak. I grew up in the political left, and my parents raised me in its core values. Whatever its problems, its best people and best ideas are central to making democracy work. During the height of the McCarthy era I developed a deep appreciation for the First Amendment and civil liberties in general. I cannot imagine a good society that does not include the right to speak, assemble, organize, picket, demonstrate, and otherwise dissent. Last, I owe a great debt to the religious people with whom I spent much of my work life. While they arrived at their commitments via a different route than my own, their passion for justice and democracy is an enduring inspiration.

Finally, of course, are the leaders, members, and staff of MCO, who are the real story of this book. In the very nature of a powerful community organization, there are many leaders and activists who make the organization work. I have introduced the most important of them in the text, but to limit mention only to that central, but relatively small, group would be to ignore the fact that literally hundreds of people participated, many on a weekly or even more frequent basis, in building MCO. You will find some of them listed in the appendix.

Organizers in those days were by intent publicly invisible, so I'd like to give them special mention here: Luis Alberti, Spence Limbocker, John McReynolds, and Elba Tuttle (now Elba Montes Donnelly) were the organizing staff during my tenure as MCO's staff director/lead organizer. Charles Bolton was our researcher and dug up a lot of what became "tactical intelligence" for us. Even less visible were the support staff who made our office hum and kept my head on straight. Each of them worked solo, coordinating volunteers and cranking out the work herself. They were Dolores Abeyta, Ann Drury, Elba Navarro, and Marina Amaya.

Introduction

This is an "organizer's tale"—an analytic history based on my experience from 1968 to 1971 as "lead organizer" (called "staff director") of the San Francisco Mission Coalition Organization (MCO), and from 1964 to 1966 in work that laid the foundation for MCO. Widely recognized as San Francisco's most powerful grassroots organization, MCO was the subject of many local media accounts and sociological and political science studies.

An organizer's job is to assist people to build a powerful voice through which they can effectively speak on their deepest concerns. An executive director works for a board of directors; the board makes policy and the executive director (and a staff) implement that policy; an organizer, on the other hand, assists leaders and members of a democratic organization to make—and implement—their policy and programs. In current terms, the iron law of organizing is not to do anything for people that they can do for themselves.

MCO grew out of a successful campaign that took place from 1964 to 1967, culminating in a 6-5 San Francisco Board of Supervisors vote against the city's Redevelopment Agency proposal that federal funds be sought for urban renewal in the Mission District. Having beaten the "federal bulldozer," Mission District residents went on to dramatically slow the gentrification tendencies that were already present at that time. They accomplished this by creating a broadly based, internally democratic, multi-issue organization whose membership included, at its peak, more than one hundred civil society organizations ranging from formally structured churches and a few unions to relatively informal block clubs, tenant associations, and youth groups—some of which were organized by MCO's full-time organizers.

Community Organizing

Community organizing is a process to build people power. It is deeply rooted in democratic values and the moral, economic, and social justice teachings of the world's great religious traditions. Community organizing today is making regional, state, and national challenges to the present "power structure." While I sometimes think these challenges are too timid, this current activity is a major part of the tradition I come from.

This particular approach to people power addresses all the issues stemming from inequalities of wealth, income, and power. It solves or ameliorates specific problems for specific constituencies and tackles big issues that affect most of the American people.

Community organizing process shifts people who think of themselves as, and who in fact often are, powerless, helpless victims of unaccountable power to become active participants in civic life. It often brings together diverse groups, replacing suspicion of "The Other" with mutual respect and cooperation. This diversity can be of race, ethnicity, religious belief, age, neighborhood, income, gender, citizenship status, or any of the other sources of conflict that typically divide people.

Community organizing deepens the experience and meaning of "community"—whether inside an already existing organization, like a religious congregation or a union or among residents on a block, tenants in an apartment building, or any other group that might have some weak sense of common identity but little means to express it.

Community organizations like the MCO typically bring together low-to-middle income people so that they can negotiate with decision makers in the public, large-scale nonprofit and private sectors. When good-faith negotiations fail to take place, these organizations use the pressure of people power to compel such negotiations. That pressure can be expressed through political action (lobbying, testifying, and nonpartisan electoral work that inserts key issues into election campaigns), economic action (boycotts, strikes), social pressure that shames or embarrasses public figures before their peers, or nonviolent disruptive action that seeks to make it impossible to conduct business as usual and focuses public attention on an issue (perhaps best illustrated by the demonstrations in Birmingham, Alabama, at the height of the 1960s civil rights movement).

The vision of community organizing is grounded in the capacity of everyday people to democratically participate as co-creators of civic life, not merely as consumers who occasionally choose among competing candidates and their programs. It imagines:

> Vital neighborhoods in which people know, and watch out for, one another instead of walling themselves off either in gated communities or behind bars on their windows and doors
>
> Meaningful and well-paying work for all capable of employment

No great disparities in wealth or income

Diverse, locally owned business enterprises that make neighborhood business strips vital places to shop, hang out, and visit

A multiplicity of voluntary associational life in which people express their interests and values

Health care and other necessities of life available to all

Public services that work and treat people with respect

Quality public education that graduates all students who learn the basics and are ready to be democratic citizens.

Present concentrations of wealth and power are the major obstacle to realizing this vision. Presidents as early as Thomas Jefferson warned of this. So did Lincoln and Franklin Roosevelt. Community organizing, like a vital and democratic labor movement, offers the possibility for effectively challenging this concentration.

Everything changes. The more things change, the more they remain the same. Both propositions are true. Labor and community organizing have to change to fit a new global economy, different politics, changing demographics, and a culture that is far more quiescent than the one present at the time of this organizing story. At the same time, principles, strategies, and tactics used by MCO are applicable today if they are modified for the new context. Those who learn from mistakes made then can avoid mistakes that will otherwise be made today.

Obama Puts Community Organizing on the Map

Barack Obama put community organizing back in the national conversation about how change happens. The work he did on the South Side of Chicago is similar to what I did in the Mission. If the past is any indication at all of the future, the debates that took place in the MCO, in San Francisco's local government, and in Washington, DC, about how to solve social and economic problems hold important lessons. Failure to heed them will lead to their repetition and a new cycle of disillusionment with government, and a new withdrawal of citizens from public life.

The incubators for protest against injustice—and support for new policies to remedy it—are the various forms of civic life that are the hallmark of American democracy. MCO embodied the best of a tradition that includes the most vital elements of the labor movement, the Deep South civil rights movement, and other social movements that spring from poverty, discrimination, and alienation but are born in the hope that powerful citizen action can change things.

The Setting

The setting is the framework in which an organizer works. It defines possibilities and creates constraints. For example, in the quiet 1950s, a picket line was a far-out tactic. By the late 1960s it was ho-hum. In 1955 before the civil rights movement began to take off, snail's motion characterized progress for minorities, yet minority communities were not up in arms. By 1965 the pace of progress had radically increased but minority community aspirations for equality and justice were moving even more rapidly. When the Mission Coalition Organization was launched, the country was in turmoil—the optimistic early 1960s were being replaced by the contentious late sixties.

The Country

These important things were part of the setting for my work in the Mission District; they were the context in which it took place:

The civil rights movement in the Deep South made national and international news with its massive demonstrations and efforts by Blacks to break legal barriers against their right to register and vote. In 1964 the Mississippi Freedom Democratic Party challenged the seating of the white racists of the "regular" Democratic Party at the national convention in Atlantic City; their challenge was denied.

The northern, mostly white student movement was escalating its protests against the war in Vietnam, and a steadily growing number of Americans opposed the war. By 1968 the country's polarization over Vietnam forced President Lyndon Johnson to withdraw from seeking his party's nomination for a second term as U.S. president. Senators Eugene McCarthy and Robert Kennedy both ran on platforms to get the country out of the war; Hubert Humphrey got the Democratic Party's nomination at a deeply divided convention in Chicago.

Ghetto and barrio communities across the north were organizing and engaging in protests against slum conditions, un- and under-employment, poor schools, bulldozer approaches to slum clearance that destroyed neighborhoods, highways that did the same, de facto housing and school segregation, and other social problems. Anger in the Black community erupted in urban riots, first in Watts, California, then in the next several years in ghettos across the U.S.

Urban community organizing, ranging from timid to militant, took place across the country. Saul Alinsky was the nation's most prominent organizer. Those who took conservative approaches thought you could have change without conflict; they called what they did "consensus organizing" to distinguish it from Alinsky's tactic of "rubbing raw the wounds of resentment" in order to stir people from passivity into action. The federally funded Poverty Program claimed to support serious organizing, and in a few places it actually did. On the left end of the political spectrum, the Black Panther Party, Brown Berets, Young Patriots, and other youth-led groupings mixed direct action, social services, and issue organizing in Black, Chicano, and Puerto Rican neighborhoods.

▧ The Poverty Program

The Office of Economic Opportunity (OEO), the agency running what was generally called "the Poverty Program," was President Lyndon Johnson's pet project. Willard Wirtz, Johnson's labor secretary, called for legislation and appropriations to create full employment in the country. This, he argued, was the only real way to end poverty. Years later Black scholar William Julius Wilson echoed Wirtz's case. Johnson didn't agree; the Wirtz program was too expensive—it certainly couldn't be funded along with the war in Vietnam. OEO was doomed from the start by a Congress that wouldn't appropriate funds sufficient to create real employment opportunities for those who could not find decent jobs in the private sector.

In place of full employment, OEO offered what appeared to be a major innovation in public policy—"maximum feasible participation of the poor." Poverty program architects persuaded Congress that the residents of low-income neighborhoods across the country should be able to actively participate in programs designed for their benefit. For example, in Project Head Start, an early-childhood education program for low-income children, parents often elected a board of directors for the local Head Start center. It was a good idea, but not one that would reform education or end segregated schools. In many communities, locally elected advisory or policy boards decided what government programs to bring into a neighborhood, monitored their performance, and evaluated them for further funding. A good idea, but not one that would change private employers' discriminatory hiring practices or stop urban renewal.

In some instances, such participation was a cruel hoax. Congress mandated participation by tenants in a public housing "modernization" program but failed to appropriate funds anywhere close to what was needed. In local project participation groups, tenants would fight about whether roofs leaking water or stoves leaking gas should be fixed! As one friend of mine put it, "These forms of participation are like asking a prisoner in a concentration camp whether he wants to be murdered by gassing or rifle fire." A bit exaggerated, but the point is valid.

The Bay Area

Though San Francisco and the Bay Area were already among the most liberal cities and regions in the U.S., there were pockets of segregation in towns and neighbor-hoods, and conservative political leadership. The period of quiescence that hung over the nation's politics, inspired by the often hysterical anti-Communism of Senator Joseph McCarthy and his state and local imitators, never fully took hold in the Bay Area. The political left here had strength in the region's maritime and warehouse unions as well as among liberals, who resisted efforts to purge left-wingers from their organizations. As a result, discussion and debate, while faint, still existed.

A bitter loyalty oath fight at the University of California (UC) joined liberal faculty, graduate students, and undergraduates together in a defense of civil liberties. By the mid-fifties, students at Berkeley were beginning to break out of the Cold War atmosphere that hung over most campuses in the country. In 1957, SLATE, a new liberal-to-radical student political party took aim at elected campus government offices. I was among its founders. Influenced by the student sit-ins and freedom rides in the South, and moved to act by the massive 1963 Birmingham, Alabama, demonstrations led by Dr. Martin Luther King Jr., students at UC and San Francisco State, joined by others, engaged in massive protests, sit-ins, shop-ins, and other direct action at San Francisco's Sheraton-Palace Hotel, Auto Row, and Mel's Drive-In, and Lucky's supermarket in Berkeley.

In 1960, when the House Un-American Activities Committee came to town with its trick-bag of subpoenas and intimidation to curtail the First Amendment, it was greeted by massive student protests culminating in a sit-in at San Francisco's City Hall, with hundreds of protestors arrested. Capping all this, in 1964 the UC campus was transformed by the Free Speech Movement, during which thousands of students protested against university-imposed limitations on the students' ability to support off-campus issues, notably the civil rights movement in the South.

San Francisco

In the early 1960s, the federal War on Poverty was getting its start in San Francisco. In city after city, poverty-program confrontations took place between emerging activists in low-income, often minority communities and the older political organizations and leaders who controlled city hall and its patronage. San Francisco was no exception to these battles. The issue in San Francisco was whether there would be elections in which residents of neighborhoods targeted by the Poverty Program would select their representatives to shape or influence the program. Herman Gallegos was instrumental in citywide resistance to then-Mayor John Shelley's view that the mayor should appoint a majority of the members of the poverty program's citywide board of directors. Shelley finally agreed to a two-thirds-neighborhood, one-third-mayor appointee formula. Five "target areas" (Chinatown/North Beach, Western Addition, Bayview/Hunters Point, South of Market/Tenderloin, and the Mission) were mapped out. Each was to have its own neighborhood nonprofit corporation whose board would be elected from among the poor of the neighborhood. The neighborhood corporations, in turn, would name representatives to the citywide Economic Opportunity Council (EOC), the nonprofit corporation designated to receive and administer War on Poverty (OEO) funds. The neighborhood corporations would have a budget to hire their own organizing and social service staffs and to provide funds for projects in their neighborhoods that were approved by EOC and OEO.

The Mission

If by "community" we mean something cohesive and conscious of its identity and interests, there was no community in the Mission prior to the development of the Mission Coalition Organization (MCO). For that matter, there are very few communities in this sense anyplace in this country. Indeed, as a nation we are plagued by the lack of community and the presence of social and personal isolation.

The Greater Mission District is located in the heart of San Francisco. "The City," as its natives proudly refer to it, is a forty-nine-square-mile peninsula roughly square in its shape. If you put a bull's-eye in the middle of the square, the Mission District is a little below and to the right of it. Nature favors the neighborhood with warm, sunny skies—often in sharp contrast to the fog that enshrouds San Francisco's western half. Even before the arrival of BART—the underground mass transit system begun in 1964, with Mission stops opening in late 1973—public transportation and proximity made the area fifteen minutes from Downtown, even without a car. The neighborhood gave the main street its name, or perhaps it was the other way around. In any case, at one time Mission Street in the Mission District was the city's "miracle mile," filled with affordable department stores and specialty storefronts catering to working-class customers from all over town.

By the mid-1960s, the Inner Mission was the major place of residence for the City's Spanish-speaking/Spanish-surname population. They replaced Germans,

Russians, and Italians, but mostly the Irish, who had been there from the turn of the twentieth century until its midpoint. The neighborhood also included a number of other racial and ethnic minority groups (Samoans, Filipinos, Native Americans, Blacks, and a scattering of others).

Still in the Mission were a number of older white ethnic elderly people who hadn't left in the white exodus to the suburbs and more middle-class neighborhoods in the City. A newer, younger group of Anglos was also moving in. These were the people who would much later gentrify the Mission. ("Anglo" was the term the district's predominantly Latino population used for whites, even though many of the people referred to in this way had no English heritage. For convenience and to reflect the times accurately, this is the term I've used throughout most of this book.)

By the 1960s, the Mission was a polyglot. It had little to identify it as a neighborhood other than its geographic boundaries. The "Greater Mission" was MCO's turf. Besides the Inner Mission, this included the following neighborhoods: Potrero Hill, immediately to the east; Bernal Heights, immediately to the south; Noe Valley, immediately to the west; and part of St. Mary's Park, to the southwest of Bernal Heights. The Inner Mission itself had distinct pockets, or subneighborhoods, including East Mission and North Mission.

The Mission District's poverty program was incorporated as Mission Area Community Action Board, Inc. (MACABI)—the Mission arm of EOC. Its initial leadership included people who had a background in and were sympathetic to the kind of organizing I do.

Saul Alinsky and the

Organizing Tradition

Saul Alinsky was the late-1930s founder of a theory and practice of community organizing that borrowed from the tough approach of the industrial union movement (Congress of Industrial Organizations—CIO), grafted its strategy and tactics onto the poor, working-class communities that surrounded the great industrial stockyards of the Midwest, and found in local traditions and values the ideas that supported organizing. Alinsky's approach built community power on the strength of existing formal and informal social relationships and institutions within these communities. Without power, such communities were at the mercy of unaccountable government and profit-at-any-price businesses. With power, local people could influence and negotiate with politicians, bureaucrats, business executives, and administrators of large nonprofit organizations like hospitals and universities. A community organization in the Alinsky tradition was flexible; its democratic character meant it could address whatever were the principal concerns of the people who made it up. Churches, fraternal and sororal organizations, athletic and social clubs, retiree, small business, youth, ethnic, labor, and other voluntary associations were the building blocks he used to develop community power.

Chicago Origins and Beyond

In Chicago, in the stockyards made infamous by Upton Sinclair's muckraking book *The Jungle*, Alinsky brought the Catholic Church and the Packinghouse Workers Union, whose principal organizer there was openly a member of the Communist Party, along with a multitude of smaller associations together in a powerful grassroots organization called Back of the Yards Neighborhood Council (BYNC). The organization's major contribution was to align the community with striking packinghouse workers, tipping the balance of power in their favor so that their employers recognized and negotiated with the union. But BYNC also improved city services, and got public health care for residents, hot lunches for schoolchildren, neighborhood recreational programs, and more. Soon Alinsky was invited to other industrial cities in the Midwest to replicate what he'd done in Chicago. With support from progressive Catholic bishops and the CIO—led by United Mine Workers President John L. Lewis—Alinsky was propelled to prominence. His 1946 book, *Reveille for Radicals*, was a best seller.

The post–World War II McCarthy era placed a chill on both community and labor organizing. Alinsky managed to survive but was very low on the public radar screen. When unions purged their radicals, the labor movement's support for Alinsky disappeared. However, in its place a new approach to "mission" was growing in both Catholic and mainline Protestant churches. This approach said that justice, not simply charity, was a religious concern. Alinsky, his philosophy, and his methods became a vehicle for the expression of this understanding, which, in fact, was rooted in long-standing Christian traditions, teachings, and the Bible itself.

In the early 1960s, an Alinsky critic said that Alinsky "has the smell of the thirties," meaning he thought that Alinsky was passé. The reality is that poverty, marginalization of "The Other," exclusion from full democratic participation, and discrimination—things that also have the "smell of the thirties"—were as present in the sixties as they had been in the thirties, and they all diminish America's democratic tradition. Indeed, as we watch the disappearance of the country's middle class, the growth of poverty, and the increasing concentration of wealth in the hands of a few, we are reminded daily of the Gilded Age of the 1920s and the Great Depression that followed.

Alinsky remains a mystery to many because he didn't fit typical left-right dichotomies of thinking. Alinsky was radical: he believed that vast inequalities of wealth and income contradict democracy; that they are representative of inequalities in power and mightily contribute to that inequality. He sought to organize the powerless so they could use "people power" to counter concentrated "money power." At the same time, he was a small-d democrat, and in some ways a conservative. He believed that the strength of the people was to be found in the indigenous institutions they created or to which they gave their loyalty. He worked, as he put it, "within the experience" of people, building on their beliefs and traditions, and framing these in the American democratic tradition, to create something totally different and new. In Chicago, at the height of power of the Democratic Party Machine—an organization built on accommodation of the business sector, city jobs and contracts for loyalists, ethnic politics, and trickle-down favors to the neighborhoods—Alinsky was able to organize people power that could negotiate with the machine.

In most northern cities, such machines grew among newly arrived immigrants. New York's Tammany Hall was among the most famous. Chicago's endures today. But every major city had one of these organizations. Typically, the machine ran on favors. The politician provided services in exchange for votes. The services covered the entire range of concerns that a constituent might have: getting a job with the city, or a work permit; translating; determining eligibility for welfare; intervening for teenagers in trouble at school or with the police. Precinct captains connected the voters to the politician; they were his face in the neighborhood. Precinct workers were on the city payroll, and sometimes worked at regular jobs. But at election time, their job was to get the vote out for their patron.

Most of the machine politicians made deals with the business community. In exchange for money for his campaigns and jobs for his constituents, the politician got contracts, licenses, permits, waivers, tax breaks, relief from regulation, and favorable legislation for his business supporters. That meant that some of the urban machines were anti-union, though not all of them. While these political machines often helped immigrants and others, they were not internally democratic organizations. And their deals with business interests often placed severe restrictions on what kind of reform they would support. In fact, they were often mechanisms for trickle-down economics.

In the stockyards, Alinsky's community organizing strengthened the Packing-house Workers Union so that it could negotiate with the industry's "Big Five"—the companies whose huge meatpacking plants dominated the neighborhood. If you want to imagine conditions in these plants prior to the union, picture the TV news exposés you've seen on working conditions, pay, and benefits in Haiti, Thailand, Mexico, or China. BYNC was a democratic voice independent of the Chicago political machine, which finally made peace with it because it couldn't destroy it.

At the core of his being, Alinsky had confidence that "given the opportunity," most people would make the right decision most of the time. But his idea of democracy was far deeper and richer than voting every two years. His experience bringing racist Eastern Europeans together with Blacks and Mexican-Americans told him that no "ism" or stereotype of "The Other" couldn't be overcome. But to do so, a combination of shared values and mutual self-interest had to be articulated in a highly participatory "mass-based" organization. In such an organization, diverse people would develop face-to-face relationships, struggle together to realize common interests, and support each other on particular concerns in a "you scratch my back and I'll scratch yours" give-and-take exchange. In the course of this engagement with each other they would discover their common humanity. Priests, ministers, and secular labor leaders would articulate a framework of common values drawn from the Western small-d democratic tradition and from the moral teachings of the world's great religious traditions. This approach depended on building relationships that cut across historic lines of antagonism among people. And it depended on articulating and fighting for those small-d democratic values, but doing so in contexts where people could work together.

Alinsky was explicit in his opposition to racial discrimination and segregation. "You can't," he said, "have one group of people meet and by majority vote decide to segregate another people." That, in his judgment, would vitiate the entire democratic idea. It was unacceptable. But he was pragmatic in his efforts to fight racism. For example, to the horror of most liberals, he advocated quotas to integrate Chicago's lily-white neighborhoods and suburbs. This was tried in Oak Park, next to Chicago, and worked. Quotas were, he thought, the only way you could prevent massive white flight after the first Blacks moved in.

By the late 1950s and early 1960s, Alinsky-related community organizations had emerged in several Chicago neighborhoods and in cities elsewhere in the country. Organizers trained by him continued to work and, in turn, trained still more organizers. Amoeba-like, organizing spread across the country. It was these community organizations that identified and made a national issue of blockbusting and redlining. Blockbusting was the way unscrupulous realtors got whites to sell cheap. "Sell now," the realtors said to white homeowners, "because Blacks are moving in and your property values are going to plummet." Realtors then sold at above-market price to Blacks, who had the money to buy but were excluded from most markets. While this vicious practice made it possible for Blacks to move into better housing, it also created urban turmoil and heightened racist feelings among whites threatened by such neighborhood turnover. Banks, savings and loans, and insurers cooperated by the procedure of redlining: if you lived in a neighborhood that had a red line around it on an undisclosed map, you either couldn't get financing or insurance, or you paid dearly for them. Homeowners in a redlined neighborhood couldn't get home improvement loans. As deterioration and decline became noticeable, the blockbusters moved in. Planning, zoning, code enforcement, and urban renewal officials played their part as well by failing to enforce codes, designating neighborhoods as "deteriorating," or targeting them for urban renewal projects. This process went on all over the United States. In different neighborhoods, different interests took the first step. But the participating parties were usually the same. Each part—blockbusting, redlining, public action or inaction—reinforced the other. Though now illegal, these practices still go on.

Soon after World War II, Alinsky hired West Coaster Fred Ross to organize Mexican-Americans in California and the Southwest. Ross was already organizing in the 1930s. His postwar work for Alinsky led to creation of the Community Service Organization (CSO), in which Cesar Chavez, Dolores Huerta, Gil Padilla, and others who were later to form the United Farm Workers union first learned organizing. Like other Alinsky-related organizations, CSO was to be a voice for the concerns of its members, whatever they happened to be. Unlike other Alinsky organizations, CSO started as a statewide effort, with chapters in cities across California. Any given chapter might focus on job opportunities, education, immigration and citizenship, police practices, urban renewal, or affordable housing. All of them were "multi-issue"—open to whatever the interests of the members were. All of them were interested in having a voice in decision making.

Ed Roybal, California's first Mexican-American member of the U.S. House of Representatives, emerged from the East Los Angeles CSO chapter. CSO trained many other Mexican-American urban leaders as well, some of whom played a major role in creating the powerful grassroots organization in the Mission District that is the subject of this tale. Though CSO was never as important in the Mission District as it was in Los Angeles and other parts of California, important leaders there were trained in CSO, including Herman Gallegos, Alex Zermeno, and Adan Juarez.

▉ Alinsky and the Churches

The mainline Protestant churches of this period were going through the great internal revolution of consciousness brought about by the civil rights movement and the dramatic changes in the population of northern inner cities. Past "mission" programs were under fire for paternalism and failure to challenge racial and other injustices. Young clergy in the mainline Protestant churches were demanding new forms of participation to solve the problems of the poor and oppressed. In the debates on how this participation was to be achieved, Saul Alinsky played a major role. The Board of National Mission of the United Presbyterian Church was deeply committed to Alinsky and his approach. This meant that Presbyterian funds were available for Alinsky-directed or oriented organizing efforts across the country. Presbyterian inner-city churchmen became advocates of Alinsky's approach, and he traveled across the country leading seven-to-ten-day clergy workshops on the strategy and tactics of mass organization. Nationally, Congregationalists, Episcopalians, Disciples of Christ, Methodists, American Baptists, and different strands of Lutherans debated whether to follow the Presbyterians. Many did. In each of these traditions, the battle raged over whether or not the church should align with Alinsky's organizing efforts. In local, regional, and national decision-making bodies, clergy and laity argued over whether their denominations would sponsor and fund organizing projects of Alinsky's Industrial Areas Foundation, and whether local congregations should join these organizations once they were formed. Alinsky's approach was applied in Black, Mexican-American, Puerto Rican, and white ethnic working-class communities in the north. His major support came from churches.

Catholic churches varied from diocese to diocese, and the level of support for Alinsky largely depended on the local bishop. But even where the bishop was hostile, socially concerned priests, women religious (nuns), and laity became involved in efforts to develop "mass organizations" à la Saul Alinsky.

The fundamental issue was whether church organizations and funds would support the development of independent, militant, mass-based organizations in low-income and minority neighborhoods. The debate raged in U.S. journals of Christendom. *The Christian Century* (Protestant) vigorously opposed Alinsky; *Christianity and Crisis* (also Protestant) supported him, as did the *National Catholic Reporter*, while conservative Catholic journals of opinion called him a Communist and moderates questioned his uses of conflict. Alinsky's influence in American Christendom was ironic: he was a Jew and an agnostic!

■ Alinsky to the Bay Area?

The debate over Saul Alinsky that raged in the country was intense in the Bay Area as well, and it was of crucial importance to the development of the MCO. Rev. William R. Grace, a devoted adherent of Alinsky's, directed the Department of Urban Work of the United Presbyterian Church, Synod of the Golden Gate. Rev. David Knotts, similarly committed, was Grace's assistant. Herman Gallegos had been exposed to Alinsky's approach, though he was not an Alinsky advocate. In varying degrees, the Episcopal Diocese, the United Church of Christ, and the American Baptists were supporters of the Alinsky approach. On the other hand, the Methodists and the Methodist-related Glide Foundation, led by Rev. Lewis Durham, were anti-Alinsky and provided funds for different approaches to community action. Grace's primary agenda for the Department of Urban Work was to bring Alinsky into the San Francisco Bay Area and to have one or more of his organizing projects sponsored by the Golden Gate Synod. Grace sought support for such a project in the Oakland Black community and in the Mission District.

Both Glide and Grace were committed to community organization, civil rights, and the fight against poverty. Alinsky was the source of disagreement. His approach to organizing embraced conflict as a necessary part of the struggle of the powerless to gain recognition and a seat at decision-making tables. His use of militant tactics appalled Christians who sought consensus and who believed in "reasonable" dialogue.

Grace assigned Knotts to work as a detached minister (without a church) in the Mission District. The assignment gave Knotts carte blanche to learn the Mission, gain the trust of its people, and, as he learned how, to work as a community organizer. Such an assignment was part of the new view of what church mission should be. Detached from building a specific congregation, Knotts could view his "church" as the people of the Mission. With no obligation to build a specifically Presbyterian church, he could earn the trust of all lay and clergy, as well as those with no church affiliation at all.

In 1966, before I left for Kansas City, I was working as the Student Nonviolent Coordinating Committee's (SNCC's) representative in the Bay Area. I knew both Knotts and Grace through my organizing efforts and worked with them. Through Bay Area Friends of SNCC, I arranged a meeting in San Francisco for Alinsky. The meeting was at the home of Robert and Naomi Lauter. Robert was the chairman of the city's Human Rights Commission; Naomi was a highly respected leader in the Jewish community; both of them were close to Leo McCarthy, a member of the San Francisco Board of Supervisors and later speaker of the California State Assembly—the second most powerful position in state politics. Herman Gallegos chaired the meeting. Its purpose was to get key liberal, church, and labor leaders in town exposed to Alinsky and his approach, so that if a local organizing drive were to take place they would be among its sponsors, helping to provide funds and generate citywide support for a community organization—or if not sponsors, at least not opponents. This was part of Alinsky's standard operating procedure. For him to work in a community, two conditions had to be met. First, he wanted a widespread "invitation" from the people who would become members of the organization his organizer would build. Such an invitation was demonstrated by resolutions from churches, civic associations, and other groups in a targeted area and by petitions signed by residents of the community. Second, there had to be funding for the project safely deposited in his foundation's account prior to the initiation of the organizing work. The first of these conditions was meant to establish legitimacy for the presence of Alinsky, the "outside agitator." The second was to insure adequate financial support through the two-to-three-year development of the organization. Such financial support typically came from some combination of church funding agencies and a handful of liberal-to-radical foundations.

In the fall of 1966, the United Presbyterian Church Department of Urban Work and its Episcopal Church counterpart sponsored a separate meeting with Saul Alinsky in the Mission. They invited Mission neighborhood activists. The purpose of the meeting was to introduce neighborhood leadership to Alinsky and to lay further groundwork for an Alinsky project in the Mission. Some leaders actively opposed Alinsky at this time, including the Maoist Progressive Labor Party on the left, some church people, and some minority community leaders.

The Alinsky idea was moving on several tracks. In the largely Latino Mission District, and in the Black community of Oakland, across the bay, Alinsky was being introduced to local leaders. In the wider Bay Area, Alinsky was being introduced to religious, labor, civic, and other leaders and "influentials" who could fund organizing projects, or whose opposition would make it difficult to launch them. In regional mainline Protestant denominations and in the Catholic Diocese of Oakland, the step-by-step process of obtaining support and funds was underway. (San Francisco was considered less likely because of the conservatism of the archbishop.)

Bill Grace, David Knotts, and I each recognized that efforts to defeat urban renewal would benefit greatly from Alinsky's presence. In my conversations with Alinsky and Ross, I was learning what I could from their experience in earlier urban renewal fights across the country. Grace and Knotts were similarly learning from Presbyterian counterparts across the country about the devastation of low-income communities caused by the federal bulldozer. Together we concluded that Alinsky's presence would be a good antidote to San Francisco Redevelopment Agency Executive Director Justin Herman and his urban renewal bulldozer. Further, we agreed that Alinsky's multi-issue approach to organizing offered the possibility for a stable continuing voice in public life for otherwise marginalized people.

Grace was ultimately unable to raise the money needed to bring Alinsky to organize in the area, but with Alinsky strategy and tactics, Grace, Knotts, and I were building the relationships that could lead to a mass organization in the Mission. I had by this time learned a fair amount about organizing in general and dealing with urban renewal in particular.

Alinsky's Impact

While Alinsky was not formally working in the Bay Area, his impact was felt in the Mission, and in the Bay Area as a whole. Churchmen and women, clergy and laity, people in the pews, pastors, and major decision makers in dioceses and Protestant denominational offices did not abandon their commitment to his ideas simply because there was no formal "Alinsky project" in the Bay Area. As Alinsky continued to agitate for his vision of a small-d democratic America, his influence expanded.

By March 1970, Saul Alinsky was featured in a *Time* magazine article titled "Radical Saul Alinsky: Prophet of Power to the People." His thinking influenced most of America's Catholic and mainline Protestant churches. At the local level, these churches were core participants in community organizations. At the regional and national levels, they were funding his work and shaping implementation of their social justice teachings around his thinking. He was speaking to enthusiastic student audiences across the country. Major organizations like the Commonwealth Club of San Francisco invited him to be a featured speaker. He even discussed organizing the alienated middle class nationwide in a program he called "proxies for people." The idea was to collect individual and institutional corporate proxies and show up at annual meetings representing tens of thousands of people on corporate reform issues. Alinsky hoped that churches and unions would assign proxies for their pension funds to his new organization. Maybe they would win on a given issue that mobilized them. But if they lost, it would be because a handful of very wealthy people or financial institutions were voting against many, many people. That would provide a framework for either greater government regulation or democratizing the corporation.

Then, on June 12, 1972, before his latest project could get off the ground, he suddenly died of a heart attack. The Industrial Areas Foundation, the base of operation Alinsky developed after his initial Chicago Back of the Yards organizing work, continued under the direction of his associate director, Ed Chambers, and remains a major organizing center today.

Urban Renewal

Urban renewal plans provide a special threat and opportunity for an organizer. They can lead to dislocation and disruption of an entire neighborhood, adversely affecting local institutions, businesses, residents, and neighborhood facilities. And they can provide the necessary stimulus to action that brings the people of the neighborhood together in a people-power action organization. The job of the organizer in this situation is two-fold: on the one hand to make clear the external threat to the interests of the people and, on the other, to convince people that it is possible to do something about the threat. The very talk of urban renewal studies begins to change a neighborhood. In the absence of confidence that such plans can be controlled, people think they will have to move. They start looking for a new place to live and stop thinking about where they are now living, other than how to sell a house or get out of a lease. Landlords, other property owners, and city agencies stop providing services, or the quality and quantity of services decline. The study of a neighborhood that is labeled "deteriorating" becomes a self-fulfilling prophecy. The neighborhood starts to deteriorate because it is being studied by the urban renewal agency.

What Is Urban Renewal?

Urban renewal was a post–World War II federal program with a mixed and contradictory agenda. Slum clearance, affordable housing, the revival of decaying central cities, and the restoration of a tax base to local government were among its legislative mandates. In legislation, and in Department of Housing and Urban Development guidelines, residents of an urban renewal site were supposed to be relocated to housing that was decent, safe, sanitary, affordable, and not too distant from the home the bulldozer forced them to abandon. Parallel relocation provisions existed for businesses and local institutions.

For the most part, residential housing wasn't sufficient to restore a declining city's downtown or its tax base. Thus urban renewal also included the power of eminent domain (which allows public acquisition of private property) to assemble large parcels of land that could be used for convention centers, sports arenas and playing fields, first-class hotels and tourist facilities, and high-rise office buildings. Federal subsidies would assist in their construction.

Federally funded urban renewal projects drastically altered their sites; they also had major spillover effects on adjoining areas because land values increased as a result of new developments underwritten with federal dollars. Speculators often bought these properties and let them deteriorate, anticipating that new construction in the adjoining area would vastly increase their value. At this point, a speculator could either sell at a dramatically higher price or demolish and become the new developer himself.

In fact, relocation guidelines were often ignored. Small businesses, dependent on a geographically specific clientele with whom personal relationships had developed over the years, couldn't relocate. Nor could many churches and other local institutions. The dense, yet fragile, web of relationships that creates urban neighborhoods was the victim of planners who had little idea how real neighborhoods worked. Sociologists and social critics like Herbert Gans, Nathan Glazer, and Jane Jacobs developed a blistering critique of these destroyers of urban villages. But for the most part the destruction continued—for two reasons.

The people in neighborhoods targeted for urban renewal were relatively powerless. Typically they had low incomes and were often racial or ethnic minorities. The businesses and institutions that served them weren't the dominant players in a city's business community, social welfare establishment, or religious circles. They lacked political and economic clout. Further, when site residents and local institutions did organize, they typically limited their organizing work to the confines of the urban renewal agency's targeted area—even though people in surrounding areas would also be dramatically affected by substantial changes in the targeted area. Single-issue, anti–urban renewal organizing was itself problematic. Residents were forced to defend neighborhoods that really did require changes to make housing decent, safe, and sanitary. A broken-down home is better than none, but planners, politicians, investors, and their allies were able to paint opponents of urban renewal projects as defenders of slums who had narrow, parochial interests and didn't see "the big picture"—the supposed overall good of the city or even region.

The second reason for urban renewal's momentum was that large financial and business interests, as well as major nonprofit and public institutions like universities and hospitals, were often the major supporters of urban renewal projects. There was money to be made, often big money. Or, as in the case of public and nonprofit institutions, expansion property could be obtained or "undesirable" low-income neighbors could be eliminated. Urban universities, for example, wanted a *cordon sanitaire* to "protect" their students and staff from crime. Using the power of eminent domain, urban renewal agencies could assemble large parcels of land and force recalcitrant owners to sell whether they wanted to or not. In addition, the property could be "prepared" (leveled and new infrastructure built at public cost) and sold to a developer at below-market price, presumably because the developer was building something that was in the broader public interest. As further enticement, cities offered big developers tax breaks and other incentives if they would build on an urban renewal site.

Urban renewal agencies themselves were typically more powerful than any other city agency. In fact, they were a mix of local, state, and federal authority. While local governments had to authorize them and approve their applications to the federal government for planning money, once that money was granted the urban renewal agency had funds with which to buy allies. Few local governments were prepared to turn down the possibility of a large federal grant to rebuild a slum neighborhood and bring new tax and spending revenues, and resources, to the city.

Across the country, community organizers worked with people who were trying to stop, slow down, or alter urban renewal plans. They were woefully underfunded and typically made the mistake of defining their organizing turf on the urban renewal agency's terms, instead of drawing surrounding residents in as well. The constituency they were trying to organize was like water in the palm of your hand; it would be there one minute and gone the next. Those able to relocate on their own typically did. Those left were soon demoralized by the elaborate and lengthy (five to ten years at a minimum!) urban renewal process. Single-issue, anti–urban renewal organizing meant long periods of time with no action and hoped-for victory in the distant future.

Poverty Program lawyers helped, particularly around the failure of urban renewal agencies to implement adequate relocation plans. Courts were often outraged by the arrogance of urban renewal planners who flagrantly violated relocation guidelines. But court orders don't fix broken toilets; building owners often simply stopped making repairs in neighborhoods targeted for urban renewal. Nor do court orders move people.

A handful of "advocate-planners," usually funded by a patchwork of Poverty Program and foundation grants, made themselves available to help low-income communities in major cities develop alternative plans, rather than simply defend an existing slum. In some cases, lively partnerships developed between architects, planners, lawyers, community organizers, and local people. But these were few and far between.

Parenthetically, freeway construction had the same destructive impact on many American cities. In a few cities, major anti-freeway fights were mounted and won—but they were the exception that proved the rule. Maryland's Senator Barbara Mikulski rose to prominence in a successful anti-freeway campaign in white-ethnic Baltimore led by the Alinsky-tradition South East Community Organization.

Urban Renewal Reshaped San Francisco

San Francisco's urban renewal agency was well known across the country. Its executive director, Justin Herman, was a West Coast counterpart to New York City's infamous Robert Moses—subject of Jane Jacobs's *The Death and Life of Great American Cities* and Robert Caro's scathing indictment, *The Power Broker: Robert Moses and the Fall of New York*. The San Francisco Redevelopment Agency (SFRA) was active in this period, using its own ongoing core budget and staff as well as federal funding for specific projects. By the mid-1960s, SFRA was reshaping the very character of the city.

Just north of Market Street, along the Embarcadero, on the city's eastern edge, urban renewal bulldozers demolished what once was a longshoremen's, seamen's, marine cooks, stewards, and related waterfront workers' neighborhood, as well as the once flourishing downtown flower market. Many of the workers were single men living in affordable apartment hotels in the area. It was dotted with inexpensive restaurants, bars, and barbershops that were part of working-class life, and churches and social service agencies. These were replaced with a first-class hotel (Hyatt Regency), upscale high-rise rentals, even more expensive townhouses, and new skyscraper office buildings.

A few years later, in the South of Market area, not too far from the scene just described, SFRA would plan a new convention center, more hotels, more high-rise office space for the booming downtown financial and commercial district, and additional cultural facilities to draw tourists and conventioneers to spend more money in San Francisco.

SFRA gutted the center of the once vital Fillmore District as well. Prior to their forced relocation to concentration camps in World War II, Japanese-Americans called this home. It was also the center of the city's African-American population. Stores, churches and temples, and local institutions reflective of the makeup of the neighborhood dotted the streets of the Fillmore. When the bulldozer was done, more expensive high-rise apartment buildings, another fancy hotel, and a tourist-oriented Japanese-American center had risen in their place.

SFRA later targeted the much larger surrounding area, by then predominantly Black in its makeup and the cultural heart of the African-American community, for bulldozing as well. Also on SFRA's drawing board was Hunters Point, by then also largely Black, where temporary public housing built during World War II for workers in the adjacent shipyards had become semi-permanent, near-slum housing. The pre-dominantly Latino Mission District was soon targeted for urban renewal as well.

But by the early 1960s the city's Black community was up in arms, claiming "urban renewal is Negro removal." And in the Mission District, Latino veterans of the Community Service Organization knew urban renewal as removal as well—having seen its impact on chapters elsewhere in the state and having watched it in San Francisco.

Opposition to Urban Renewal Was Weak

Urban renewal agencies enjoyed a powerful argument in their arsenal. The neighborhoods they wanted for their projects were often blighted. They could convince the broader public that slum renewal was a good thing—even if for the people, small businesses, and local institutions that were "renewed," the opposite soon proved true.

In each of the neighborhoods demolished by the urban renewal bulldozer, opposition was organized too late. It is worth understanding how urban renewal worked, because the general principles behind its particulars are common to all big development plans. Within the urban renewal agency itself, using in-house staff architects, a preliminary "sketch plan" was produced. This plan, and the drawings associated with it, were sufficient to show to key potential allies in a targeted area and to present to city government. Public hearings would follow. If the city government approved, the urban renewal agency could apply to the U.S. Department of Housing and Urban Development for a planning grant. These grants were substantial, providing their recipients with funds sufficient to hire staff and begin serious conversations about renewal plans with both citywide and target-area leaders. The agency could also contract with noted architects to develop more elaborate plans and designs for a renewed neighborhood. Once a planning grant was awarded, the process was well underway. The city government was itself committed to urban renewal.

Learning from the lessons of other San Francisco neighborhoods, key leaders and organizers in the Mission District got active prior to the planning grant award and, as the reader will soon see, defeated the effort to obtain one. This prevented SFRA from getting the funds to make private deals with various constituent groups in the Mission, deals which would have silenced them on the larger urban renewal question or even made them public allies of SFRA.

The Mission Anti–Urban Renewal Effort: The Seed Is Planted for MCO

In the spring of 1966, so the story is reliably told, conservative populist Jack Bartalini learned that SFRA, the city's urban renewal authority, was seeking funds for a study in the Mission District, focusing on the so-called "Bay Area Rapid Transit (BART) corridor," that strip of land above the rapid transit route in the Mission District going from 16th to 24th Streets on Mission Street. The study area was to include Mission, Valencia, South Van Ness, and two smaller, in-between, parallel streets. Bartalini's first act was to call Maoist John Ross with the information.

BART was one of the country's early rapid transit systems, promising to relieve the clogged freeways of the Bay Area with quick, clean, inexpensive public transportation that would link surrounding counties to downtown San Francisco's shopping, government, and financial centers. Within the city, several additional stops made the system accessible to Mission and Outer Mission neighborhoods. Some city and regional planners imagined many middle-class people who had abandoned the city for the suburbs moving back and living close to these urban BART stations; BART would bring the middle class back to the core city. BART's routes were themselves controversial. While they brought suburbanites to the central city, they did next to nothing to take central city minorities to jobs in businesses that were fleeing to the suburbs and beyond.

Bartalini and Ross were not the only ones talking about urban renewal. Mission District Latino leaders and Alinsky-oriented churchmen were as well. They formed what became the Mission Council on Redevelopment (MCOR). Its campaign against urban renewal sowed the seeds for what later was to be the Mission Coalition Organization.

Opposition to urban renewal ranged from the far left "Maoist" Progressive Labor Party led by John Ross to the populist right and its Mission District leaders Jack Bartalini, who had been a San Francisco leader in Alabama Governor George Wallace's campaign for president, and local realtor Mary Hall. From different points of view, each opposed urban renewal in any form. In an earlier San Francisco urban renewal fight I had seen this same alliance. At a meeting to build opposition to San Francisco's Yerba Buena Center project (which ultimately built the Moscone Convention Center), a right-wing apartment building owner who could have been Jack Bartalini called urban renewal "socialism." An Italian immigrant retiree shot bolt upright and interrupted him, shouting in a heavy accent, "It is not socialism; it is fascism!"

Because of their "extremism," Bartalini and Ross were unacceptable as leaders to the majority of the Mission's leaders and activists, though they worked with them. At the same time, this majority recognized that urban renewal had to be confronted.

The earlier described pro-Alinsky forces also saw urban renewal as a perfect setting for their agenda of mass organization. Presbyterian Urban Work clergymen Dave Knotts and Bill Grace and I began to work with community leaders to put together an organization through which the issue of urban renewal could be handled, one that would have the power to deal with Mayor John Shelley, the board of supervisors (San Francisco has a combined city and county government) and the redevelopment agency. My move to Kansas City was not yet on the horizon.

The first organizing meeting took place in late spring of 1966 and included key clergy, leadership from two influential Latino community-based social service organizations—OBECA and Centro Social Obrero—and Mission Poverty Program (MACABI) representatives. Founded in May 1965, the Organization for Business, Education and Community Advancement (OBECA) offered job training and other programs in the neighborhood. (In 1967 the name changed to Arriba Juntos, Spanish for "upward together.") Key in the Mission among its founders were Leandro Soto and Herman Gallegos. Centro Social Obrero was both a Latino caucus in the Laborers' Union ("obrero" is Spanish for "worker") and a Latino community center offering various social services to its members and others. Its leader was Abel Gonzalez, himself a business agent in the Laborers' Union.

At this first meeting, Alex Zermeno, then head of the MACABI staff, agreed to allocate some of his organizing staff's time to such an organization. Zermeno had the confidence of Centro Social Obrero. Grace released Knotts to work almost full-time on the enterprise. I became involved too. Though my role was not so defined, in some ways I played the organizer in this meeting, raising questions about strategy and sharing my anti–urban renewal experiences from other neighborhoods in the city. We asked trusted lay Catholic leader, CSO veteran, and OBECA founder Herman Gallegos to become temporary chairman, and he agreed.

Zermeno's willingness to cooperate was important. The Poverty Program organizing staff had been through a training session with Fred Ross Sr., the organizer of the Community Service Organization, who had trained Cesar Chavez and was viewed with confidence by many Mexican-Americans throughout the Southwest. Chavez later referred to Ross during the farmworkers' strike as "my secret weapon."

Also at the time of this meeting, the concept of a neighborhood coalition to seek city recognition on the urban renewal issue was agreed upon. The initial organizing committee developed what was to become the guiding strategy of the fight against urban renewal in the Mission: its position was not to oppose urban renewal, but to seek veto power over its planning, development, and implementation. The veto power idea had two major strengths. First, it made it clear that the community wasn't opposed to change; however, second, it wanted to have a decisive voice in any urban renewal plans. This made it possible for people who weren't completely opposed to urban renewal to participate in the coalition. If recognized by the city and granted these powers, the community would cooperate in the development of an urban renewal plan.

■ The Base for Organizing against the Bulldozer

The organizing coalition was to be made up of these groupings and their key leaders:

The Catholic "network" of clergy, parishes, and lay organizations. (Gallegos had key connections here, and Knotts was developing them.)

The Centro Social Obrero (Abel Gonzalez) and OBECA (Herman Gallegos, Leandro Soto) networks.

Unaffiliated residents to be organized by MACABI (Alex Zermeno) neighborhood organizers and other community organizers in block club, tenant, welfare rights, and other groups. These new groups would also work on other issues of immediate importance to them, not just urban renewal.

The Protestant churches (Bill Grace, Dave Knotts)—mainline as well as Evangelical and Pentecostal.

Existing Latino organizations and others.

Any other group that genuinely had a constituency in the Mission.

While they were not viewed as central to the strategy, John Ross and Bartalini were also to be invited to participate in the developing organization.

■ Where Am I in This Picture?:
The Initial Organizing Question

The errors and activities of the opposition provide the organizer with his most powerful weapons. To pursue his Mission District agenda, in the early 1960s Justin Herman created the Mission Renewal Commission, but he and SFRA made a fundamental error. Commissioners represented almost no one but large-scale Mission Street merchants and the locally based but absentee-run community center. In addition, a "sketch plan" of what the Mission might look like was commissioned by the redevelopment agency. This plan showed a "new" Mission Street, but for local people, it left unanswered the question "Where am I in this picture?" And it was this question that organizers and community leaders asked Mission pastors, tenants, homeowners, small businessmen, community-based agencies, and others. In fact, in the "renewed" Mission many of them would be left out. Nice new buildings weren't going to provide low-rent space!

Pointing to the membership of the Mission Renewal Commission and the evidence of earlier urban renewal projects in the city, we could readily convince those with whom we spoke of the threat. Whether it was interpreted as a conspiracy or simply the workings of economic forces, the conclusion was the same: urban renewal, combined with the completion of BART, would mean high-rise fancy apartments, new stores and businesses, and the massive dislocation of the people who now made up the Mission. We rapidly proceeded with our contact work and saw the pieces of our strategy begin to fall into place.

The Mission Council

on Redevelopment

In a late spring 1966 meeting a new organization was born—the Mission Council on Redevelopment (MCOR), and the demand for veto power over Mission District urban renewal plans was adopted. Without this power, MCOR would seek to defeat any request for federal planning funds because these funds would almost inevitably open the door to a later bulldozer.

Initial Problems

The organizing work was not without its problems; it never is. Key to the Mission Catholic community was Msgr. John Murray, pastor of St. John's Catholic Church and a leader of the Catholic pastors in the Mission District Deanery, which encompassed all of MCOR's turf. The deaneries were administrative units below the San Francisco Archdiocese, which included the City and County of San Francisco, San Mateo County to the south, and Marin County to the north, and was headed by the cautious Archbishop Joseph McGucken. MCOR never won a firm commitment from Murray. Perhaps one of the reasons was the fact that Mayor John Francis "Jack" Shelley came from his parish.

Shelley was as indecisive in the urban renewal development fight as he had been in the struggle around the War on Poverty. San Francisco then was not the liberal/ progressive bastion it is today. His predecessor as mayor had been a Republican. The western half of the city elected a Republican to Congress. The city's Democrats ranged from centrist supporters of Lyndon Johnson to those who would later elect the unquestionably liberal Mayor George Moscone.

Out of a trade union background himself, Shelley was not unfamiliar with conflict and organization. He had gotten his start in the 1930s as president of the Bakery Wagon Drivers' Union and was elected president of the San Francisco Labor Council in 1937. Elected to the state legislature in 1938, he served there until, ten years later, he was elected to Congress, serving eight terms and representing the largely working-class and minority neighborhoods in the eastern part of the city. In 1964 he defeated conservative Republican Harold Dobbs in the mayoral election.

Shelley was not an administrator and vacillated when faced with the new conflicts emerging in American cities. Even his critics generally thought his heart was in the right place. But the new minority forces in the city's political structure were operating outside the framework of the older labor/ethnic politics of the Democratic Party. Shelley came from that older group; he sought to accommodate the new forces but could not reconcile MCOR's demands for veto power over urban renewal with the interests of other Democratic Party leaders and groups—particularly the construction trade unions—who were backing urban renewal in the Mission District.

In this context, Msgr. Murray faced cross-pressures. As a civic-minded priest, he enjoyed having the ear of Mayor Shelley—his own parishioner. He was also respected in the community and acknowledged to be a man of integrity. He now faced the dilemma inherent in his position: he tried to play the role of honest broker between the community and the mayor, but MCOR wanted a face-to-face negotiated agreement with the mayor. It didn't want to rely on the goodwill of one priest, no matter how decent he might be. Murray, acting on his own, sought to bring about a compromise that all parties could live with; but he did not have the mandate of MCOR to be its representative in negotiations with the mayor. The "good man" acting on his own initiative, outside the framework of a negotiated settlement between an organized community and "downtown," can suddenly be viewed with distrust. From MCOR's point of view, the demand for recognition would allow it to negotiate an agreement and enforce it. It is precisely because Murray was so unlikely to be a sellout that his situation so clearly illustrated the limits of solo action.

MCOR Progress

By mid-1966, MCOR was making a dent in the politics of urban renewal. To respond to its case for veto power without granting it, two liberal members of the combined City and County Board of Supervisors, Jack Morrison and Terry Francois, sought a compromise renewal package that would begin work on vacant sites, emphasize low- and moderate-priced housing, make use of rehabilitation wherever possible (as opposed to demolition), and otherwise be more responsive to the interests of low- and moderate-income residents as well as businessmen and other institutions in the neighborhood. By the end of November 1966, the board of supervisors was considering a sixth draft of urban renewal legislation, titled "Establishing Policies of the Board of Supervisors regarding Inner Mission Renewal to Further and Safeguard the Interests of the Present Residents, Businessmen, Property Owners, and Organizations and to Insure Citizen Participation in Planning."

Morrison and Francois warned that with the opening of BART stations in the Mission, private developers and speculators would take over: "They will build for their own profits, not for the sake of the people. Therefore, redevelopment, even if the present laws do not guarantee protections for the residents, is better than private speculation." This view was echoed by the citywide, downtown-oriented San Franciscans Planning for Urban Renewal: "The natural forces of the private economy responding to rapid transit along Mission…will dislocate many more residents than carefully controlled public action in accordance with an acceptable plan."

But MCOR had done some homework. It cited a study done for the SFRA by Development Research Associates of Los Angeles. In effect, the study said that rapid transit alone would not radically change the character of a neighborhood. "Finally," MCOR's newsletter said:

> The report…concludes that one of the major factors spurring development activity is the availability of large parcels of land under single ownership. The Redevelopment Agency's land buying operations make large parcels of land available to developers. Therefore, it can be concluded that it is the activities of the Redevelopment Agency, much more than the presence of a rapid transit system, which stimulates economic and residential activity and results in the eviction of low-income tenants, homeowners, and small businessmen.

Put another way, the urban renewal agency would label a neighborhood "deteriorating" or "dilapidated." Because of the label, property owners would stop or slow maintenance and repair of buildings they owned in that neighborhood; lenders and insurers would make it more difficult to obtain loans and policies—causing deterioration. The urban renewal agency would then use the deterioration that its label had created in the first place as a basis for saying the neighborhood needed to be "renewed," and would take steps toward obtaining city approval for an urban renewal grant. Those steps would lead property owners to cease maintenance and repair, and lenders and insurers would stop their activity, making the neighborhood even more deteriorated.

A weak campaign was waged by the liberals to win victory for their package. MCOR concluded that the new proposal also had Mayor Shelley's support. This legislation included a number of nominal guarantees to protect the interests represented by MCOR. In exchange for these protections, Morrison and Francois wanted MCOR to sacrifice veto power. The MCOR leadership refused to accept, arguing that guarantees would only be enforced if an ongoing neighborhood organization were recognized and granted the authority to do the enforcing. Having contacted the Alinsky-related Woodlawn Organization, in Chicago, which had negotiated a similar arrangement there, MCOR thought such an agreement was feasible.

As an alternative, these battles might be fought in court, but they took too long to win, and the victories would be hollow if they came after people, businesses, and institutions had moved from the area. MCOR said that urban renewal had to be watched at every step by local people with power to stop the process if it violated the agreement.

MCOR Wins

MCOR kept the fight going through 1966 and into 1967, until the issue of the development of the Mission BART corridor finally came to the board of supervisors; the question actually came before the board twice because SFRA modified its proposal in hopes of picking up a majority vote. Each time, by different 6-5 votes, the supervisors rejected the urban renewal agency's proposals for a grant to study the Mission corridor. Each time, MCOR brought out a couple of hundred people to the meeting.

One of the votes against urban renewal involved a bit of luck. The Catholic Archdiocese had noted the agitation in the neighborhood, including the parishes. When Herman Gallegos asked conservative Archbishop Joseph McGucken for a last-minute support letter, the archbishop told him, "You can't change much with a letter" and called William Blake, a moderate Irish-American Democratic Party politician, and asked him to oppose urban renewal in the Mission. As the roll-call vote proceeded alphabetically in the supervisors' chambers, Blake's name was called first. "Nay," he responded. Justin Herman, sitting in the audience, jumped to his feet and yelled out, "But you promised me your vote!" By then it was too late: MCOR had its sixth vote.

It took two rounds at the supervisors' chambers for MCOR to win, but win it did. The political battle captured the entire city's attention. Under the February 8, 1967, headline "Renewal for Mission Back on the Track," *San Francisco Examiner* urban affairs writer Donald Cantor opened his story with these words: "The politically explosive issue of Mission redevelopment will be revived by the Board of Supervisors within the next few weeks…Just how explosive the Mission renewal issue is became clear when some attending the [Mission Merchants] dinner passed out badges urging the recall of both [Mayor] Shelley and [Supervisor Jack] Morrison for their support of the redevelopment scheme."

After the second vote in 1967 (I was by this time already working in Kansas City), the dramatic headlines read, "Mission Renewal Bid Killed," "Stormy Session," and "Supervisors Kill Mission District Renewal Project." The *San Francisco Chronicle*'s Mel Wax told the story:

> SF Board of Supervisors, by a 6-5 vote, yesterday turned down an ambitious
> $2 million two-year plan to create an Inner Mission Redevelopment project.

The vote, at the weekly Board meeting, climaxed six months of hearings. It came before a raucous, standing-room-only crowd, which had to be gaveled to silence half a dozen times by Chairman Peter Tamaras.

As Supervisor Kevin O'Shea, who earlier had indicated he would follow the plea of Mayor John F. Shelley, who had appointed him, and vote for redevelopment, switched sides and voted against it, the crowd erupted in a loud roar of victory. In addition to O'Shea, voting against were Supervisors McCarthy, Moscone, Casey, Ertola and Boas.

Voting for it were Supervisors Morrison, von Beroldingen, Francois, Blake and Tamaras.

Casey and O'Shea were last-minute switches. Both, in public and private conversations in recent weeks, indicated they would go along with redevelopment.

In addition to the MCOR crowd inside, another three hundred opponents of urban renewal picketed outside City Hall.

In the Mission District, urban renewal in San Francisco suffered its first and only defeat. Indeed, urban renewal was rarely defeated across the country. The MCOR battle was won, but the army that won it was unable to continue its fight to improve the neighborhood. MCOR went the way of most single-issue organizations; having killed urban renewal, the organization itself died. MCOR's orientation was not to build permanent people power in the Mission, though it made some motions in that direction. Some of its organizers and leaders had this idea in mind, but they lacked the influence to transform the urban renewal victory into a new and continuing voice for the Mission District's people, one that could address the multitude of problems in housing, education, employment opportunities, health care, community services, recreation, police practices, small business development, neighborhood investment, child care, and more.

Lessons from MCOR

While the Mission Council on Redevelopment (MCOR) died soon after its victory, it set an important precedent for the people of the Mission.

MCOR Strengths

MCOR's accomplishments were major. By establishing a wide base of formal membership, it became the unquestionably legitimate spokesman for the neighborhood on urban renewal. That base was sufficient to force the San Francisco Redevelopment Agency (SFRA) to make modifications in its plan, to seek adherents in the community, and to attack its opponents. To put it simply, SFRA ran scared. Its handpicked businessmen's front in the neighborhood made it vulnerable. And the more SFRA attacked MCOR, the more people in the neighborhood looked at MCOR and compared the two. MCOR did well in the comparison.

Beside its representative character, MCOR could show that it was not this representation was not simply on paper. When people were needed, they came. Two to three hundred of them turned out for major community or board of supervisors meetings in the urban renewal fight.

Key breakthroughs occurred with the Catholic community, especially through the Catholic Council for the Spanish Speaking (Concilio) and its leader, Eduardo Lopez, and with Catholic clergy. The Concilio, a gathering of Latino parish-based groups in the Greater Mission, was funded by the Archdiocese so that it could have its own staff person.

MCOR Weaknesses

The Abel Gonzalez/Centro Social Obrero forces never really came into the coalition; they were nominal members. As a business agent in the Laborers' Union, with a base of members who depended on construction work, Gonzalez's interests were divided between the promise of work for his people and his broader political role in the community—a community now generally hostile to urban renewal.

While important breakthroughs were achieved with Catholic lay and clergy leadership, the people in the parishes weren't really reached by MCOR's campaign.

MACABI organizers were unable to develop ongoing organizations of the unaffiliated. With the exception of two organizers—Elba Tuttle and John McReynolds—the Poverty Program staff built few new organizations. However, they and others, such as Joan Bordman and Ed Sandoval, all played roles in building MCOR. Continued support came from MACABI Executive Director Alex Zermeno.

Mainline Protestant clergy continued to play an important role in MCOR, but like the Catholics, they too failed to get their congregations involved in the campaign.

Jack Bartalini and his merchant and homeowner allies, opposed to urban renewal in any form, remained outside MCOR. It was not simply a matter of the community having a voice in the urban renewal process; from their point of view, the process itself was against the interests of those they represented. There was no way small businessmen and homeowners could benefit from urban renewal.

John Ross and the Progressive Labor Party (PL) forces joined MCOR and continued active for some time. Ross was elected to the MCOR steering committee and was a constant critic of the rest of the leadership of the organization. His style and demands isolated him from most of the organization's leaders and base. During this period, the Mission Tenants Union and a committee for fair taxes, both led by PL and its allies, started a ballot initiative for a rent control and tax reform measure that would both stop the already increasing rents in San Francisco and shift the property tax burden from individual homeowners to large businesses. But most MCOR members would not support anything involving PL, no matter how legitimate the issues.

▓ Multi-issue versus Single-issue

MCOR was a single-issue organization, wholly focused on the urban renewal threat to the Mission. I have on several occasions referred to single-issue versus multi-issue organizing. A discussion of each is in order.

Different people experience different problems with different intensity at different times in their lives. The working single mother with preschool-age children is deeply interested in child care but probably not too concerned about the local high school—at least not yet; she will be in twelve years. The teenagers who hang out at the local park and don't do too well in school are angry about being rousted by the cops. With decent job opportunities, some respect, and a voice in the community, their group could become a positive young men's club. Without, it could become a delinquent gang. The seniors who've had their purses snatched and homes broken into, and who may have been hurt in one or another of these encounters, want police protection. Tenants are concerned about their landlords; homeowners about property taxes.

If the goal is to build a people-power organization among low-to-moderate-income people, all these groups should be involved. This makes possible new relationships developing across constituency lines; of moving from one issue to another when timing is good for one but not so good for the other; and of the salience of a hot issue resulting in a shift from passivity to action. Perhaps most important, the multi-issue approach offers the opportunity to talk about power. An organizer can ask, "Isn't the common experience on most of these concerns that the community is powerless to move decision makers to respond to them?" That strikes a responsive chord because of its fundamental truth.

Further, if you don't want differences of interest to be magnified and to become barriers to groups working together, you need a forum within which they can compromise with one another in order to achieve the unity they will need to build the kind of power that will get good jobs, reduce property taxes, shift the tax burden to those who can most afford to pay, create affordable child-care centers, protect people on the street and in their homes, and respect youth. That forum is a multi-issue organization.

In the absence of such an organization, older homeowners and childless singles may only focus on their taxes and vote against school bonds. The "off the pig" shouts of youth hassled by police will only alienate other constituencies. Anglo parents may get upset when bilingual programs or racial justice curriculum materials are introduced into the schools. Each constituency can view The Other as a potential ally or as an adversary. The forum of the multi-issue organization affords them the opportunity to work together on their separate as well as common interests. The problem with a group limited to common interests is that these are usually so large—not enough income, for instance—that tremendous power is required to make a dent in them. And the very people whose participation is essential to build such power don't join in because they believe "you can't fight the powers that be."

Sometimes a single issue comes along that by its very nature unites large numbers of people because all of them are adversely affected. Urban renewal is a prime example. Given the scarce resources available, it made sense for MCOR to focus on a single issue. But when the issue was won, the possibility that people power could defend and advance the interests of the Mission District's low-to-moderate-income residents and give voice to the neighborhood's minority communities was lost.

Organizing versus Mobilizing

Once an issue is decided upon, a campaign has to be mounted to win it. In the same way that a candidate for office tries to put together a majority to win an election, an organization tries to put together the constituency to win its issue. There may be room for discussion and debate on tactics, but the issue has been decided upon. Whoever made that decision "owns" the issue. Others may be drawn into the battle and even become co-owners of it. But those drawn in will be limited to those who are interested in the issue and think their participation will make a difference. With great effort, MCOR could draw a representative group of several hundred people to a community meeting or board of supervisors meeting. But its ongoing activity was limited to a relatively small group. That small group "mobilized" the community on the occasions when large turnout of people was required; people were convinced by arguments about why they were needed, or they came out of trust and respect for those who asked them.

Organizing does something different. The organizer's first tool is his or her ears, not mouth. A respectful listener finds out what people care enough about to shift from passivity to involvement, from complaining to participating, from being victims to becoming actors. But there's more: the organizer has to challenge people to act on what they care about. Years of butting their heads up against the walls of indifference and antagonism, of voting because of promises that then go unfulfilled, can lead people to withdraw from public life. The organizer has to challenge them to act despite past experience that suggests action is a waste of time. Then the organizer has to think through with people what can be done. Examples from elsewhere in the neighborhood or, at the very beginning of an organizing drive, in other places, paint a picture of hope. Maybe this time will be different. Finally, organizers train people in the skills required to build an effective organization.

All organizations engage in mobilizations if they are worth their salt. It is possible to use a mobilization to build ongoing organization, though it is very difficult. But the typical single-issue mobilization ends when the issue is won or lost. (The same principle, by the way, applies to mobilizations around elections: a candidate wins or loses, but usually the organization formed in his campaign dies.) Typically, the people who are still involved toward the end of a campaign like MCOR's are the "activists"—good people who care about changing the world but who, too often, aren't rooted in the constituencies needed to bring that change about.

▨ Where the Sixties Went Wrong:
A Different Urban Coalition Was Possible

Each of the board of supervisors' 6-5 votes was split along lines having little to do with normal liberal-versus-conservative voting. In his *San Francisco Chronicle* story, Mel Wax observed, "Mission redevelopment created odd alliances. Liberals...found themselves playing on the same team as conservatives." Indeed, the complexity was even greater: liberals Francois and Morrison voted for urban renewal; liberals McCarthy and Moscone voted against. Conservatives Casey and Ertola voted against; conservatives von Beroldingen and Tamaras voted for. Another dimension of analysis is needed to explain how members of the board voted on this issue.

The peculiarity of the San Francisco Board of Supervisors' vote distribution holds a clue to potential urban coalitions that might have changed the future of American politics. Post–World War II and subsequent anti–urban renewal and anti-freeway struggles in American cities sometimes brought together white, blue-collar, urban ethnics with African-Americans, Puerto Ricans, and Mexican-Americans. Had these coalitions endured and become multi-issue, the subsequent polarization that led to white backlash and flight of whites to the suburbs might not have happened. "Majority constituency" organizations might have supported full-employment legislation, national health insurance, major public funding for affordable housing, and big grants to urban schools and public transit systems—all paid for by highly progressive income taxes that were redistributive in character. In this context, racism and sexism might have been challenged in ways that paralleled their challenge in such 1930s industrial unions as the United Packinghouse Workers of America—where "Black and white/Unite and fight" was a slogan that took on reality, and women's rights became an important part of the union's program.

A different form of the New Deal coalition, one that rejected the racism of the 1930s, might have been revived. Thanks to the civil rights movement that took place in the Deep South from 1955 to 1965, the Dixiecrats—white, racist southern Democrats—lost the power they had in the Democratic Party from the 1930s to the mid-1960s, when their congressional representatives blocked progressive legislation particularly in, but not limited to, the South. By 1968 their supporters and politicians had become Republicans. A "new New Deal" that combined economic and racial justice might have taken root. This alliance might have led to a different future for politics in the United States. It didn't happen. With the 2008 election we can again see its possibility on the horizon.

The struggle against racism in the United States had several central and radically different approaches. Separatists, whether militant or moderate, advocated building up the Black community through self-help, mutual aid, and local economic development. Liberal integrationists relied on courts and legislative battles that were far removed from the daily lives of people who would be affected by their outcomes. Urban political machines sought to incorporate Black and other minority communities into their cities, and used patronage to build an electoral base among their voters. A small-d democratic organizing tendency was present as well. It included the late-nineteenth-century rural populists who were antiracist in their early period. Their slogan then was "Race has kept us both in poverty." The urban Knights of Labor, one of the most important labor organizations of the late nineteenth century, opposed both racism and discrimination against women. In the twentieth century, this tendency was present in some of the industrial unions that made up the Congress of Industrial Organizations (CIO). The 1930s Packinghouse Workers Organizing Committee, with which Saul Alinsky worked in Chicago, was as progressive on the issue of race as any union. In the postwar period, the San Francisco Bay Area's International Longshoremen's and Warehousemen's Union carried on this tradition.

In a well-known 1971-72 Chicago fight, such a coalition was successful in defeating then-Mayor Daley's pet Crosstown Freeway project. Puerto Ricans, Blacks, and white ethnics along the proposed freeway corridor, joined by small- and medium-sized businesses and local institutions, involved tens of thousands of people in the anti-Crosstown fight. During the 1972 national election, whose Chicago ballot included local contests as well, the Crosstown Freeway issue was used as a test of where any politician stood. A "For the People" column on a widely read flyer included the Democratic gubernatorial candidate, Daniel Walker. "Against the People" was the Republican incumbent, Richard B. Ogilvie. Walker won and later attributed his victory margin to the Crosstown Corridor vote.

Perhaps even more interesting in that race was the fate of State's Attorney Edward Hanrahan. He was directly involved in the police killing of Chicago Black Panther Party leader Fred Hampton, and popular in white ethnic precincts in part because of that involvement. But in the white precincts along the Crosstown Corridor, Hanrahan was "Against the People," while Bernard Carey, his Republican opponent, was "For the People." Even in normally racist Crosstown Corridor precincts, Hanrahan was defeated—another indication of the potential for a different urban coalition.

Barack Obama's March 2008 speech on race in America highlights the promise of rebirth for this alliance. His community organizing background increases its possibility.

Each of these examples illustrates the possibility of a different kind of coalition based on a different vision of a good life: an affirmation of the positive values of neighborhood living—local institutions, small businesses, neighborhood merchants, ethnic and racial identity, and neighborhood preservation—in contrast to downtown-oriented development and social engineering by remote planners; justice popularly agreed upon, rather than decided in court.

After Urban

Renewal's Defeat

Between the defeat of urban renewal, with the subsequent dissolution of the Mission Council on Redevelopment (MCOR), and the rebirth of a Mission coalition, a major electoral development took place. And the name of Saul Alinsky was also coming into greater prominence in Mission District conversations.

Joseph Alioto: Mayor of San Francisco

Joseph Alioto, running as a moderate Democrat with strong support from Laborers' Local 261 in general and Abel Gonzalez in particular, became mayor of San Francisco in 1968, defeating Jack Morrison—though early polls showed Morrison winning. Alioto was an accidental mayor. He had been chairman of State Senator Eugene McAteer's mayoral campaign. With only two months left before the election, McAteer suddenly died from a heart attack. Alioto stepped in.

By this time San Francisco had become an overwhelmingly Democratic city. Since the election of John Shelley, there hasn't been a Republican mayor or significant Republican minority on the board of supervisors. By 1968, San Francisco politics of any importance took place within the Democratic Party. Alioto was part of its centrist grouping; Jack Morrison was aligned with the liberals led by Congressman Phil Burton—though they had their own important disagreements.

Alioto was a brilliant antitrust lawyer, a truly cosmopolitan man who played the violin and wrote poetry, a skilled negotiator and power broker, and a man who loved politics and his city. As a two-term (eight years) mayor, he managed the city through some of the nation's most polarizing conflicts—the Vietnam antiwar movement, student protests and strikes at San Francisco State University, militant Black and Latino community protests over police brutality, the American Federation of Teachers' first strike in the city's public schools, and more. He created an electoral coalition among labor unions and the Black, Latino, and Asian communities that won, by substantial majorities, the two mayoral campaigns he ran.

Mayor Alioto was the keynote speaker at the February 1968 Spanish Speaking Issues Conference held by Mission Area Community Action Board, Inc. (MACABI). He dropped a bombshell. He said he would seek Model Cities funds for the Mission District—if so requested by a broadly based group representative of the neighborhood. To many present, this looked like a sneak attack to bring urban renewal back to the Mission. (Prior to becoming mayor, Alioto had been on the San Francisco Redevelopment Agency Commission.) The core leaders of the now-defunct MCOR came together to form a new coalition that would seek the mayor's recognition and preempt the possibility of urban renewal supporters doing the same thing.

Mayor Alioto was the Mission District's adversary and negotiating partner from the immediate post-MCOR period through development of the Mission Coalition Organization (MCO) to its most powerful point in 1971, and into its decline and fall by the mid-1970s. MCO went to the mat with Alioto on more than one occasion. Out of its struggles with him there emerged a mutual respect that was responsible for one of the nation's best Model Cities programs.

Keeping the Organizing Idea Alive: After MCOR, before MCO

While MCOR disappeared, Presbyterian minister Dave Knotts remained. Without a local church, on the Department of Urban Work staff, he continued to be a "detached minister" in the Mission District. He developed a wide base of confidence among Mission activists and churchmen, including Catholics and mainline, Evangelical, and Pentecostal Protestants, and became involved in a number of specific-issue fights that took place after the MCOR victory.

Knotts epitomized the new breed of young Protestant clergy who were shaped by the student, antipoverty, civil rights, and antiwar movements and who learned the social gospel in the country's mainline Protestant seminaries. His boss, Bill Grace, provided the protection and backup for him to continue working in the Mission with few administrative or denominational responsibilities. The two of them and I were also talking about Saul Alinsky, and ways to bring his approach to organizing to the Bay Area. In 1965 and 1966, Bay Area clergymen participated in two of Alinsky's ten-day community organizing workshops. As much as anyone, Knotts kept the organizing flame burning in the Mission District between MCOR's demise and the birth of MCO.

Though the Poverty Program's "maximum feasible participation" accomplished little in the way of grassroots organizing, Poverty Program staff developed and began to win recognition as leaders and organizers in the community. Among them were Elba Tuttle, a tough Puerto Rican single mom living in the East Mission who sponsored a slate of candidates in one of the MACABI board of directors elections (against an "Abel

Gonzalez slate") and won. The young Anglo organizer John McReynolds was getting involved in some issue-oriented activity in the neighborhood. The Poverty Program itself bogged down in internal fights over who was going to get funded to do what and in what amount. These bitter internal struggles drove away those who did not have a stake in funded programs. Turnover of key staff was continuous. No matter who "controlled" the program, its limitations seemed to control the controllers.

Also, a new personality emerged on the Mission stage. Ben Martinez was hired by OBECA (Organization for Business, Education and Community Advancement, later renamed Arriba Juntos), sent to a national workshop to learn the Model Cities program, and began working as a community liaison, or organizer, for the community-based agency. A recent graduate from San Francisco State, he was to become a key person in the future of the Mission.

Activity in the Mission during this period included affirmative action picketing by the Mexican American Political Association; housing and recreation demands from groups organized by Tuttle and McReynolds out of the East Mission MACABI office; some tenant organizing, with most of it done by Progressive Labor's John Ross through the Mission Tenants Union; homeowner involvement with a federal grants and low-interest loan program to rehabilitate owner-occupied property, led by Bartalini; and a committee for bilingual education. A major preoccupation for many activists was dividing the underfunded War on Poverty pie. And because of these fights, groups defined by neighborhood, race, ethnicity, age, and program interest divided and opposed each other.

I have never been able to decide whether the Poverty Program was deliberately conceived to divide people or simply had that effect. In the Mission, that effect became increasingly clear. Certainly the urban reformers who designed these programs thought they were doing good. At the same time, I have no doubt there were others in politics and the power structure who knew how to make use of the reformers' work for different ends. Understanding how this all works is essesntial for those who want to understand power in the United States.

In this milieu, Dave Knotts was a quiet but continuous presence. He supported local struggles with his time, advice, and limited resources—and kept the idea of a powerful alliance of local groups alive.

▨ Model Cities: Threat or Promise?

Model Cities could become a vehicle for urban renewal, but not necessarily. It could also bring across-the-board improvements to the quality of life in low-income neighborhoods. Which course would be followed varied from city to city and depended on the relative strength of neighborhoods in relation to mayors.

Unlike the earlier War on Poverty, Model Cities was designed by its social planners to be a mayor's program in neighborhoods rather than a neighborhood program that bypassed mayors. Bending to pressure from big-city mayors who threatened to kill the Poverty Program, Congress in 1967 passed "the Green Amendment" (authored by Congresswoman Edith Green). Its intent was to give mayors the power to block earlier Poverty Program activities that bypassed their authority. In a number of cities, older white ethnic (Italian, Irish, Polish, and other) political machines discovered that Blacks, Puerto Ricans, Mexican-Americans, and other "new minorities" were using the Poverty Program to build their own political organizations. (These minorities, I would argue, later inherited many central city governments when the resources to solve their cities' problems had all but evaporated after private industry and the white middle class abandoned them and the government cut funding.)

Model Cities explicitly lodged authority for its administration in the hands of mayors. Besides this element of political caution—giving control back to mayors—the Model Cities design was born of rational planning considerations supported by urban-reform social planners—coordinating services, avoiding their duplication, and strengthening the capacity of mayors or city managers to solve urban problems. Many urban programs designed at the federal level had ended up "on the ground" in a multiplicity of efforts that either duplicated or competed with one another or, even worse, operated at cross-purposes; in the planners' view, a centralized authority was needed. The idea was also that a "citizen-participation component" would be created out of negotiations between mayors and community groups and would work with mayors, not independently of them.

People-Power Leadership Steps Up:
The Creation of TMCO

As a building needs a strong foundation to stand, so too does a social creation. Building the MCO was as difficult as building a strong building on landfill. The contradictions and diversity of the community had to come together.

MCO got its kickoff, ironically enough, from Mayor Alioto's speech—though he had little idea at the time what he was unleashing.

Dave Knotts and others who shared the larger, people-power vision were among those who responded to Alioto's invitation. They saw it as an opportunity to act. Knotts, Tuttle, Joan Boardman (MACABI), Ben Martinez, and others gathered in a small Mission planning meeting reminiscent of the meeting that gave birth to MCOR. Their purpose was to move early and preempt the field of entrants who might step in to accept the mayor's invitation. Their reasons were basically two: first, they wanted to be assured that control of such an organization remained in the hands of those who demanded neighborhood veto power over urban renewal; second, they saw the Model Cities program as a new opportunity to build an ongoing, people-power, action organization that would have the popular participation necessary to win campaigns on issues that couldn't be resolved with funded programs, or by the Progressive Labor Party and its coterie of organizations, or by the small civic and issue organizations of the neighborhood.

This core group began to expand, inviting key figures in the Mission to join with them to respond to the mayor's invitation. Soon more than twenty-five groups came together in the Temporary Mission Coalition Organization (TMCO). (The "T" was dropped at the organization's founding convention. It had been important because it made clear to anyone not yet in the organization that there was plenty of room to help shape it.) Included were the primary community-based service agencies of the Mission, several of the churches, several block and tenant organizations organized under the Poverty Program, some predominantly middle-class Latino organizations, and some active individuals. While some of the organizers spoke of a multi-issue action coalition, it was clear that Model Cities brought most of the groups together.

Knotts was the key person putting the coalition together. He had the time and a basic understanding of the ideas, and he was not identified with any particular faction or interest group that had been involved in the Mission's internal fights. Joining forces with him, and elected president of TMCO, was Ben Martinez. They, with Elba Tuttle, John McReynolds, and Joan Boardman, whose Sioux roots connected her to the Native American people in the district, were the core of the TMCO organizing team.

To anticipate and avoid some of the problems of the Poverty Program, Knotts recommended that TMCO plan a community convention at which officers would be elected, a constitution adopted, and a platform established. Knotts envisioned a large number of vice presidencies to represent different area, ethnic, racial, and interest groups. That way, should the internal fighting that existed in MACABI occur, it would at least take place in a body whose legitimacy as the elected voice of the community was established. Further, an action organization, acting outside the framework of dividing a federal pie, would not have the pressures that were tearing the Poverty Program apart. At this time, I was organizing a similar convention in Kansas City, Missouri, developing action on issues there, and talking or corresponding with Knotts about what I was learning.

■ TMCO Gains Mayor Alioto's Recognition

TMCO gained rapid recognition by the mayor as the neighborhood group with which he would deal; it was broadly based, had no rival claimants, and wasn't yet doing anything that might upset the politicians with whom it had to deal. Martinez and

Knotts did their organizing homework well. The key groups in the Mission were represented, and TMCO looked like nothing more than what the mayor had requested. Martinez understood the Model Cities program, and emerged as a capable leader. He had a good relationship with Abel Gonzalez who was, as a result of his involvement in Alioto's election, crucial to the mayor's recognition of the new organization. With Martinez as leader and Knotts as informal organizer, there existed a team that had good credentials with all the Mission's key players. Tuttle had strong reservations about working with Gonzalez, but she could not deny that he had to be in a coalition, and she could readily see that if he was going to be in it, she had to be in it as well.

Among other things, coalitions of this nature are built on the interests of those who join them and the fear that "If I'm not in it, those who are will run it for themselves and cut me and my people out." For Tuttle, "my people" were the smaller, grassroots organizations, in particular single-building tenant associations and block clubs that she was organizing in the East Mission.

TMCO began to develop its negotiating position on Model Cities only after winning recognition from the mayor. Thus Alioto would have to back away from recognition he had already granted if he wanted to start dealing with a new group. Furthermore, one could presume that the mayor had learned the lesson of MCOR and was not interested in a big fight with the community. The TMCO-developed proposals for Model Cities now took what could be argued was a step further than the demand for veto power. In effect, TMCO was calling for community control of the program—something antithetical to the views of the Department of Housing and Urban Development (HUD). But TMCO thought the mayor could live with it and it might slip by a federal review. This was expressed in a series of formulas for governance of the Model Cities planning and implementation process. TMCO wanted Model Cities funds for neighborhood improvements, including social programs, but feared Model Cities as a front for unrestricted urban renewal.

TMCO's activists argued the relative merits of four alternative proposals for the structure of Model Cities in the Mission, each sharing the feature of community control of the program. Since no one had a crystal ball, it was impossible to know whether urban renewal was on a hidden agenda. TMCO wanted to make sure that if it was, it would be erased.

On the other side of the negotiating table when meeting with city hall was John Anderson, the mayor's representative for the program. Within TMCO, lengthy debates took place over what the precise language proposed to Anderson would be. In part, I think the arguments were spurious. What is written in agreements is only as good as the enforcement power of the parties to those agreements; that is the record of broken treaties among nations, the failure of the U.S. government to live up to equal rights commitments in the Thirteenth, Fourteenth, and Fifteenth Amendments to the Constitution, employer abuse of workers when unions don't have the power to enforce their contracts, and the many other examples that demonstrate the point. The question of how the power would be built tended to be lost as TMCO argued about what the words in the agreement would be.

My Return to the Mission

While TMCO was forming, I was directing Saul Alinsky's Black community organizing project in Kansas City, Missouri. In a phone conversation with Martinez and Knotts, I had agreed to temporarily work for TMCO when I got back to the Bay Area. Martinez, Knotts, and Ed Sandoval made arrangements for a late-summer meeting upon my return, in 1968. While Martinez's experience was in a community-based agency, he was clearly interested in Alinsky's approach to mass action organizing, such as I'd been doing in Kansas City.

The best community-based agencies sought to provide sensitive and relevant programs, like culturally sensitive tutoring for inner-city children. At minimum, they simply provided jobs for minorities who had less opportunities in "downtown" agencies. At worst, they were neocolonial buffers between those in power and low-income, typically minority communities. In contrast, Alinsky-tradition mass action organizations wanted to influence major decision makers in government, large nonprofit organizations like hospitals and universities, and big business. This influence extended to the nature of service programs in their neighborhoods. They weren't averse to participating in programs, but at least in theory, they sought to retain an independent power base.

By the time I returned to the Mission from Kansas City, I had fully internalized the role of the outside organizer. Both SNCC and Alinsky made organizers the catalysts to build local people-power organizations. SNCC's Bob Moses was one of the people I came most to admire for his embodiment of the role. By the time I got to know Alinsky, he was a nationally known, and very public, figure. But he was organizing national religious denominations, not local communities.

In Alinsky's days, the outside organizer worked only three years in a project, then moved on after training a locally recruited successor. He was:

Invisible in the news media

Silent at decision-making meetings, and often didn't attend them

Trusted sufficiently by different factions within an organization to have access to all of them; they all wanted the benefit of conversations with him about everything from broad ideas of democracy to strategy and tactics

Committed to building the power of the organization, keeping it democratic and united, and teaching local leaders to view issues in the context of building the organization, not simply on their "merit." (As an organizer, I knew that almost any problem could be defined as an issue that would either build or weaken an organization. I will later elaborate on this organization-building process.)

Rewarded by developing action by people who were accustomed to being passive objects of the decisions made about them, rather than with them, and

Excited to see local leaders confront and challenge people in authority who thought they didn't have to pay attention to such challenges.

Organizers recognized that strong egos were a given when power was at stake. The main brake against the abuse of power by ego-driven leadership would be the checks that leaders placed on each another. People power required many leaders with diverse constituencies, and leaders who wanted serious people power came to recognize that. Better to have rivals in the same room, where roles that gave everyone recognition could be created, and internal compromises could be hammered out to satisfy all constituencies, than to have them separately holding their own news conferences or seeking deals with "downtown" and getting crumbs or nothing. I emphasized the legitimacy of internal caucuses within a large democratic organization.

▓ I'm Officially Hired

At our July meeting, Martinez confirmed our earlier phone conversation. I would assume the position of staff director on a temporary basis to put together a first community convention, with the idea in mind that if the community liked me and I performed well in putting the convention together, a longer relationship might be worked out. I indicated interest in the proposition under two conditions: first, that a broad-based group of neighborhood leaders ask me to work as their organizer; and second, that initial agreement be reached on the proposition that we were building a multi-issue mass action organization, not just a coalition to deal with Model Cities. Such a meeting was held with a dozen or so key Latino leaders and a few others in the early fall of 1968, and agreement was reached. In addition to those who attended the meeting, Knotts and Martinez "cleared" my hiring with Herman Gallegos, Abel Gonzalez, and some key church leaders in the Mission.

Far from meeting Alinsky's ideal beginning point of having enough money in the bank for two to three years, we started with two thousand dollars (over twelve thousand, in 2009 dollars) in our treasury from the Laborers' Union Local 261, a slightly larger amount from the Presbyterians, and a small grant from the Episcopal Diocese. Dave Knotts continued as an almost full-time staff worker—an in-kind contribution of even greater value than the money from the Presbyterians; and OBECA, newly renamed Arriba Juntos, released Ben Martinez to work half-time with TMCO. Filling out the "inner circle" was Elba Tuttle. Abel Gonzalez held informal veto power over major decisions in the development of the organization—important decisions were "checked" with him before they were made; generally he would acquiesce to whatever Martinez and Knotts had agreed upon. By this time, the Centro Social Obrero, which he had initially organized as a Latino caucus within the Laborers' Union, was a major force in Mission community politics.

My first job was to assemble a staff to put together a founding convention. This was done with support from MACABI director Adan Juarez, who had replaced Alex Zermeno when he went on to another position. Like his predecessor, Juarez was committed to community organizing, and he acknowledged that the internal intrigue of dividing up Poverty Program funds precluded MACABI's becoming a powerful grassroots organization. Through Juarez, Tuttle and McReynolds were released for almost full-time work with TMCO. Two young workers from VISTA (Volunteers in Service to America—the domestic equivalent of the Peace Corps), Ann Drury and Spence Limbocker, joined the staff. Eduardo Sandoval had opened an office and started some of the administrative machinery rolling for the new organization.

There were, as of September 1968, some thirty member organizations in TMCO. With our initial staff we began working to build for the first convention. Our objective was to increase organizational membership to sixty, and to begin to increase the involvement of the "grass roots" of the neighborhood: the people who were unlikely to be involved in civic life and were in fact often labeled as "apathetic," typically of low to moderate income with modest formal education—not the employees of community-based agencies. Every conceivable neighborhood contact any of us had was listed on a chalkboard and I made assignments to pursue these leads. Our definition of an "organization" was so simple that someone who could bring ten people together in his or her home for a meeting would be able to obtain recognition and seating on the convention floor. This allowed, for example, an extended family, a group of neighbors, or a clique at a neighborhood park to be an "organization" for the purposes of TMCO's founding convention.

■ The Lay of the Land

The first requirement for a people-power organization is people. Who are they? Who should be in the organization for it truly to be *the* "voice of the people" of a particular constituency? Beyond the broad demographics, one prerequisite to knowing who the people are is understanding the patterns of relationships that exist among them. Who knows whom? Who respects whom? Who follows whom?

People are connected—both in formal and informal organizations. The connections aren't random. Typically, there are patterns of deference and respect. The informal "mayor of the block" may be key to building a successful "block club"; if the mayor is not involved, many of the people on the block won't join. And there may be more than one mayor on any given block. These leaders, in turn, may want to know what the pastor of their church thinks of a larger organization before they lend their support to it. The same patterns of relationships exist within churches, and they may or may not be reflected in the official decision-making structures of a church.

At the same time, there are people who are outside these webs of relationship—newcomers, loners, late bloomers, or people connected to networks and organizations beyond their blocks or even their neighborhoods. They might welcome the opportunity to be part of something with a purpose larger than themselves that involves the people next door. A new organizing effort might create the social space in which they can develop relationships and see their talents develop and blossom in a new setting.

The group of people who hired me to be the organizer in the Mission included many of the respected leaders there—but not all of them by any means. My first job was to learn how the neighborhood ticked, to go far deeper into the patterns of relationship among its people than ever was done during the MCOR fight. The result of that digging was a community analysis, a road map to the texture of the area in which I was organizing. Without this information, an organizer is like a driver in a new city without a street map to guide him.

The Spanish Speaking/Spanish Surname/Latinos

The "Spanish," "Hispanics," "Mexican-Americans," "Mexicans," "Chicanos," or "Latinos"—the preferred name varying with the age, nation of origin, and militancy of whomever you were asking—who made up about 30 to 40 percent of the population of the Greater Mission area and 60 percent of the Inner Mission, were beginning to develop a variety of civic participation organizations. But they were a complicated group. They included substantial numbers of Nicaraguans, Salvadorans (both subgroups outnumbered other Latino groups), Mexican-Americans, Mexican nationals, and Puerto Ricans. Most of the other nations of Latin America were also represented in the Mission. Some of these residents were citizens, but a large number were not; and some of these were "undocumented." Among the early groups were MAPA (Mexican-American Political Association), LULAC (League of United Latin American Citizens), GI Forum (a World War II veterans organization), Spanish Speaking Citizens' Foundation, Catholic Council for the Spanish Speaking ("Concilio"), Mexican-American Unity Council, Puerto Rican Club of San Francisco, and a number of primarily social nationality organizations. There were also athletic clubs, including Deportivo Peru, Deportivo Colombia, and those of a number of other nations of Latin America. Each club sponsored a soccer team; together they were in a league.

MAPA and LULAC specifically involved themselves in issues affecting the Latino population and had a centrist-to-liberal political orientation. The Catholic Church included parishes in the tradition of Catholic self-help and self-education and some that were more action-oriented. The latter supported Cesar Chavez's efforts to organize the farmworkers of California. Some of the nationality organizations were led by the conservative middle class of their countries. These groups came together in the Spanish Speaking Citizens' Foundation, the conservative political voice of the community.

Catholic Charities, the social service arm of the Archdiocese of San Francisco, supported by the Catholic Council for the Spanish Speaking—indeed, at its urging—provided a financial base for the creation of OBECA/Arriba Juntos, the locally based community service agency, which was led by liberal Mexican-Americans. For a long time this was Herman Gallegos's base in the Mission. He was a key figure in the Community Service Organization (CSO), which had once been a vigorous statewide organization of Mexican-Americans. Cesar Chavez had been its director. By the 1960s, CSO was tremendously weakened. Many of its key people had moved into government or labor union jobs. The San Francisco chapter never was large. Gallegos was at the center of the San Francisco CSO-Catholic Council-OBECA/Arriba Juntos network, making him one of the most influential figures in the Latino community and a recognized spokesman in San Francisco politics. He was a leader in the fight to keep control of the War on Poverty program in the neighborhood.

The Centro Social Obrero, which by 1965 had become a major Latino organization in the Mission, had gotten its start in the early 1960s as a caucus in the building trades unions (AFL-CIO). Many a building tradesman in the Mission claims to have been the founder of the Obreros. Whatever its origins, the man who emerged as its clear leader was Abel Gonzalez. The Obreros provided English-language classes and other services. With the help of Bethany United Methodist Church and its pastor, Rev. Bill Miller, they gathered volunteer tutors to hold the classes. Soon their base narrowed to the Laborers' Union, and Abel Gonzalez became their undisputed leader in Laborers' Local 261. Gonzalez surrounded himself with a talented group, including people not in the union. But the base was the Laborers, and Abel Gonzalez had the followers in that base. Many who worked with him would later leave him, claiming that he ran a one-man show. But they didn't take any of the base with them. Many who rallied around the Obreros held the anticlerical views that had come out of the Mexican Revolution.

MACABI (the Poverty Program) rapidly became an arena of struggle for Latino leadership in the Mission, with the major protagonists being aligned with OBECA/Gallegos, Centro Social Obreros/Gonzalez, and MACABI staffer Elba Tuttle. MACABI also became the center of struggle of other divergent interests in the Mission. Each saw in the Poverty Program an opportunity not only to fund needed services in the community, but also to build a power base.

Control over War on Poverty funds was at stake in these conflicts. Much of the money available was for specific programs or services. A smaller amount was for organizers. Low-income communities struggled to control an amount of money totally inadequate to the tasks that had to be undertaken if poverty were to be abolished. Further, legislative and administrative guidelines for the use of the funds were established outside the community. This struggle for funding was at the heart of Poverty Program politics.

MACABI funded a number of organizing offices in sub-neighborhoods of the Greater Mission. It funded the Obreros' English Language School, the Organization for Business, Education and Cultural Advancement (OBECA, Herman Gallegos's base), Horizons Unlimited and the Mission Rebels (both youth-serving agencies), and other projects. Out of each of these agencies were to emerge people who would play key roles in the development of the Mission Coalition Organization.

■ Country of Origin Politics

All the immigrants in the Mission brought with them a way of thinking about politics that was rooted in their homeland experience. The Mexican PRI (Partido Revolucionario Institucional, Institutional Revolutionary Party) and its labor arm, CTM (Confederación de Trabajadores de México, Confederation of Mexican Workers), were by the 1960s highly bureaucratized and corrupt. Many Mexicans were initially suspicious of labor unions and revolutionary language. Others had been in real revolutionary parties or labor unions.

The Mission Coalition Organization would include pro- and anti–Ferdinand Marcos Filipinos, pro- and anti–Sandinista Nicaraguans, pro- and anti–rebel Salvadorans, pro-commonwealth, statehood, and independence Puerto Ricans, exiled pro–Salvador Allende Chileans, refugees from Guatemala's dictatorship, and others who brought vivid ideas to the U.S. from their homes.

Inner Mission "Anglos" and White Ethnics

The older white ethnic homeowners in the Mission were represented by old-line conservative homeowner organizations. The older stores on Mission Street had their own merchants' association, as did those along 24th and Valencia Streets. In the "hill" sections of the Mission, liberals and centrists had their own organizations. Some were Democratic Party clubs, remnants of the once active and powerful liberal California Democratic Clubs (CDC). Others were in independent neighborhood organizations.

A number of elderly people were relatively isolated and had no organizational representation except through the staff of one or another local community center. They did benefit from the special interest shown them by the offices of Congressman Philip Burton and Assemblyman John Burton. Others were in clubs of elderly people—either in churches, park and recreation centers, or union retiree groups. A number of churches and related service organizations provided social services to the elderly, but no grassroots organizations that engaged in civic action for the elderly were evident.

Most of the elderly were the Irish, Italians, Germans, and Russians who had remained in the Greater Mission after the exodus of their children to other, "better" parts of San Francisco or farther south into suburban San Mateo County. Some of them were veterans of San Francisco's militant maritime labor movement of the 1930s including the 1934 General Strike that demonstrated working-class power in a way matched by few other strikes of that period. Others had worked in the building trades and brought the conservatism of their trades with them into community life.

Other Anglos

The remaining Anglos of the Mission were more likely to be found in the neighborhoods surrounding the Inner Mission—Potrero Hill, Bernal Heights, Noe Valley, and beyond. They were influential in a number of civic associations, and many had a strong feeling for urban living. They included artists, professionals, blue-collar workers, and public employees.

Other Ethnic Minorities

While relatively small in number, there were other groups in the Mission to consider: Filipinos, Samoans, Native Americans, and Blacks were the most important of them. They were in churches, they were major participants in community-based agencies, they were active in multi-ethnic and multi-racial organizations, and sometimes they were in important leadership positions.

For two reasons, MCO made a special effort to reach these groups. MCO's initial leadership deeply believed that MCO should include all people of the Mission. This belief was expressed in all aspects of the work to build MCO. There was a pragmatic reason as well. Though the numbers of a particular group might be small within the Mission, their presence was important for decisions made outside the Mission. Two examples are illustrative. While there were few African-Americans in the Mission, their presence in MCO was important to key Black allies in San Francisco, where there were already tensions between Latinos and Blacks, and to getting the vote of the African-American member of the Board of Supervisors. While there were few Samoans in San Francisco, the First Samoan Congregational Church's pastor became an important advocate in his denomination's decision to fund MCO.

The Churches

The churches of the Mission reflected its diversity. Examples were numerous. Often nationality groups brought the politics of their countries of origin to the United States. Anti-Marcos Filipinos tended to be in one Catholic parish, while pro-Marcos Catholics were in another. Pro-Somoza Nicaraguans (there weren't many) were in one church, while Sandinista revolutionaries were in another. And so it went throughout the organizational life of the District, whatever the larger questions might be.

In addition to whatever they thought personally, the mainline Protestant and Roman Catholic clergy who led their churches to join MCO were deeply pastoral—concerned about the daily material and spiritual lives of their people. Some of them shared also in the prophetic tradition—wanting to challenge their people to act on the social and economic justice teachings they found in the Bible. But whether prophetic or not, pastors who led their churches to consider membership in MCO cared deeply about the life circumstances of their people and the neighborhoods in which they lived, even if that caring was limited to acts of charity. In many cases it was possible to extend their pastoral care to a larger vision—as long as that vision wasn't couched in language they viewed as liberal or radical. If an Evangelical pastor understood membership in MCO as a service for his people, and a liberal Protestant saw it as action on the social gospel, and a Catholic saw it either as an expression of charity, liberation theology, or the social justice Catholic encyclicals, it was all right with me. I thought that out of the action they would experience in MCO, some new theological thinking would take place. And if it didn't, that was okay too.

The Catholic Church in the Mission was the clear majority church. Some of the pastors were on the fringes of social action in the community; others had contacts in city hall, reflecting the old Irish and Italian connections of the community—and the fact that the Irish and Italians now dominated the Democratic Party in San Francisco. These pastors also related to the newer Latino developments in the churches through Latino "círculos," and these, in turn, related to the Catholic Council for the Spanish Speaking.

Catholic churches in the Inner Mission usually were predominantly Latino, but older Anglos often held key leadership positions—especially when the pastor was an older Anglo who was fairly conservative. Pastors and the old guard who had once been the dominant ethnic group in the parish held on to control of budgets and other important aspects of parish life. The newer Latinos in these parishes developed their own groups, such as the Guadalupe Societies and other "círculos," and this was sanctioned by the church.

In a church like St. Peter's, where Pastor Jim Casey and the young, liberation-theology-oriented Fr. Jim Hagan were the clergy leadership, the picture was different. The Anglos there were much friendlier to the new Latino presence. Yet even here, a group of older, conservative, Anglo members opposed MCO. As you got further out from the Inner Mission, the percentage of Anglos increased—that was especially true in Bernal Heights, Potrero Hill, Noe Valley, and at St. John's, which was really on the edge of the Mission.

Each Catholic parish had its own character, and an organizer who failed to learn and understand it missed opportunities and made mistakes. Begin with the pastor, who was the main figure unless he chose not to be. Pastors had different theological orientations, political views, social orientations, and administrative styles, and these weren't necessarily in a consistent pattern. A relatively authoritarian pastor might also have strong, positive views on economic and racial justice. A more passive, "laissez-faire" pastor might be more conservative politically. In almost every Catholic parish there was a multiplicity of groups, each of which had its own leadership and character. In the same parish, a Father's Club might be very conservative, while the Parish Council might be liberal. While Catholics were supposed to attend the church of their geographic area ("parish"), not all did. Some gravitated to a church because their particular ethnic group was dominant, because of the pastor, because of the parish school, or for any of a number of other reasons.

The mainline Protestant churches were still overwhelmingly Anglo. Each of the local churches had a unique character shaped by: the denomination of which it was a member; the history and social character of the congregation; the particular interests of key lay leaders; and the interests and theological orientation of the pastor. Some pastors were looking for ways to keep what they had, hoping to stem the exodus of members from the neighborhood to the Outer Mission or beyond. Others were looking at ways to relate to the new Latino population, including offering bilingual services, service programs, church-related schools, and participation in local issue activities.

In both Catholic and mainline Protestant churches, we found that "social action" or "social concerns" or "peace and justice" committees weren't necessarily the places to seek participants in MCO. Often, the people in these committees had global interests (war and peace, global economic and social justice, and national immigration policy among them). But more to the point, they were often relatively uninterested in local community concerns and isolated from most of the members of their church. While this was not always the case, it was common enough to be worth noting.

The newer Evangelical and Pentecostal churches, some still storefronts, others in developed church buildings, were Latino, usually a specific nationality, and conducted their services and business in Spanish. Their theological orientation was other-worldly; ideologically they were conservative, but they had practical concerns for their members' lives, including education, immigration, and job and housing concerns. They had institutional interests as well for joining MCO. A pastor might be drawn into MCO because of parishioners' problems with landlords or immigration papers or some other issue. For one pastor, it was a zoning issue affecting whether he could expand his church or not. Once in, he learned that his members might get jobs through the MCO Jobs and Employment Committee. When they did, he joked about becoming a radical (he didn't).

Founding the Mission

Coalition Organization

For the organizer, a community convention (or congress) is at once a dull and tedious process and a theatric production. Much of the work is standard and routine, but the convention is the big annual meeting of the organization and makes its major decisions. If successful, it brings together, in one very large meeting, representatives of all the segments of a neighborhood's life. At the convention, the delegates decide upon basic policy and elect the people to implement it. A series of preconvention committees prepare for the meeting. I had organized a major convention of the Black community in Kansas City, Missouri, that was attended by about one thousand delegates and alternates.

At weekly meetings, TMCO's Steering Committee, made up of representatives of each of the affiliated organizations, heard reports from the preconvention platform, nominations, and arrangements committees, and acted as the preconvention Constitution and Bylaws Committee. It devoted a major portion of its meeting time to issues of governance for the newly forming organization. The constitution and bylaws proposed to the founding convention included a structure that was implicit in the way TMCO was organizing: a federation of existing and newly formed organizations that together expressed the values and interests of the people of the Mission.

The structure presented to, and adopted by, the founding convention had these elements:

An annual convention, designed for maximum participation, of delegates and alternates from already existing and newly formed organizations, that elected MCO's officers, adopted platforms on issues, and adopted and later modified a constitution and bylaws. Each participating organization named its own convention delegates. Delegation size ranged from 20 percent of the membership of a small organization (defined as ten or more people who regularly met) to fifteen delegates for organizations with more than two hundred members.

Monthly meetings of a smaller number of delegates from member groups, at which policy decisions could be made between conventions.

A large (thirty-five positions) Steering Committee, elected by the convention, that conducted ongoing business and coordinated organizational campaigns. These were the officers elected at the convention plus committee chairs, who were appointed by the president but had to be confirmed at the monthly delegates' meeting.

A strong elected president who, along with five elected "executive vice presidents," key committee chairs (some of whom were elected members of the Steering Committee), and leaders of key member organizations, were the major MCO leaders.

Committees on housing, jobs and employment, education, police-community relations, and anything else that affected the lives of the people of the Mission, that were open to anyone in a member organization.

What the new structure meant in actual operation became the source of internal conflict. This question will reappear in this text, as it reappeared periodically in debates within MCO.

Preconvention Tensions

As the founding convention drew near, there were political problems in policy and resolutions. There were deep conflicts on two issues: the organization's stance toward Model Cities, and its position on tenant organizing and rent strikes. In both cases the centrists wanted conciliatory language. Delegations influenced by the Progressive Labor Party (PL) were pushing the most militant rhetoric and radical program. By this time, PL had indirectly joined TMCO by way of three organizations its people led; their base was expanding in the Mission. (Because political parties couldn't join MCO, PL was not formally a member.) Handling this conflict was the first key job of the organization's inner leadership circle. From years of dealing with conflicts of this type in the student and civil rights movements, I had some ideas, which I discussed with MCO's leaders. We developed a strategy which was to characterize the leadership's relationship to those both to its left and to its right.

To deal with PL on the left, the leadership decided to adopt most of the PL platform because the issues and interests represented in that platform were precisely those that TMCO's key leaders wanted to work on: tenant rights, unemployment, police-community relations, and education among them. However, the leadership reformulated PL's language in such a way that the resolutions could be supported by a majority of the delegates at the convention.

At a tense lunch meeting at Bruno's Restaurant, located on Mission Street in the heart of the Inner Mission, PL's John Ross and one of his associates met Ben Martinez and Elba Tuttle to discuss the coming convention and their resolutions. I was there as well. Vito Saccheri, a cook at Bruno's, shuttled back and forth between the grill and our table. Martinez and Tuttle offered this proposition: Bring your resolutions to the preconvention platform committee. We will support their substance, but not their current language. They will be adopted. If you choose not to go along with compromise language, we will inform the grassroots groups in whose name you claim to speak that you are more interested in making noise at the convention than solving community problems.

The threat was not an idle one, because the people in TMCO leadership who were dealing with PL also had the confidence of the emerging leaders in the tenants' organizations and block clubs that were joining TMCO. If PL was interested in promoting the substance of its resolutions, its leaders would have to go along; if, on the other hand, it was using the resolutions to divide grassroots people from leaders it viewed as sellouts, that would become clear as well.

Bruno's was a classic neighborhood Italian restaurant. Historically a gathering place for the many trade union leaders whose headquarters were in or near the Mission, it had become a hangout for TMCO's leaders as well. Because we were regulars at Bruno's, and owner Virgil Dardi was already friendly, he didn't mind his cook taking breaks to be a community leader. At lunch, dinner, and long after formal meetings were adjourned at 9:30 or 10:00 at night, TMCO's active members gathered at Bruno's or Kerry's, also in the heart of the Mission. These comfortable, low-pressure (you could nurse a cup of coffee or soda for hours) neighborhood hangouts were important to building the social glue that held TMCO together; they were the headquarters for TMCO's informal business and my "educationals." In these informal conversations, I could talk about political theory, strategy, tactics, values, and whatever else seemed appropriate to broaden the worldview of those present, or elaborate on what had happened at a meeting, negotiation, or action earlier that day.

To deal with centrists and liberals who might oppose agreements struck with the PL people, MCO leaders argued that if the interests of the lower-income groups that made up the majority of the community were not recognized by the convention, we would not be able to expect their participation—and the centrists and liberals wanted them to be involved. Further, we argued that we could deal in an effective and responsible way with issues of landlord-tenant relations, which the liberals and centrists wanted to steer clear of because it might involve militant mass action, like public embarrassment of landlords or rent strikes. The choice was clear. Finally, Martinez and his core leaders argued that if MCO didn't work with them, low-income people would follow the leadership of PL, since it would be the only organization advocating for, and acting in, their interests.

On Model Cities, the leadership's position was relatively moderate. Debate on the Model Cities program and guidelines did not follow any predictable political lines. Here the issue was over what language our leadership should employ with the mayor. The leadership wanted flexibility. As things turned out, the majority of the delegates wanted strong language. The memory of urban renewal was too recent for them to want anything less than a specific mandate to MCO's elected leadership. As a struggle over Model Cities later emerged, these strong words would become a reference point for those who didn't want to compromise.

■ The Role of Externally Funded, Nonprofit, Community-Based Agencies

Another issue ran through the debates that preceded the convention. It was subtle, but of deep importance for the future of the organization. A number of funded community-based agencies (the so-called nonprofits) participated as member organizations in TMCO. Unlike long-established nonprofit service organizations like the Boys Club, YMCA, Catholic Charities, nonprofit hospitals, and others, they were often the recent creations of Poverty Program or foundation grants. Their paid executive-level leadership often had an activist orientation. They were vehicles for newly emerging talent in minority communities. Some of the representatives of community agencies began insisting on language that would make TMCO "support" the activities and programs of member organizations. What they sought to do was limit TMCO to a support role. They were beginning to see that a strong federation of organizations, with a constantly growing base of its own in grassroots groups organized by its staff, along with an increasingly active clergy and church-related organizations, could become their rival for funds and also represent the community to city hall and to other institutional decision makers.

On the one hand, these agencies simply provide services and may be viewed as social service organizations; but on the other hand, they are political organizations. Their funds come from political bodies. To obtain these scarce funds, they need political allies, and they need politically skillful executive directors to win support from these allies. And politicians ask as well as give. If one receives from the politicians, then one must deliver for them. Votes and campaign workers are what the politician is most interested in from a minority, low-to-moderate-income neighborhood. These community-based agencies, then, become the brokers for the neighborhood.

Because they are dependent on outside funding, and because this money is political in its distribution, and because politicians rely on these agencies to manage conflict that could emerge from a constituency that is oppressed or discriminated against, these agencies can have what Alinsky called a "welfare colonial" role. Just as neocolonialism substituted a new class of local administrators for the direct presence of the colonial administrator, so, Alinsky argued, welfare colonialism in the U.S. created a group of local people who kept the lid on ghetto and barrio neighborhoods. An agency could be rhetorically and tactically militant but do nothing to substantively challenge the status quo.

Further, because the amount of money available is nowhere near enough to solve the problem(s) community-based agencies seek to address, this funding process causes endless fights in these neighborhoods. The agencies created by foundations and government to administer funds during the height of the War on Poverty became rivals for continued and expanded funding. The inadequacies of the agencies, often staffed by good people, led many residents to view them with suspicion, even though the constraints at work were beyond the agencies' control. The effect of the whole set of relationships established in this process undermines real people power. Foundations may also play a domesticating role as they seek to channel protest into acceptable mainstream programs. Once an agency is dependent on external funding, particularly if it has little or no popular base in the community, it is highly unlikely to support larger social change.

But the problem is not limited to a conservatizing or domesticating role. It is replicated with militant or radical agencies, but in a different way. Their funding sponsors may support radical programs and militant rhetoric and action, but the broad base of support required for significant social change is lacking here as well. Radical policy and analysis and militant rhetoric or action don't necessarily build people power, though they may satisfy a nominally radical funding agency or a wealthy, ideologically left-wing donor.

Adding to the sources of tension, continued funding in most instances requires of the agency that it distinguish itself from other claimants for funds. The process encourages invidious distinctions, rivalry, and competition where mutual support and cooperation are called for to solve significant problems.

While the central leadership made clear that MCO's function would not be to administer social service programs, the community agencies could not be sure. They sought a typical "community council" approach—an organization that would simply be a vehicle of communication for its members, incapable of developing an internal life and political base of its own.

The question of base is critical to a mass organization. If it is based primarily on externally funded agencies—whether their funds come from government, foundations, or corporations—and their program beneficiaries or presumed beneficiaries, then the issues that characterize the organization will generally be the problems of legislation, guidelines, funding, and administration faced by these agencies. Both social service agencies and community development agencies have to operate within such constraints. And those agencies that engage in "advocacy" often speak for people who could and should be organized independently to speak on their own behalf.

On the other hand, if a mass organization is based in churches, block and tenant associations, the unemployed, seniors, youth clubs, parent groups, neighborhood merchant associations, and other voluntary associations—whose funds come primarily from their members—then a very different set of issues will define the organization's agenda.

No federal or foundation programs provided for rent strikes or job-related sit-ins; nor did they envisage hundreds of residents marching on City Hall to stop urban renewal or to stop a highway from destroying a neighborhood. It was precisely this latter agenda that people like Knotts, Tuttle, and Martinez had in mind when they started TMCO. At least in their early thinking, they had little idea that the new neighborhood coalition would become involved in the details of administering the Model Cities program. No doubt they wanted to control its policies and character, but that was far different from its daily administration.

The externally funded agencies were a double-edged sword. Their very presence in TMCO because of Model Cities inhibited the leadership in its effort to develop a wider base of new constituencies. At the same time, had they quit TMCO at the very fragile period of its initiation, the organization might have collapsed. Certainly the Mission Area Community Action Board, Inc. (MACABI, the Poverty Program) and the Organization for Business, Education and Community Advancement (OBECA) provided critical resources for TMCO, and later MCO. MACABI provided VISTA volunteers and assigned two of its field organizers to my supervision. OBECA gave Ben Martinez, its community liaison worker, almost free reign to spend his time as MCO's president. In each case, leaders with earlier experience in the Community Service Organization (CSO), Alinsky's earlier statewide organizing effort among Mexican-Americans, recognized the limitations of their programs and sought ways to strengthen an independent organizing effort. MCO could not have been born without these more visionary agency executive directors.

Implicit in TMCO's preconvention structure and the platform positions taken by most of the externally funded, nonprofit, community-based agencies was the view that TMCO should not develop a base in the churches, block clubs, tenant organizations, and other independent groupings that might move the organization into the role of primary voice for the neighborhood on issues that affected general life there. As we shall see, MCO did grow to do just that, not without creating friction with some of the neighborhood agencies. At this point, however, given the fact that Model Cities was the initial program bringing these groups together, it was impossible not to expect these agencies to take an active role. Model Cities, after all, was the new source of federal program money for all of them. They legitimately had a concern and interest. If TMCO was going to be the voice on Model Cities, they wanted to know that it would not usurp their role as the dispenser of funds in the community and, in some cases, as political broker between "downtown" and the neighborhood.

The Role of Unions

Like agencies that felt threatened by what TMCO might become, public employee unions might also consider a strong organizational voice for the beneficiaries of public services (public schools, neighborhood parks, public health services all being likely examples) to be a potential threat to the union's relationship with its members' employers. On the other hand, the union could recognize such a voice as a potential ally with whom it might be able to make members' work more meaningful, and the services they provided more appropriate, effective, efficient, and of higher quality. With the help of such an ally, the public agency's budget might be made more adequate to the need it was supposed to meet. The power of both the union and the community could be enhanced so that each could better serve the interests of its members and those it served.

Other unions, notably those in the building trades, wanted MCO's community voice so that Model Cities funds (which they erroneously understood as being primarily for construction) could come into San Francisco. But they were nervous about being pressured to increase the number of racial and ethnic minorities in the crafts. When a formerly powerless social group gains power, it presents new proposals to those whose decisions affect its interests. The question for those who already have some power is whether they will oppose such new entries to the bargaining arena or welcome them, recognizing that adjustments will have to be made to take the new voice into account. In the U.S., craft unions had a history of excluding the unskilled, Blacks and other minorities, and women from their ranks, and opposing equality of opportunity and affirmative action. But the example is not limited to these historically conservative unions.

An industrial, service, or public sector union might organize all workers in an industry, whatever their race, ethnicity, gender, or occupation, and adopt progressive policies in the political arena. Nonetheless the union might be opposed to effective organization among the consumers or beneficiaries of whatever product or service its members' employers provided—whether they be private, nonprofit, or public. The profitability of their firm or industry, or the budget for their particular public or nonprofit organization, would be more important to them than an effective voice for consumers.

As things played out in the Mission, the San Francisco teachers' union departed from the usual course.

I hoped that unions would at least support if not join MCO. I grew up with the idea that unions were a good thing. Nothing in my college education or the student movement persuaded me otherwise. At the same time, as the Student Nonviolent Coordinating Committee (and I) learned in the civil rights movement, most of organized labor was deeply intertwined with the Democratic Party's established leadership. I brought the idea that a balancing act was required into my MCO work.

Within the MCO, leaders like Abel Gonzalez and Herman Gallegos, pastors of key churches, and people like Bill Grace and Dave Knotts also had hopes that labor could be an ally. We worked at making that happen.

New versus Old Organizations

Every organizer must deal with the relationship of the new and old action organizations; it is difficult to effectively work without some support from what already exists. On the other hand, most of the existing organizations have a focus that is too specific, or a constituency that is too narrow, to build the power needed to deal with major issues. Further, many of these organizations are simply not set up for that purpose. Balancing the new and old took up a good deal of time in the beginnings of MCO. The existing social and service organizations had to be bypassed because action on issues was not their purpose, but they had to be involved because their participation was needed to give legitimacy to MCO.

In my view, our job was to simultaneously build the structure that included everyone and, within that structure, build a new constituency that was not dependent on external funding and that would democratically control the mass organization and begin to hold accountable the agencies that were funded by outside sources. Building the new constituency would take place around the immediate and specific issues that organizers found as they went door to door, church to church, block to block, school to school, and association to association in the neighborhood. Grievances against city government, the school district, landlords, employers, cheating merchants, and others would provide the issues around which new organizing would take place. Out of the new organizing would come the central base of the coalition. And, out of the churches that became involved as their members won benefits from the organization would come an additional base of legitimacy and participation.

Our immediate organizing problem was that the founding convention was too close for us to be able to move into action on issues and at the same time organize the convention. Our compromise was to find out what the issues were, promise people that they would be worked on after the convention, and, by getting them into the excitement of a community convention, try to overcome their suspicion that this was just another talk-talk operation.

Further, we had to convince many people that there was in fact something that could be done to change living conditions in the Mission. Behind the mask of apathy, every organizer knows, is a backlog of experience that leads people to conclude that there is nothing they can do to "beat city hall." In this kind of setting, the organizer is a hope peddler, agitating for the idea that if people come together they can have power and they can do something about the conditions in which they live. In making this argument, we had the advantage that activists and clergy in the neighborhood supported Knotts and Tuttle. Their past participation in issue battles gave them the credentials to convince people that the convention was going to be more than a talk shop.

Top Leadership

Another problem was posed by nominations for Steering Committee offices. I initially argued, and the core leadership agreed, that a large top leadership body, numbering as many as thirty-five to forty people, was essential for several reasons:

> We had to have room at the top for all key groups to be represented, including both the organized forces of the neighborhood and the varied ethnic, geographic, age, racial, and interest groups.

> A large leadership body would allow the organization to lose elected leaders without sacrificing its effectiveness. Since there had not been an opportunity to test leadership in action, I anticipated that some leaders would fall away as MCO's character as an action organization developed.

> Finally, a large leadership body provided the opportunity to train more leaders.

These arguments flew in the face of traditional wisdom that argues for a small, efficient group as the top leadership body. To answer this objection, the Constitution and Bylaws Committee proposed a group of five executive vice presidents who, along with the president, could be an emergency body to meet and discuss an important issue. This group could convene the large elected leadership with little effort—five phone calls by each member of the small group could reach and brief everyone about the issue and get them to a meeting. Finally, this group would serve as a planning body for the Steering Committee.

A second major Nominations and Constitution/Bylaws issue had to do with ethnic and racial vice presidencies. The core leadership proposed numerous vice presidencies. Much of the division of the community was along ethnic, racial, and interest lines. It was a fact that Mexican-Americans tended to head most of the funded agencies of the Mission. Many of the activists in the Mission saw politics in terms of nationality and/or race. In recognition of this, it was essential to have ethnic vice presidents who could give each of these groups a voice in MCO's top leadership body. This problem had to be solved before other interests could be effectively pursued. Adding insult to injury, in the view of some, was the fact that Nicaraguans and Salvadorans far outnumbered other Latinos in the District, but were in hardly any key positions in existing agencies.

Who was to represent the ethnic minorities? Tuttle cut the issue as grass roots vs. middle class, and she demanded the right to fill three of the top executive slots. Puerto Rican herself, at the time she saw ethnicity as irrelevant to the more basic issues that she posed. For her, the grass roots were the people whose problems the organization could focus on. The main threat she saw to the interests of these grass roots was a combination of the agency people and the middle class.

Naming the other major executive slots was Abel Gonzalez, an archrival to Tuttle in the Mission. Gonzalez looked at Mission community politics in a very different way. The object was to develop a center of power through which funding had to go; he was building that center of power in Centro Social Obrero. With programs that would serve needs of the community and patronage that could be developed through hired staff, such a center would be able to demand more from the city, because it would be able to deliver politically. At election time, Gonzalez's forces would line up behind a candidate who made commitments to the Mission. Indeed, after primary elections, the victor would court Abel Gonzalez's support, even if he had supported a rival in the primary—Gonzalez had get-out-the-vote troops, and any nominee wanted to benefit from their work. If one were to summarize these views, Tuttle's approach was issue-oriented politics, and Gonzalez's was ethnic, ward-style politics.

Other key interest groups in the Mission were represented on the slate of officers presented by the Nominating Committee to the founding convention. Heading the list, as the nominee for president, was Ben Martinez, a delegate from the Catholic Council for the Spanish Speaking as well as an OBECA/Arriba Juntos employee. This nomination assured links to both the Gallegos network and the Catholic Church.

Through this period, I was raising only one question. Granting that nominations had to be representative, I wanted to see where potential nominees would stand on a mass action approach to the issues that would emerge when we began organizing after the convention. It was clear that within a given ethnic group there could be both an agency-oriented representative and an issue-oriented, people-power representative.

As an Anglo organizer, the situation presented me with some difficulties. But Cesar Chavez was clearly cutting the issue of Anglo organizers in his organizing among the farmworkers and making them a legitimate part of the movement. That gave me a handle, especially in dealing with Mexican-Americans who identified strongly with Chavez.

The issue of ethnic representation was resolved by nominating people from ethnic organizations or agencies, and others from block club, tenant, religious, or other issue-type organizations. To challenge the Nominating Committee's list of candidates then became difficult, and potential criticism was neutralized. If, for example, a nominee for vice president was a working-class, Nicaraguan Catholic layman who wanted to work across nationality lines, and someone wanted a middle-class nationalist representing Nicaraguans on the Steering Committee, s/he couldn't complain, because the complaint wouldn't be supported by the large majority of the organization.

Anglo Activists

TMCO's active Anglos, both liberal and centrist, had a good deal of organizational experience. They did not identify with the Mission's remaining Irish, Italian, and other ethnic organizations. Many had ties to citywide politics and politicians. They disliked talk of confrontation, conflict, and power. Their general view was to try to cooperate with the city because the city government was trying to do something good for the neighborhood. Power and self-interest were not major components of the way they thought about politics. "Reasoned discourse" and "competency" were their favored terms.

Further, they were either unsympathetic or hostile to the kind of ethnic/poverty politics that was going on in preconvention TMCO. At this stage of organization, no defections could be afforded, and it was a difficult organizing task to keep these groups in.

Knotts and I used two major arguments with the Anglos. One was that if they wanted their views represented, they would have to be in the arena of discussion and debate; this was tied to their hostility to John Ross and PL. A democratic organization was going to be open to the left; if the liberals and center wanted to debate him, the forum was in the organization. Given growing Latino participation and the fact that TMCO was the only avenue of access to the Latinos for many of these Anglo groups, the argument to stay in was persuasive. Further, leaving TMCO would contradict their purpose of achieving an interracial organization in the Mission.

Avoiding Splits

Many of the early efforts to keep people in TMCO might be viewed in retrospect as a waste of time. Quite the opposite was the case. A coalition that has not yet established itself and its ability to represent people and mobilize them for action cannot afford to have people getting off before the train has left the station. Many of the people with whom we spent a good deal of time turned out to have no real constituency in the community, but they had access to politicians and news media. Time and the development of new leadership took care of them. Either they developed follow-ings in the community or they were displaced by rivals who challenged their roles as representatives of a particular point of view or constituency. In the absence of alternative leadership, however, organizers had to deal with who was there.

In retrospect, the liberal, non-church-related Anglos who were interested in neighborhood issues were never successfully recruited to TMCO, except through its Planning Committee (which dealt with land use and related matters). Their absence from the organization is explained by their general disagreement with ethnic politics on the one hand and their distaste for power struggles and confrontation on the other.

Remember that TMCO was still less than a year old. It was ad hoc in char-acter. Until its founding convention, scheduled in the late summer to take place in October 1968, it was unclear whether many people would even pay attention. While TMCO's letterhead of organizations and leaders was impressive, and broad enough to gain recognition from Mayor Alioto, that only assured the organization a role in Model Cities planning. It was sufficient neither to win desired veto power nor to build a successful mass action organization that could address the interests of the Mission District.

Summing Up the Preconvention Period

This picture emerged as the date of the founding convention approached: At the center of TMCO were its organizing staff, including Dave Knotts and me, and a key group of leaders, particularly Elba Tuttle and Ben Martinez. Surrounding the center were key people who held, in effect, veto power over major decisions: Gonzalez, Gallegos, and, to a lesser extent, Alex Zermeno, Adan Juarez, and Joan Bordman in MACABI. Barely developing within the organization was a base that identified primarily with TMCO, as opposed to one of the long-standing organizations in the community.

Another twenty or so people in secondary leadership positions made up the rest of the core of the organization. Of these, few were employees or members of boards of directors of funded programs; some were clergy. Clearly the pastors' institutional interest was their churches, and their pastoral and prophetic concerns were with their members and how to make them effective Christians engaged in community life.

Issues of poverty and racism were high on the agendas of the social gospel Protestants and Catholics influenced by the tradition of justice-oriented encyclicals that began in 1891 with Pope Leo XIII's Rerum Novarum. The other clergy were more cautious about civic participation. But whatever their theological orientation, the clergy who became involved in TMCO were pastoral—they cared deeply about the lives of their people. Some of the lay leaders worked for community-based agencies in program or policy positions. Others worked in "regular" jobs—as carpenter, realtor, cook, and laborer.

It was this group that moved the organization toward its first convention. Every effort was made to insure that key groups of the community were given some role and recognition in the convention. The complexities of the community were reflected in the number of roles created to give this recognition. If a Catholic gave the invocation, a Protestant gave the benediction. If he was a mainline Protestant, then somewhere else there was a Pentecostal. It was similar with the ethnic groups, though there was still a problem of "over-representation" of Mexican-Americans in top organizational slots. By the time the convention rolled around, most of these problems were ironed out. Race, ethnicity, and religion were largely eliminated as underlying tensions of the convention.

Two other problems existed and were not resolved. Progressive Labor continued to look for issues that it could raise at the convention, to make itself the vanguard force for the grassroots constituency. And young people were not adequately involved in preconvention plans. The second of these errors led to near disaster on the convention floor. That is the next chapter of the story.

MCO Birth Pains

An organizer imagines that, just as the founding convention after the American Revolution gave birth to a new nation, so a community convention will give birth to a new voice for a previously voiceless constituency. And that voice retains its legitimacy through regular conventions that represent a broad base of the people for whom the organization claims to speak.

Community Conventions

On Friday, October 4, 1968, about eight hundred delegates and alternates from sixty-six organizations met at the Centro Social Obrero hall to form MCO—the Mission Coalition Organization (the "T" for "Temporary" was dropped). The hall was fully wired with headsets at each delegate's and alternate's seat, courtesy of Pacific Bell—the local phone company—to provide simultaneous English-Spanish translation. (The simultaneous translation offered a bit of humor to the proceedings. Many of the delegates were bilingual. They would listen to speakers with one ear and translation on their headsets with the other. When they thought the translation was in error or missed a nuance, they would raise "point of order" objections to the proceedings. Only skillful chairing kept the meeting from being bogged down in the translation process!)

An organizer looking at a convention of this type would imagine it to be completed in three or so hours. It expresses, to a great degree, the democratic thinking of "the community." It is the first time that so many representatives from so many groups within an area (actually several neighborhoods, in the MCO case) gather to determine what their goals will be for the year and who is to implement steps toward those goals. Ideally, the convention is highlighted by a major resolution declaring war on one of the community's most bitter foes—a recalcitrant school superintendent, a discriminatory employer with a large facility in the district, a major property management firm that handles the worst slums of the neighborhood, a mayor who refuses to deal with the community in good faith—any of these would be good targets.

With appropriate "Whereas" and "Be It Therefore Resolved" statements, the community names its adversaries and vows action against them. By and large, consensus characterizes most of the resolutions that are passed. In some cases, preconvention committees may submit majority and minority reports to the floor. Constitution or bylaw amendments may be presented and vigorously debated, but it is unlikely that the report of the Constitution and Bylaws Committee will be rejected. Similarly, the Nominating Committee will present a slate of candidates, in some cases more than one for an office, and it is from these nominees that the winners will most likely emerge—though it is also possible to be nominated from the floor by petition—in MCO's case, fifteen delegate names were needed, and they had to come from three or more organizations.

The convention typically ratifies a series of agreements, negatively characterized as "deals," made in preconvention committees. It is within the committees that compromises are made, power relations among the various groups tested, leadership recognized. Such is the case in a neighborhood organization or in the conventions of major unions, political parties, or any other kind of democratic organization. In the committee meetings, and prior to and after meetings in informal discussions, a process of reaching agreements emerges. Ideally, each of the preconvention committees should be a miniature convention, except that groups with particular interests in particular outcomes will play a disproportionate role in deliberations most affecting them. The key forces and points of view necessary to make the organization viable should be represented in these committees and should use the formal committee meetings and informal pre- and post-committee discussions or caucuses to work out whatever agreements are essential for the continued cooperation of the members of the organization. In some cases a formal minority report might be presented from a committee—but it too is part of an agreed-upon process.

Bitter and organizationally disabling floor fights do not emerge if there has been an adequate, democratic preconvention process. The democracy of the organization is not demonstrated by the arguments on the convention floor, but by the operation of a principle of majority rule and minority rights and widespread member participation in the preconvention period. The members seek resolutions and candidacies that will allow all of them to work together in the coming year. It is only under severe external pressures, or when preconvention democratic procedures are violated, or when a group with a strong interest in a convention outcome refuses to participate in the preconvention committees, that negative floor fights begin to emerge. When they continue regularly, there lurks in the wings the possibility that the organization will split, because a major group might leave if its views are not given recognition by the organization as a whole. Compromise, in this perspective, is not a dirty word but a constructive recognition that we need a big tent under which we can all work together. On the other hand, clear majority and minority reports to a convention allow for vigorous debate before the body as a whole.

The fundamental guarantee against bitter divisiveness is recognition by the members of the organization that it is in their self-interest to stick together and create a powerful instrument to defend and advance their interests and values. Unlike its predecessor the Mission Council on Redevelopment, which formed in the face of an urban renewal threat to the Mission, MCO was born without a looming, visible, threat to the interests of the community. Only those who thought that Model Cities might be urban renewal with another name saw a threat. Thus nothing from the outside was pushing people toward cooperation and compromise.

MCO was born without a riot, a clear urban renewal bulldozer threat, a precipitating action, such as Rosa Parks's refusal to give up her seat on the bus in Montgomery, Alabama, an already existing social movement, or any other major rallying point that might have galvanized the community. Quite the contrary, the birth of the organization resulted from an invitation from the mayor to participate in the Model Cities program; though this wasn't the mayor's intention, MCO's leaders created a mass action organization in response to his invitation. But the members of MCO who participated in the founding convention didn't yet fully appreciate the implications. Only when MCO actually moved into nonviolent direct action would they.

The preconvention process was in many ways less than ideal. Participation in preconvention committees was relatively low. Key organized blocs were represented at most stages, and recognized in resolutions and nominations. But no major controversies emerged that required compromise except for Model Cities and housing resolutions. A major accomplishment was that church, Poverty Program (MACABI), Obrero, grassroots, and other key groups were represented in the list of nominees presented to the convention.

■ MCO's Founding Convention Almost Falls Apart

Our first indication of trouble came from a warning given us by a friendly MACABI staff member. She told TMCO President Ben Martinez that the youth-serving, community-based agency called Mission Rebels was unhappy with the way things were going and was planning something disruptive for convention night. We were in a panic, wondering whether to have the police or muscleman bodyguards there or not.

The convention gavel sounded at 7:15 p.m. and the meeting was called to order. The Credentials Committee gave its report; it was adopted without controversy—the delegates and alternates from sixty-six organizations were duly seated. The hall was filled. We had the makings of a solid organization. The chairman moved the body to the Constitution and Bylaws report. About this time, the Mission Rebels made their grand entry. Led by their African-American executive director, Rev. Jesse James, they occupied the chairman's platform, took over the microphone, and stopped the proceedings. They were roundly booed by most of the delegates, but they did not surrender. James attempted an impassioned plea aimed at showing the people they were being sold out by this "phony organization."

The confrontation was on the edge of violence when a specially installed long-distance phone hookup rang and Cesar Chavez, leader of the growing farmworkers' union, was on the line to give the convention keynote address from his hospital bed. Chavez was probably the only person who could upstage James—and James knew it. (Chavez had just ended one of his lengthy fasts and was in the hospital recovering.) A number of us used the occasion of the Chavez remarks to go into a caucus room with James and some of the Rebels. Roberto Vargas, then Mission District Brown Beret coordinator and later cultural attaché to the U.S. for Nicaragua's first Sandinista government, managed to convince the Rebels to leave the stage. Ben Martinez, Elba Tuttle, Herman Gallegos, and others tried to arrive at a common understanding in the caucus room. However, it was clear that nothing could be done. When Chavez was finished, some of James's supporters came to the caucus room and told him that the meeting was resuming. James returned to the stage and microphone. But this time Herman Gallegos upstaged him in a move that saved the meeting.

Gallegos was serving as parliamentarian for the convention. He stepped to the microphone and began an exchange with James based on the theme of brotherhood and mutual respect that had been central to Chavez's speech. James had to agree that the people of the community needed to work together. Once they agreed, Gallegos extended his hand and James shook it. The convention, now delayed by well over an hour, resumed. But the meeting had been shaken. To get things moving again, the delegates suspended the rules to allow the Rebels to make last-minute nominations from the floor for MCO offices.

Adding unintended humor to the Rebels' challenge, one of their delegates said he could prove that the coalition was controlled from "outside the neighborhood" because one of the delegations came from the upper-middle-class suburb Los Gatos, thirty-some miles south of San Francisco. Not a Spanish speaker, he was unaware that "los gatos" means "the cats," which was the name of a Mission youth group. When he said this, great laughter erupted from the Spanish speakers.

The hour was late, and because we were so far behind schedule, all platform (issue) resolutions were postponed for one month. The three hours planned for the meeting had already passed before the Platform Committee could even give its report. The Rebels ruckus ruled out completing the convention's agenda at one meeting. Regular working people were leaving the building before the recess was called. I feared that if the number of delegates was radically diminished, the remaining few would be activists who would adopt positions that put MCO way out of touch with the people who were its base—with the result that the organization wouldn't see them again.

◼ Loyal Opposition or Destructive Disruption?

In preconvention work, the organizing staff and leadership had carefully informed all potentially dissident groups of deadlines, procedures, meetings, and other convention requirements. This was done precisely to eliminate any legitimacy to claims they might make that they were excluded from the development of the organization. Yet the Rebels, joined by Progressive Labor and a couple of other youth delegations, about 10 percent of the delegates on the floor, acted as if they were the righteous force for the community in a sea of alien interests.

How does an organizer deal with this kind of situation? In retrospect, it is clear that some errors had been made—youth contingents had not been sufficiently involved. With a limited staff and a priority of organizing the community as a whole, we could not give great attention to youth organizing. Yet we had gone out of our way to give notice to all the youth groups of the preconvention meetings and processes, and to meet individually with their key people to invite their participation. Given our errors in combination with the youth militancy that characterized the times, the possibility of disruptive factions in a mass organization should have been anticipated.

Having provided the Rebels with an opportunity equal to that of everyone else to participate in the convention, and having made sure that formal notice was given of all preconvention events, I concluded the Rebels were looking for a reason to disrupt the convention. But I may have been wrong about that. Let us assume that the Rebels did in fact believe that we were "fronting for Mayor Alioto" and that we were going to "rip the neighborhood off." And let us assume that they were wrong in this belief. The sincerity of their beliefs is not the issue. Given the nature of the emerging organization, we now had to discredit those who sought to destroy our credentials as a bona fide representative of the community. The Rebels' effort to disrupt the convention was likely, if successful, to have precisely that effect on MCO. It was in the interest of MCO therefore to widely advertise the facts of who participated in the founding convention, and of how few votes were given to the Rebels' nominees for MCO offices. This was done and had its intended effect.

▨ Gesture Politics, Symbolic Confrontations, and Real Negotiations

The Mission Rebels disruption came when "mau-mauing" was at its peak. In the moment, we weren't sure whether the convention would hold together under a youth delegation's disruptive tactics. (The term "mau-mauing" came from Tom Wolfe's *Radical Chic and Mau-Mauing the Flak Catcher*; Wolfe humorously examined the fear-generating, though nonviolent, confrontation tactics initially used by militant Blacks, then borrowed by others.)

Characteristic of this period were the phenomena of "gesture politics" and militant rhetoric. The War on Poverty seemed to have a fondness for funding youth groups that talked in radical terms and acted in a militant style. This was a national pattern; as one examined what these groups did, it became clear that they simply provided services to their members and gave them an identity in the community. And, at times, they played a political role such as that just described. MCO was to dramatically improve its relations with youth in the district, but it took a year and a half for that to happen and required bypassing most of the youth-serving agencies.

My observation is that symbolic confrontation as a style is one of the responses to powerlessness. At the peak of the urban crisis, Black, Latino, and other minority group leaders or activists were suddenly meeting face-to-face with mayors, top public administrators, and corporation executives. Often these were delegations of newly active groups from the ghettos and barrios. Lacking the experience of dealing on the basis of equality, because it had never been accorded them in the past, they had never sat across a negotiating table from a mayor or CEO and made a deal. At the same time, self-image demanded rejection of the servant-master role exemplified in the old style of dealing with "downtown." Symbolic confrontation served this purpose. Symbolic confrontation functioned to replace servant-master roles, particularly the stereotyped Uncle Tom shuffling, hat in hand, into "The Man's" offices. Perhaps it is equivalent to the violence that Frantz Fanon's classic anticolonialism book *The Wretched of the Earth* argued was necessary for the mental liberation of the colonized. (In my U.S. experience, nonviolent confrontation serves this function as well.)

When "the Establishment" was willing to simply capitulate, symbolic confrontation showed that militancy could win. When the Establishment wasn't willing to deal, the tactic confirmed its user's allegation that the power structure wasn't responsive and allowed for a walkout and continued demands. But when the Establishment wanted to bargain, often after successful mass action made bargaining necessary, the tactic was not very effective, because the back-and-forth of real negotiations was not part of it. Ironically, symbolic confrontation can become a self-fulfilling prophecy: its practitioners may force the Establishment to act just as predicted.

■ The Founding Convention: Part Two

As we feared, attendance was drastically down at the resumption of the convention, which saw as its most dramatic moments the resolutions introduced by groups related to the Progressive Labor Party and other self-styled radicals. However, Mayor Alioto's recognition of the organization and the promise of Model Cities (or its potential threat) somehow gave staff and leadership a basis to get a reasonable turnout for the meeting a month later and keep most of the member groups from pulling out of MCO.

The convention adopted a number of resolutions which indicated the interests of the district in housing, employment, education, police-community relations, city services and community maintenance, health, and the remaining range of concerns of the people of the Greater Mission District. A major dispute arose over a resolution for community control of police introduced by Progressive Labor, and it was defeated. Thirteen "non-negotiable" demands for participation in the Model Cities program were passed, with MCO veto power and funding priority to locally controlled agencies as two of the most important. Several amendments to resolutions were passed which stressed MCO's supporting member organizations rather than taking initiatives on its own. The convention went on record against the war in Vietnam and for a shift in taxes from homeowners to large corporations.

Exhausted by two huge meetings held one month apart, MCO was off to a weak start. Several important internal tensions arose at and between the two conventions: some argued for the loose-knit structure of a confederation, while others desired a federation's ability to produce central initiatives while protecting member group autonomy; some argued for a focus on "community control" rather than pressure-group politics (that is, getting existing institutions to become more responsive to neighborhood interests—what later came to be called "institutional change"); some supported rhetorical militancy (gesture politics), which would have isolated MCO from its church, labor union, and new grassroots organizations constituency, over a more moderate style that could become militant in the face of arrogant resistance to efforts at good-faith negotiations.

These were not simply abstract differences. They were also reflections of social differences within the organization—differences of age, ideology, race and ethnicity, class, and more. These tensions plagued the organization for over a year and were only resolved when MCO finally developed a working strategy in housing and employment.

The Shape of People Power:

MCO's Formal Structure

While hundreds, and at its peak thousands, of hours were put into the Mission Coalition Organization by its members and leaders, none of them were paid. Some were able to make participation in MCO part of their paid jobs (clergy, staff of nonprofits, and a few others). Most participants in MCO gave their time voluntarily. These included students, youth, retirees, "homemakers," and many people who worked full-time. All their activities took place within the organization's formal structure, which gave MCO shape and focus for the informal structure of caucuses and conversations.

In adopting a constitution, the founding convention created the formal, continuing organization. The formal structure provided the shell in which MCO's politics took place. The importance of the democratic form is that it has the mechanisms for self-correction and for holding leadership accountable to those they are elected to represent. Typically, the formal organization simply ratifies what key leaders and members in a democratic organization have informally agreed to. Various interests and views are discussed and argued in numerous informal settings—phone conversations, coffee shops, restaurants and bars, after-church social get-togethers, union hiring halls—before they are on the agenda of a formal meeting. In addition, leadership takes these interests and views into account when it formulates proposals for action. When, at any particular level, the informal process doesn't work, then the formal structure is used to resolve the question. For example, at various times in the development of issues in the MCO, sharp disagreement in committee made it impossible to reach a consensus or compromise among those with strong views on a particular issue. In such cases, the minority view had the right, through the vehicle of a "minority report" to state its case before the next level of the organization—the Steering Committee. And in some cases, a minority report went from the Steering Committee to the Delegates Council. And a member could always raise a matter from the floor of a meeting.

It was within the formal structure that MCO activities took place. Here I describe that structure so that terms have a "constitutional" reference point for the reader.

▪ Community Conventions

The annual convention was clearly MCO's most important meeting. The leadership and organizing staff made every effort to achieve widespread attendance at this gathering. Full-time staff started work on the convention two months before it convened. About a month of the organization's staff time was primarily dedicated to the convention. For two weeks prior to its convening, almost nothing else was done. For many MCO delegates and alternates, the convention was the only activity relating them to the federation. As the constitution and bylaws adopted at the founding convention provided, each convention was organized and prepared by preconvention committees: Nominating, Constitution and Bylaws, Platform, Credentials and Elections (counting close votes or secret ballots), and Arrangements. Preconvention committees were open to any member of a member organization, except for the Nominating and Credentials and Elections Committees, which had specific numbers of members who were approved by the monthly delegates' meeting.

In addition to proposals from these committees to the convention, the constitution provided for platform resolutions and nominations from the floor. A minimum number of delegates from a minimum number of organizations were required to make proposals from the floor. A petition form was available in the convention hall for such floor action and had to be filed with the temporary chair by a specific time of the meeting.

During this period, organizations in the Alinsky-tradition typically came together annually in such conventions to elect officers, amend their constitutions and bylaws if they so chose, and adopt a platform. Representation in the annual convention was based on a formula. In the case of MCO, organizations with ten to fifty members could send 20 percent of their membership as delegates; fifty-one to two hundred members, twelve delegates; over two hundred members, fifteen delegates. Large organizations frequently sent two or three delegations. For example, a church might have a choir, an usher board, and a parent-club delegation. In addition, groups could send alternates. Since a federation is interested in using the convention to show its power and maximize participation, the possibility of duplicate membership is of no great importance. It all evens out.

In MCO's history, caucuses formed prior to each of the conventions for the purpose of supporting slates for office. In the first convention, there was just one caucus and it devoted most of its attention to the top slots of the ticket. (Later, in the second convention, there was again only one caucus, though the League of United Latin American Citizens (LULAC) ran its own slate for some offices. In the third convention, when issues had heated up and known personalities were vying for top slots, there were three slates. One was organized by Tuttle, the other by Manual Larez of LULAC, and the third by Ben Martinez.)

Delegates Council

Between annual conventions was a monthly Delegates Council. It could become a mini-convention, as each member group was entitled to send five delegates to it. Typically, attendance was light, considering the number of eligible delegates. Only a hot issue in the organization brought out two to three hundred delegates, and even then probably no more than 60 percent of the organizations were represented.

Major interim issues were decided in the Delegates Council, usually on the basis of a recommendation from the Steering Committee. In addition, the Delegates Council approved nominations for committee chairpersons. The president submitted these, usually with concurrence from the rest of the officers. In the case of preconvention committees, the Delegates Council approved all the chairs. The Delegates Council approved new member organizations, who would present themselves for approval at its meetings. Finally, this body set the date and issued the call for the annual convention.

Steering Committee

Between Delegates Council meetings, on a weekly basis (except for the week of the Delegates Council meeting), was a meeting of the elected officers and appointed committee chairpersons who together formed the Steering Committee. This body of about thirty-five could be brought together quickly; its members were those most active in MCO. The primary business of the Steering Committee was presented to it either in recommendations from the action committees or in the president's report. On some occasions, a member group came directly to the committee with an issue.

Standing Committees

Over a dozen standing action committees were provided for in MCO's constitution and bylaws. While not all were active at any particular time, they had the potential to deal with the issues that might come to the organization from newly formed groups (like tenant associations) or from already existing member organizations.

The organization's platform, adopted at the convention, provided policy guidance to the committees. Committees were open to all members of member organizations. The committees tended to reflect particular constituencies of the organization. Homeowners were in Community Maintenance (potholes in streets, traffic control, abandoned buildings, homeowner loans, street beautification, and similar issues were its jurisdiction). Tenants were in the Housing Committee, which primarily dealt with tenant-landlord matters. The unemployed, those who wanted to help them get jobs, and agencies operating manpower programs were in the Jobs and Employment Committee.

The Steering Committee acted as a balancing forum for the interests of different committees that, in turn, represented different constituencies. Committees came to the officer body for approval of action recommendations. While it was rare for the Steering Committee to reject a committee's report, it was possible. Informally, the officers learned if a committee had actually been stacked. If this happened, and if the "stacking" was by an organized faction seeking to raise an issue in a way that was inconsistent with what MCO stood for, the Steering Committee could reject the report; during my years in MCO this seldom happened.

■ The President and Executive Vice Presidents

The president was the daily operational leader of the organization, handling any items that came up from the mayor's office or news media. He also was general media spokesperson, though whenever, throughout MCO's development, there were issue campaigns, media recognition was spread to include committee leaders and activists and, when appropriate, leaders of member organizations who were particularly involved in the issue at hand. None of the persons so far mentioned were salaried by MCO. The president received a small (fifty dollars a month) expense account, which he usually spent on lunchtime planning meetings with his executive officers and me.

Informally, prior to Steering Committee meetings, the president and his executive vice presidents met to review the evening's agenda and to discuss priorities for the organization. The meeting was open and sometimes attended by committee chairs who had particularly lively issues that were going to involve the whole organization in some kind of direct action.

■ Formal Structure Facilitates Unity

This structure is the means by which unity is maintained. These are the rules of the game. All parties acknowledge them as the legitimate means by which internal disagreements are resolved. So long as these rules are not used to exclude a particular group from expressing its views, their legitimacy can be maintained. And, so long as no one group is so powerful as to walk out of the organization and make its view prevail in the neighborhood or with an adversary, then this process will work.

It was common in the MCO for the more established groups to seek their own avenues of access to institutions and forces with which MCO was in negotiating and conflict relationships. In the organization's early period, such relationships were not challenged. To have done so with, for example, a vote on a particular issue in a committee would have been to place the legitimacy of the organization's procedures on the line against the power and autonomy of a member group. The rules of the game do not, in themselves, assure that all participants will adhere to the outcome of a vote. It is the combined recognition of the legitimacy of the rules and also of the realities of power relationships in the community that assures that these democratic rules will work.

The Organizer's Role

The community organizers who worked full- or part-time for the Mission Coalition Organization were not part of the formal structure. You do not find them in the constitution and bylaws. But they were essential to the working of the organization.

Paid Organizers and Support Staff

Working on a full-time basis were a staff director (my role), a small organizing staff, and a one-person office staff. In the TMCO period, only the director and office staff were paid directly with TMCO funds. I was hired to assist local people to build a powerful organization. Paid organizers develop new groups to participate in the action and train existing and emerging leadership in how to take effective action on issues, using issues to build the organization. I hired, trained, and supervised both the organizing and administrative staff and sat in on most formal top leadership meetings; generally I was a nonparticipant in these meetings. I also sat in on many informal meetings, often actively participating in the discussions. It was understood that as the outside organizer, I would phase out in a two-to-three-year period, training a local person to take over my role.

In its first two years, the staff was quite small. An office person operated the storefront headquarters of the organization. Except for me, all of the staff were passably bilingual in English and Spanish. I learned a good idea from Fred Ross Sr.: bring someone to translate who you want to train as an organizer.

In the period of good feeling between MCO and MACABI, organizers from the Poverty Program were interned with MCO. However, this did not last very long and the staff so interned, except for Tuttle and McReynolds, were not cut out to be organizers.

Organizers Assist

I had a very definite understanding that the role of the organizer is to *assist* local people to build a powerful organization. In the typical community-based nonprofit organization, a board of directors makes policy and the staff implements it. In the MCO, the organizers assisted leaders to make, implement, monitor, and evaluate policy and take action necessary to get their policies adopted by decision makers in government and business. We sometimes don't fully live up to our standards, but the best organizers provide their assistance by a process that includes:

Listening. Empathic listening elicits the hopes, dreams, problems, and fears of local people. It draws people out, encourages them, builds trust, and forms a relationship between the organizer and the people with whom she or he works.

Challenging or agitating. When I worked in Mississippi in 1963, a very old Black man rose to speak at a small mass meeting in a Black church in Ruleville, a tiny town in the Delta. He said of the organizers from the Student Nonviolent Coordinating Committee, and his voice was trembling as he spoke, "They call you 'outside agitators.' I have an old-style washing machine in my house. It has a moving piece at the top that goes back and forth." He illustrated the motion with a rotating, dangling forearm. "That piece is called an 'agitator.' You know what it does?" He paused for dramatic effect. "It gets the dirt out." Ever since hearing that, I have been proud to be called an agitator—one who challenges people not to accept an unjust status quo.

Thinking through. What is often called "apathy" is, in fact, the resignation born of fruitless efforts to change things "downtown." This is particularly true in historically oppressed constituencies where powerlessness is a common experience. If people begin to participate because, in the course of an organizing process, they are challenged to act, organizers and leaders must have specific ideas on what can be done, or what action can be taken. These are thought through with people so that their own thinking process incorporates the results. In later years, I led four- and six-day workshops that were almost entirely taken up with participants conversing with one another to think through situations I had posed, and role-playing, with me taking the part of a representative of some decision-making authority in "the system."

The best organizers use thought-provoking questions to make people think through the options facing them. Even when he or she makes a direct recommendation and leaders accept it, a good organizer then challenges them to defend it, so that their acceptance is not simply based in their confidence in the organizer. Leaders have to "own" their decisions.

"Thinking through" was often a storytelling procedure. One of my positive Kansas City experiences provided a classic. The Paseo, a major north-south busy boulevard, cut through the heart of the Black community. At one of its intersections, elderly residents on the east side wanted to cross the street to go west to a shopping area; students on the west side had to go east to school. The residents wanted a stoplight. The city's traffic department measured cross-street foot traffic and said the volume didn't merit a stoplight. The community organization said the particular needs of the elderly and young children did. The city was adamant and refused to budge.

One late afternoon, thirty-five or so residents, some walking with canes, others holding the hands of young children, walked around the four crosswalks of the intersection, bringing rush-hour traffic to a halt. Young men ran up the line of cars and handed flyers to frustrated drivers. "If you don't want us back next week, call Traffic Engineer Falon and tell him there should be a stoplight here." The flyer provided his phone number. Two days after our action, we got a call from the traffic department: "Upon further examination, the department has concluded that the particular circumstances of the intersection require a stoplight."

The story usually brought a grin to the listeners. Creative nonviolent direct action made rush-hour motorists allies of the otherwise powerless neighbors around that street. Many a person to whom that story was told came up with a local version that could be applied in the Mission District.

Training. Having listened to people, challenged them, and thought through with them what a people-power organization could do, the organizer trains them in the skills needed to both effectively participate with one another in an organization and to engage in negotiation or confrontation with adversaries. These skills include formulating action proposals; negotiating and compromising with each other to define "lowest significant common denominators" for action; running effective meetings; negotiating with decision makers from "downtown"; planning and implementing action campaigns; and lots more. The organizer helps more experienced leaders fine-tune skills and gives them feedback that doesn't usually exist in voluntary associations. Ongoing evaluation is essential so that leaders can integrate their own way of understanding the world with events that take place in the context of the organization.

■ Organizers' Areas of Assignment

The organizing staff was assigned to member groups, committees, and the unorganized. I had the first two kinds of assignments in addition to supervising the staff. We met as a group twice a week, once Monday morning to outline the week's work and evaluate major activities of the previous week, then again Friday afternoon for a more free-floating discussion on something we had all read, or a major national or international news event. I met with each organizer individually, in two one-hour sessions, one early in the week and one toward the end. I met with the support staff as well. And, of course, I was available to any of them on an as-needed basis.

Member Groups: Working with existing member groups was typically a very flexible assignment. It might involve getting delegates to attend an important Delegates Council meeting or action; helping bring an issue from a member group into the organization's structure; trying to solve an organizational dispute between member groups, through mutual accommodation and compromise, before it became a source of conflict in the broader community; or even dealing with an internal conflict within a member organization. As annual conventions drew near, organizers worked with member groups to insure their participation in the precon-vention process. With the memory of the first convention blowup in all our minds, we knew how important this was.

Committees: Organizers worked with standing committees, offering policy ideas and strategy and tactics for dealing with decision makers. Thus, the organizer had to generally understand a range of substantive issues as well as the workings of institutions that dealt with them—housing, consumer protection, police, jobs, schools, etc. As committee members gained further expertise, they would identify technical assistance sources in whom they had confidence and become more expert than the organizer working with the committee. In some cases, committee members already had substantial knowledge in their committee's area of concern. Organizers also were assigned to preconvention committees—Nominations, Constitution and Bylaws, Arrangements, Platform, and Credentials and Elections.

The Unorganized: Finally, organizers were assigned to organize new member groups for MCO. Vague or general problems identified by activists in a new group often had to be translated into specific issues around which organization and action could take place. Overpriced, poorly maintained housing is an important, but general, topic; landlord X whose building at Y address has tenants Z who just got a rent hike presents an actionable issue, a specific opportunity for organizing. Further, groups organized around specific issues had a tendency to fall apart once the issue was dealt with, and organizers needed to minimize this tendency. This meant learning how to talk about the multi-issue approach of the MCO, as well as appealing to participants' desire to be active in an ongoing community that could add meaning to their lives.

Organizing Is a Continuing Activity

The continuous job of the organizer is to impart skills and a way of thinking to leaders who then assume the role the organizer has been performing. This leaves the organizer free to move on, into new nonparticipating groups and into new areas of activity. This is particularly true in relation to committees whose leaders have gained expertise in the substance of their community issues and in the strategy and tactics of how to deal with them.

This applies to the staff director's relationship to the Steering Committee and its leaders, as well as the individual organizer's relationship to any particular committee. The leaders of these committees become the organizers for each of them. In the course of the development of the organization, they learn the importance of keeping the organization in action on issues. If the organization does not remain in action, it will begin to chew itself up internally, as rivalries for position, tensions among groups, and disagreements on direction begin to take up the attention of the activists.

However, successfully working oneself out of a job doesn't mean the organizing function disappears. If no one is playing the role of organizer, an organization becomes stagnant and dies or gets co-opted. Organizers who stir the uninvolved to become involved, press to address more hard-to-solve issues, challenge complacent leaders, train new leaders, and otherwise prevent development of a comfortable status quo are the leaven that keeps the bread rising.

Tension between Leaders and Organizers

By the 1970s, most community organizations had been co-opted by some combination of grants from government, corporations, or foundations; they had little influence over the legislation, rules, and guidelines of the programs they were administering. Typically, the grants were insufficient to solve the broader problem their program claimed to address. Alinsky's best-known Black community organizations fell prey to such cooptation: the Woodlawn Organization in Chicago and FIGHT in Rochester, New York. The parallels for co-opting individuals were appointments to commissions or government jobs.

When the possibility of co-optation emerges, the organizer faces the greatest possibility for conflict in her job. She has to raise all the questions about co-optation and its dangers.

Many community organizers today are fond of saying that they are now "at the negotiating table" and no longer need to use the tactics that got them there. But nothing is worse than co-optation that isn't recognized by the co-opted. Being at the table means having the continuing opportunity to present proposals that ever more fundamentally address inequalities of wealth and power that undermine American democracy. When such proposals are presented, "the other side" will resist. Organizations will have to demonstrate that large numbers of people support the more radical proposals—"radical" in the sense of the Merriam-Webster's Dictionary definition "of or relating to the origin; fundamental." And this support will have to manifest itself in demonstrations, lobbying, voting, boycotts, strikes, or nonviolent disruptive mass action. Organizers who have convinced themselves that they are now "equals" at the bargaining table need to reread the Frederick Douglass quotation that opens this book.

Here is a simple illustration: An elite private high school attended by the grandson of a friend of mine has a maximum of thirteen students in each class. His fellow students come from homes where parents emphasize education; habits of study were formed at an early age; books were present in the house; TVs were turned off so children would do their homework. These were "advantaged" students to begin with. What would it take to create a public school system in which the maximum high school classroom size was a dozen students? Who would pay for it? Aren't these among the questions community organizing should be asking, if it is to address inequality in this country? But leaders tempted by sitting at the table sometimes want to ignore these questions. That means organizers have to raise them with secondary leaders and active members. That requires of organizers that they not get too close to any leaders—just as psychotherapists, for example, can't get too close to patients, or coaches too close to individual players.

Two stories about the legendary organizer Fred Ross Sr. illustrate the problem. The first one, he told me. When he was working for the Community Service Organization (CSO), the leadership in a particular chapter didn't want to raise a difficult question in a broader decision-making body. Ross told them the constitution required them to. They were willing to evade the constitution in deference to the circumstances. Ross told them that if they didn't raise it, he would. "But you work for us," one of them said. "No," he replied, "I work for the membership." He said you could have cut the tension in the room with a knife. The leaders took the issue to the next level of decision making.

An intriguing example of what happens when an organizer loses this distance is in the relationship between leader Cesar Chavez, himself a talented organizer, and Ross, who first identified Chavez as a grassroots leader and then worked closely with him to develop the farmworkers' union. Over the years, more and more decision making in the union became centralized in Chavez's hands. Many recognized this, and some tried to do something about it. Unfortunately, during his later years the way Chavez dealt with internal dissent was to purge the dissenters. When a good friend of mine who had played the role of purger, only later to find himself purged, asked Ross why he didn't support efforts to strengthen internal democracy within the union, Ross replied, "I've been too close to Cesar for too long. I'm not going to become his challenger at this stage of my organizing with him."

The staff director is the key organizer in the beginning of an enterprise (as Fred Ross was in the development of the CSO). But the organization is not his. In raising questions, the organizer forces leaders to think through options. The best organizers—having done the job of raising questions, thinking through alternatives, pointing out difficulties and opportunities, and offering skills training—assist leaders in an organization to make and implement their own decisions. Similarly, the organizer does not become involved in choosing the particular issues the organization will address. That is a matter for the members to decide. Unless some violation of basic democratic values is involved, the organizer can use any issue to do her job. Her only interest in the issues is whether or not they will build the organization. Her questions, then, have to do with building people power. The organization's formal structure is the vehicle for building power by acting on issues that are important to the people.

Growing Pains

From its spring 1968 beginnings to the end of 1969, with the exception of its dealings with the mayor's office on Model Cities, the Mission Coalition Organization worked on the agendas of member groups who sought to draw MCO into problems, struggles, issues, and policies that they had already defined. Some of these agendas had to do with a member organization wanting MCO's backing for a funding proposal. Others had to do with getting MCO backing on an issue about which there was already conflict. In either case, MCO was understood by those seeking its support to be an organization that "supported member organizations," or a confederation. As time went on, MCO leadership was able to transform the organization into a stronger federation, but it took some bitter battles.

The Confederation View of MCO

Ironically, on the question of federation versus the more loose-knit confederation, many disparate groups stood together. The Mission Merchants Association, the Organization for Business, Education and Community Advancement (OBECA/Arriba Juntos), Mission Tenants Union, and La Raza youth militants all agreed on the formula that MCO was to back the activities of member organizations when they needed such backing. Where each differed, of course, was on the substance of the issues.

African-American, Asian, and Latino student leadership at San Francisco State University wanted MCO backing for their strike and its fifteen non-negotiable demands, but they did not want MCO to formulate its own view of the strike or be in on the negotiations with university President S. I. Hayakawa. Their demands revolved around the creation of Black and Third World studies programs and the personnel to teach in these programs. MCO's leaders had no interest in being party to negotiations, but they did care what their members in the Mission thought.

Instead of supporting San Francisco State students' non-negotiable demands, MCO insisted on adopting its own position. This happened in a hotly debated

Delegates Council meeting attended by about two hundred delegates, members, and students. The MCO resolution satisfied no one fully. It called for good-faith negotiations and recognition of the students' legitimate interests; it condemned violence. The students felt betrayed by its condemnation of violence on both sides.

Student anger at the main body of MCO, and failure to recognize the ways in which MCO support could be used to provide them credibility within the community, only illustrated the student movement's inability to relate to "adult community" interests, values, and views on the issues of the day. To demand of people who do not share your experience or ideology that they fully adopt your position is to run the risk of isolation—and, in the national scope of the politics of the times, that is precisely what the student movement did.

Delegates who might have supported MCO's position knew they would get in trouble in the neighborhood by doing so. By this time they were more responsive to youth demands because they knew some of the youth leadership at SF State or those who supported them. They felt they had to identify themselves in some way with the student movement. The member organizations raised all kinds of flak about the resolution when they read about it in the next day's daily newspapers.

The Mission Merchants Association wanted MCO to back them in their opposition to pawnshops being relocated from the Yerba Buena (South of Market) urban renewal area to Mission Street, but did not want MCO leadership in on the negotiations with the citywide pawnshop association, which was trying to come up with a formula for the relocation of the pawnshops throughout the city.

OBECA/Arriba Juntos wanted MCO backing in their dealings with the phone company if its own negotiations with them for affirmative action job slots were unsuccessful, but opposed the idea of MCO's Jobs and Employment Committee negotiating a phone-company job package.

Each of these examples illustrates the confederation-versus-federation dilemma. The central MCO strategy was to build, within the neighborhood, a "majority coalition" of all the groups there, including previously uninvolved groups, to represent lower-income residents and the interests they expressed. Building such a coalition requires that the groups participating not expect the coalition to fully support their specific interests, particularly if their expression of those interests conflicts with the ideas or interests of other members. Nothing better illustrated the problems in such an expectation than the student strike at San Francisco State. At best, most Mission residents didn't understand it, and the militant style of the students didn't contribute to "educating" them about it. In fact, many—and they weren't limited to those characterized by militants as "Tío Tacos," brown on the outside but white inside—thought the students were wrong in their tactics and disagreed with some of their proposals. Many low-income MCO members, particularly many immigrants with little formal education, both in churches and in block or tenant associations, thought the students should be in class, and that teachers know more than students. They also thought an opportunity—that they had never had—was being abused by the students.

Participants in a multi-constituency/multi-issue coalition recognize that they cannot achieve their program alone; that is why they are part of the coalition. Indeed, the very notion of a coalition is that different groups join because they have more to gain by working together than they possibly can achieve working apart. But as different groups, the parts of the coalition have their own identities, ideas, and interests. These must be recognized; but a group's formulation of a particular issue may not be acceptable to the full coalition and may have to be modified if backing from the full coalition is to be won. Because some of the groups in MCO had a well-developed sense of its own identity, history, and interests, they made the situation for MCO particularly difficult.

Successful coalitions are built on a "lowest significant common denominator" notion. What constitutes "significant" is a matter for the parties to negotiate among themselves. If they are aware that there are larger adversaries out there who will only negotiate if they unite and demonstrate their strength, then the possibility of arriving at that common denominator is enhanced. When they lack that awareness, as has been the case with many of the "identity groups" now operating in the U.S. body politic, they miss the forest for the trees. What one group may consider "moral," another group may consider of dubious morality or even immoral. The art of compromise is required when building coalitions of diverse groups. So is radical patience—the recognition that once they are in a relationship, people who differ might change their views of each other.

MCO could easily call upon adversaries to meet and negotiate in good faith—with the final outcome left to the parties in the dispute. But MCO could not easily support the fifteen non-negotiable demands of the San Francisco State students, OBECA as the sole community representative with the phone company, or the Mission Merchants Association's right unilaterally to determine the rules for pawnshop relocation. In each case, other elements of the MCO membership and constituency had their own points of view, interests, or even values on the matter in dispute. The student movement's demands and tactical militancy were not supported by a majority of the people in the Mission—at least, not any majority that was discernable within the MCO. Pawnshop relocation was of interest to homeowners who were in block clubs or resident associations, not just to members of the merchants' association; they wanted their voices heard as well. OBECA's interests were not the same as those of Centro Social Obrero. The two were often rivals for funds, access to jobs, and in larger political involvement in the city. Both were members of MCO.

To give blanket endorsement of any particular member organization's approach to the issues at stake in a conflict could lead to another member of MCO quitting the organization.

Moving toward a Federation

For the MCO to develop a momentum of its own, it had to become the federation on which its formal structure was premised. It had to take action beyond supporting member groups. To achieve this, several things had to happen.

MCO had to organize a base in groups, both existing and newly created, who identified with it as their "umbrella organization" in matters of community action. The newly created organizations would emerge from the work of the MCO organizing staff. If successfully organized, they would constitute a "revolution" in the neighborhood and dramatically change the social composition of the coalition, because they would arouse the overwhelmingly low-to-moderate-income grass roots of the community from a state of nonparticipation in neighborhood affairs to one of activism—an activism that made sense to them.

MCO accomplished this by acting on issues that would appeal to this base: rents and other landlord-tenant grievances, unemployment, inadequate city services, problems obtaining home loans and insurance policies (redlining), merchants specializing in shoddy, overpriced goods, school grievances (quality of education, food and other services, student safety, physical plant, and others), park and recreation problems, and the three-hundred-dollar fees (equivalent to $1900 in 2009) that lawyers and others were exacting from immigrants who needed help with paperwork that could often be completed in less than an hour.

At other times the spark for action on issues came from a church or members within a church that was one of MCO's member organizations. In churches with social-action committees, there may have been a tendency to pass resolutions on issues but not take action on them. Or, there may have been a willingness to take action, but little idea how to get concrete results—the kind of action that will move nonparticipants into engagement.

But it took a year of near paralysis to get to this point. The pressure to keep MCO from developing its own action agenda was great. MCO had to establish a structure through which member organizations, whether existing or new, would pass in order to have MCO work on an issue, and further, it had to establish MCO's ability, within that structure, to modify the definition of the issue so as to allow the overwhelming majority of MCO members to support it. Activists from ethnic organizations, churches, and unions were recruited to the Housing Committee even if they were unlikely to have a problem with their landlord. Similarly, when an effective Jobs and Employment Committee was finally put together around the issue of summer jobs for youth, adults who weren't looking for summer jobs were recruited to the committee, including high school teachers and active church members.

As a specific example of this, consider tenants organizing a tenant association to get their landlord to repair a building. The landlord appeared before MCO's Housing Committee and said, "I can't get a home improvement loan from any of the lenders, and I can't do the repairs without one." The tenants doubted him and thought, "It's his problem, not ours." But his response struck a familiar chord with homeowners on the committee who either had experienced the same thing themselves or knew others who had. They asked, "If we support you getting a loan, will you make the repairs?" He replied affirmatively; the matter went to the Community Maintenance Committee, which dealt with more general neighborhood quality-of-life concerns. The landlord's story now triggered a totally different action. Under the joint auspices of the Housing and Community Maintenance Committees, tenants, homeowners, and landlords went to the local bank and discovered redlining was going on. That led to a campaign against redlining.

Finally, MCO had to establish itself as the key negotiating group on those issues in which it became involved, particularly those that had broad implications for the people of the Mission District as a whole. While it was agreed that MCO would not accept a settlement of any given issue that was unacceptable to the member organization most immediately affected, it had to also be stressed and understood that MCO could not simply back a member group and its issue without being involved in that issue's definition and resolution. This not only meant the definition (content) of the issue—i.e., the words used to express it and a policy solution for it—but also control of negotiations, tactics outside the negotiating room, statements to the media, and other concerns about an unfolding campaign.

■ A Different Vision Expressed in the Federation Structure

MCO had to articulate a vision of democratic participation and social and economic justice that could inspire action and create a leadership for whom MCO was an important part of their lives. Without such a core leadership, there was little hope of transforming MCO into anything more than a formal participant in the Model Cities program and a loosely knit confederation in which member organizations shared information, tried to coordinate activities, and sought support from each other on their particular interests.

The formula proposed to member groups for a stronger MCO was a joint negotiating team on issues, joint spokesmen (the relevant committee chair and head of the member organization, joined by the MCO president if it was an important organization-wide issue) to deal with the media, and tactics worked out through the MCO committee structure with final approval resting in the Steering Committee. Obviously, for this to mean anything, member groups would have to see that they could get more accomplished through the MCO structure than by ignoring it. Further, they would have to experience their own role in the victory, so that their identity as a group would not be lost and their leadership would gain recognition.

The vision that articulated what MCO might become had elements of participatory democracy, social and economic justice teachings from the religious traditions in the organization, and a strong sense of pride in the diversity of the Mission. It celebrated local character and diversity, contrasting what the Mission was and could be to the sterile "progress" that urban renewal imposed on other neighborhoods in San Francisco and other cities across the country. Nothing illustrated this better than the disappearance from neighborhoods that were "renewed" of locally owned storefront businesses and locally formed and led institutions that together had been the centers for sociability and services in the neighborhood.

For the MCO leadership, the shift to federation also posed difficulties. They had to steer through muddy waters in which some leaders preferred to be big fish in small ponds, yet not stir those waters vigorously enough to make the fish jump out. It was, after all, the present, active membership that gave MCO its strength, not some future membership that was as yet nonexistent, nor present members (as was the case with most of the churches) that were only nominally involved. It is true that MCO was guaranteed the presence of some of these fish, especially the agencies that were looking forward to Model Cities funding. But others weren't particularly interested in Model Cities, and some of them left MCO over its support of the San Francisco State student strike.

▪ Action:

Building People Power

The Mission Coalition Organization's strategy for building a strong federation was to define issues that could be won but around which there were no funded programs and out of which new bases of support for MCO could be established. For example, landlord abuses lent themselves to organizing tenant associations that operated through the Housing Committee. Negotiations with landlords and potential direct action campaigns against landlords who didn't negotiate in good faith could build MCO. When one or more of the tenants were members of an MCO church, there was an additional benefit: these members could testify to fellow churchgoers that it was a good thing that the church was in MCO. Such issues had a further advantage: they didn't fit into the kind of organizing typically done by community-based nonprofit agencies.

▪ Funded Agencies: The Non-Action Approach

Though the leadership and staff of some community-based nonprofits supported MCO and the kind of organizing it represented, the Poverty Program increasingly emphasized a very particular kind of "organizing," following these steps:

Gather a group of poor people and their allies together.

Help the group define a problem.

Incorporate the group with a self-perpetuating board of directors (i.e., a nominating committee of the board of directors proposes successors as incumbent board members leave).

Seek funds from foundations, corporations, or government, or a combination of them, to deal with the problem.

Administer the funds if granted; if not, continue seeking them from other funding sources.

A number of years later, I did what was supposed to be a one-day organizing workshop for Southeast Asian refugee leaders in San Francisco. It was funded by the government agency dealing with refugee relocation to the U.S. My orientation was toward building people-power organizations that could act on issues facing their people, and also make use of mutual aid and self-help tools. The participants' orientation was shaped by the community-based nonprofit mindset. We argued in the morning, and I insisted on laying out my framework before I would walk them through the steps to form a nonprofit corporation that could apply for grants—hoping to convince them of its merits. After lunch, not one of them returned! They were interested in grants, not in people power.

While government funding was particularly confining in this regard, the guidelines of foundations or corporate donors had similar constraining characteristics. Absent from this approach was negotiation, and confrontation if necessary, with political and economic institutions and decision makers to change their structures, practices, policies, and procedures so that the needs and interests of minority and low-income communities would be met.

There was a further problem in this dependence on external funding. Most funding sources used then, and continue to use, a "rational planning process" as the guideline for their application process. In this procedure a group defines a goal, establishes objectives for reaching the goal, and identifies activities that will be undertaken to realize the objectives. It establishes a timeline for this, as well as mechanisms to monitor progress toward the goal, and means to evaluate results. The goal might be to establish a child-care center that will serve one hundred preschool children. The objectives will include finding a site, recruiting teachers and children, creating a curriculum, developing a governance structure, and all the rest of what is involved in a child-care center. There is no sense of how to deal with unanticipated institutional obstacles. For example, if a problem occurs with zoning, the child-care provider will not be committed to the back-and-forth of an action campaign—in this case, negotiating for a zoning change and taking further action if such a change isn't granted.

▓ Action: Making Proposals to Decision Makers

A totally different dynamic comes into play if the goal is building the people power necessary to hold major institutions accountable to provide quality education and child-care; decent, safe, sanitary, and affordable housing; well-paying and meaningful jobs; affordable health care; and whatever else the people of a community or an alliance of communities are willing to struggle for. A rational planning process in the usual sense is not possible, because you cannot determine the reaction of decision makers to whom you make proposals for change, nor the tactical opportunities that will emerge in a conflict.

This dynamic is built around the idea of making proposals to decision makers in government, business, and major nonprofit sectors to change their policies, structures, and procedures. (I said "proposals," rather than "demands," which was a turnoff to some of the people we wanted to participate, or "requests," which didn't sound firm enough for many people. "Proposals" struck a middle ground.) When reasonable proposals were rejected, and no alternatives put forward, the demand was for good-faith negotiations. Since your proposal might be rejected, you must have an idea of what sanctions you might bring to bear so that good-faith negotiations take place. This, in turn, requires increasing numbers of people to shift from passivity to activity so that people power can be brought to bear on what is now a conflict. Finally, in order to bring increasing numbers of people into participation, an organization has to make the case that their participation will lead to a result. Initial small victories are needed to demonstrate the efficacy of collective action to people who think of themselves as powerless. Thus, how "the system" will respond is a prime consideration in issue selection. If an organization makes a mistake in evaluating "winnability," it must withdraw and engage in another arena; and it must withdraw in a way that doesn't admit defeat. The back-and-forth of conflict tactics does not fit into the linear "rational planning process" that is required by most government, foundation, and corporate funding sources.

▓ Defining Winnability

People in neighborhoods like the Mission don't typically get involved in things remote from their own lives. It is a concern's immediacy that makes it possible for an organizer or leader to move people whose experience has been one of powerlessness from disengagement to participation and action.

Alinsky's mandate to organizers was that organizing issues should be "immediate, specific, and winnable." Experience with defeat—expressed as "you can't fight city hall"—was the organizer's biggest obstacle to shifting people from victimhood and withdrawal from civic life to engagement. Add to this the passivity encouraged by consumer culture, including living vicariously through the TV. Add further the dependency sometimes encouraged, particularly in low-income communities, by paternalistic professional service providers whose modus operandi creates a sense of incompetence among the clients they serve.

The organizer had to identify concerns that were both important enough and immediate enough—like a dangerous intersection where a child had just been hit by a speeding automobile—for people to pay attention to and attend a meeting about.

I changed Alinsky's terms over the years to make the criteria for actionable issues even clearer. There has to be an immediate problem—an experience of pain in people's lives that is right in their faces. The problem has to be specific—it's the dangerous corner at 26th and Harrison, not "traffic safety." Having defined an immediate and specific problem, you have to imagine specific solutions to propose to decision makers with authority to do something about the problem. Implementation of the proposed solution has to happen relatively soon (how soon varies, but my experience with newly engaged groups of people is that anything more than three months into the future is too distant). And there has to be a timeline for implementation. The specific solution has to be believable (the affected people can believe in what they are asking for) and "winnable." Believability means you can't be utopian—asking for the moon—because community people aren't going to waste their time at meetings talking about something they don't think is realistic.

The careful calculation of winnability gives the organizer her "win-win" situation. I call this "win-win" negotiations—but I use the term differently than those who first authored it. If the issue is "cut" (defined) properly, there will be a victory (a "yes" from an appropriate decision maker) or a fight (a "no"). If the latter takes place, however, it will be a winnable fight and thereby strengthen the organization.

Clearly, if the traffic engineer (the person in authority in this case) said "yes" to a community proposal, that would be a victory. (In one organizing project, a city traffic engineer did exactly this with a community organization proposal for a redesigned traffic pattern. He was honored later in the year with a "civil servant of the year" award.)

■ A "No" Can Be As Good As a "Yes"

But what if he said "no"? Here a calculation had to be made: could the people with the problem mount sufficient pressure on the "target," in this case the traffic engineer, to move him from "no" to "yes," and quickly enough so that people who had previously believed you can't beat city hall would not give up and return to their private lives? A parallel illustration could be developed with a landlord who refused to fix up a slum property, or whose rent increase tenants wanted to roll back.

Much of the ongoing education within the MCO was in the tactics of negotiations. Recognizing that it is power that brings you to the negotiating table and supports the proposals you put on the table, it is negotiating strategy and tactics that get you what you want during a specific meeting. As I trained leaders in negotiations, I used role-playing to illustrate various outcomes. On the one hand, we could come to an agreement—and that could be acceptance of our proposal, a mutually acceptable compromise, or a new counterproposal that we hadn't thought of. Each of these was a "yes." On the other hand, we could end a meeting with clarity that we were far apart—a "no." Then we had to initiate or resume direct action. But care had to be taken in choosing the latter course. We had to be sure that our members would support action!

Assessing whether or not something can be won is both art and science. A formula can be defined: will the cost of refusal to implement a proposal from a people-power group be higher than the price of a positive response? People in authority have lots of experience ignoring groups that will soon disappear. Role-playing exercises included a lot of questions: "What if he agrees to meet?" "What if he refuses to meet?" I'd sit with my back toward a leadership team and say, "Ring, ring." Then I'd pick up an imaginary phone: "Hello." The team had to know what it wanted to say. If they couldn't get an agreement from me, wearing my role-playing hat, to meet, then what? I might then ask, "What would happen if fifteen different people called and said, 'I understand you're unwilling to meet with us. Is that true?'" That usually sounded pretty good, and it had an element of adventure and fun in it to add spice. But what if the response is "That's not what I said"? What do we ask the caller to do? God (or the devil) is in the details.

For each possible response to each circumstance, things have to be thought through. This is people-power contingency planning. When it is done correctly, the decision maker's reaction generates the energy for people to take a next step. When a group of people listening to a speakerphone are told by someone that he won't meet with them, it stirs up anger. That anger can either be suppressed, turned into what careless observers might call apathy and become part of internalized oppression. Or it can be turned into energy. Each of the group might agree to call five people, explain what just happened and why "we shouldn't tolerate that," and ask them to take a next step. That next step, when someone refuses to meet, is typically some kind of confrontation. Usually, when confronted by a number of people, decision makers agree to meet. A dozen to fifteen people can get a meeting with a low-level civil servant; thirty-five to fifty can get a meeting with her supervisor; and so on.

That agreement is the first confirmation that thought-through collective action can work. Winning an agreement to meet after waging a mini-campaign teaches people they don't have to accept rejection. When that face-to-face meeting with a decision maker takes place, proposals are presented to which there might be agreement or disagreement. Agreement can take the form of a simple "yes," or it can be a mutually acceptable compromise, or a new proposal that responds to the problem that brought people into action in the first place. Disagreement is a "no" to proposals that people believe are legitimate. Negotiating teams engage in careful role-playing, learning to frame proposals that will yield clear "yes" or "no" responses.

▧ Determining Winnability

The winnability calculation is essentially a cost-benefit analysis. At what cost or price would the traffic engineer change his mind from a "no" and say "yes"? We can imagine that if fifteen to twenty people showed up at his office, he might see that this corner was different from the dozens of other corners about which he'd received angry phone calls when there was an accident but then heard nothing more. Usually the little bit of "heat" would cool down. If, a week later, a larger group of twenty-five to thirty-five people showed up, the traffic engineer might now conclude that he'd better talk with his supervisor about what's going on. And if, in the following week, a "call of inquiry" came to the traffic engineer from the office of the city councilman representing voters at this corner, both the engineer and his supervisor might conclude that the reputational cost to the traffic safety department of saying "no" was higher than the dollar cost of saying "yes." Or if, as in the Kansas City action mentioned earlier, thirty to fifty people marched around the four crosswalks of this dangerous corner, tying up traffic for an hour, that might generate enough angry phone calls to the traffic engineer's office to get him to act—especially if the walkers handed out flyers to drivers telling them why they were doing what they were doing and who to call to get them to stop.

If thirty people can successfully demand the expenditure of enough money for a stop sign, three hundred people can demand even more. Three thousand can begin to command the attention of most politicians and the news media. Most organizers imagine ever larger numbers of people bringing about more and more important changes to the way dominant institutions operate, so that problems associated with unemployment, lack of decent, safe, sanitary, and affordable housing, quality public education, affordable health care, and other issues will be solved; so that the burden of paying for solutions to problems will be borne in an equitable way, i.e., so that those most able to pay taxes will do so; and so that mechanisms of responsibility and accountability will be put in place. And getting even more deeply to the root of problems, organizers imagine restructuring institutions so that the people who work in them, and the people who are supposed to be their beneficiaries, have a significant voice in how the institutions are run.

While initial issue campaigns can sustain the involvement of the powerless for a relatively short period of time (my rule of thumb was six weeks to three months), an organization that has a number of these victories under its belt can imagine longer time frames for campaigns. The process is mutually reinforcing: small victories build the confidence and skills of those who win them; they draw skeptics into the organization; with new participants, more people get engaged in action, increasing the price to a decision maker who might otherwise say "no." With more wins, the number of people involved increases, sometimes dramatically—as in the 1950s and 1960s, during the civil rights movement in the Deep South. With more people involved, the power of an organization (or social movement) increases. Thirty people can win a stop sign at a dangerous corner. Five to ten thousand can win citywide or even state-wide legislation on an important issue, or boycott a product to get its manufacturer to clean up his environmental act or stop discrimination in his hiring practices. And five hundred thousand people descending on the nation's capital can affect national legislation. Five million organized people acting in unison could begin to reshape American politics.

◼ Don't Piss on the Building; Meet with Someone Who Can Decide

There is another organizer's calculation. Organizers seek face-to-face meetings with people who have the authority to respond to their proposals. The traffic engineer could say "yes" or "no." Had the proposal been for rerouting traffic, an entirely different, much lengthier, and economically more costly governmental process would have to be initiated. For example, the fire department and health department might have to comment on access to the proposed new route for fire trucks and ambulances.

Groups with experience in winning simple issues are willing to initiate such lengthier processes, and recognize they can take a year or more for final resolution. But that's not how to energize the neighbors at the corner of 26th and Harrison. They aren't yet ready for a campaign that will take a year.

In the face-to-face meeting, when the people in the room are told "no" to a proposal in which they believe, their typical reaction is a combination of surprise and anger. Even when I had role-played the possibility of a negative response, it took the actual experience for people to say, "How could he say 'no' to something so reasonable?" The anger that is implicit in this question provides the energy that sends people back to their neighborhood to get their neighbors and friends to make the phone calls and to participate in the next delegation that visits the traffic engineer or takes some further action. As Alinsky put it, "The action is in the reaction." Instead of picketing buildings or other symbolic centers of authority and power, the organizer applying these principles always wants to target an individual who can say "yes" or "no." (As issues become more complex, the "yes" sought might be to the proposal, "Will you recommend this policy change to X?" Or "Will your department (which has a piece of the solution) adopt X if the other department will do Y (the other piece of the solution)?"

The organizer has to think about the number of people who might become involved in an issue, the nature and power of the adversary, the response of the constituency of the organization, the choice of strategy and tactics, how media might respond, possible allies, and all the other considerations that go into building people power. Success in a relatively short period of time is especially important in the beginnings of the organization. Later, the organization can take on more difficult issues. Once it establishes itself as a group that will mobilize people for action, the organization may take stands on issues over which it has no real power but on which it wants to be publicly on record. MCO did such speaking out, perhaps prematurely in a few cases, against the war in Vietnam, in support of the farmworkers' boycott, for closing corporate tax loopholes, and on other matters of public concern and policy.

▦ Calculating Price

When organizers think about "price," they see these determinants:

Elected politicians. Their bottom line is votes won versus votes lost. A politician who takes a stand on a controversial issue will win some votes and lose some, both in her present constituency and in one associated with a higher office she aspires to. Wealthy donors may cut their contributions, which translate into purchased media time to influence voters. A people's organization has to persuade a politician that it can bring both votes and machinery to reach enough voters to make up for these losses. Writ large, when Lyndon Johnson supported the southern civil rights movement, he said to his press secretary, Bill Moyers, "We've lost the South." But, at least in 1964, losing the South contributed to winning the country. Barry Goldwater, Johnson's Republican opponent, won his home state of Arizona and the hard-core Dixiecrat states—and that was all.

Corporate executives. Their bottom line is profit and a reputation that contributes to making a profit. A strike, slowdown, sickout, boycott, disruption of work, or a picket line that keeps workers or consumers out can all affect profit. But a corporation with a bad reputation for its treatment of the environment might also find it more difficult to recruit top talent from business schools.

Public sector managers. Bureaucracies depend on politicians for appropriations, so they cannot antagonize those who approve their budgets. But they also depend on a stable environment in which to operate. While the top administrators of these bureaucracies are neither elected nor dependent on profit for their budgets, they are vulnerable to disruption of business as usual. They don't want an elected official who votes on their appropriations inquiring about why their program beneficiaries are upset. Those beneficiaries are also voters. Nor do they want any potential rivals, either for their jobs or for the tasks assigned to their departments, to use public discontent against them.

Nonprofit administrators. Large nonprofit organizations, like colleges and hospitals, are also sometimes targeted for community action. It may be because of problems in the services they provide, because they want to expand their institutions into adjoining neighborhoods, or simply because their presence causes what neighbors think is excessive noise or traffic. Their price considerations include donors or public bodies that appropriate their funds, talent they might like to recruit to their staff or involve on a board of directors, and their reputation among peers and in the broader public.

In each of these settings, decision makers assess the cost of entering an agreement with a union, an environmental group, a civil rights group, or some other entity. Organizers and leaders who give careful thought to how those decision makers make up their minds can use the anticipated responses to build the numbers of people engaged in changing the status quo: "The action is in the reaction."

Decision makers of whatever institutional setting share some characteristics which lend themselves to action. They may be members of churches or social clubs, on the boards of directors of charitable associations, donors to politicians, or otherwise in positions that open the door for imaginative tactical thinking that uses public shaming to embarrass public figures. Organizers use *Who's Who* and other guides to America's elite to find points of vulnerability in decision makers who are targeted for action. A businessman who is a leader in a mainline Protestant church, for example, might feel pressure from the church's members if it became known that the company at which he's a major executive has racially discriminatory hiring practices. Here the price isn't votes, dollars, or stability—it is reputation among important peers.

Typical Patterns of Adversary Response

As I continued my work as an organizer, I got better and better at predicting responses to a community organization's efforts to get institutional decision makers to meet, negotiate, reach agreements, and implement those agreements. Community people wanted to know how I did that. Few believed I had a crystal ball, but at times they wondered. That ability enhanced my role as a teacher. People wanted to learn what I knew so they could make these predictions too, and base what they did on the anticipated reaction.

In fact, the power structure tends to respond in predictable ways. If you understand these, you can act accordingly. Interestingly enough, when you understand them, the power structure usually is one step behind you.

The first thing an adversary is likely to do is ignore you. If you're an individual making a complaint, you are likely to stop there and conclude that you've bumped into another example of "you can't fight city hall." The impetus for the call—some kind of problem—is insufficient to overcome the desire to avoid the feeling of power-lessness that rebuff or rejection engenders. People want to be somebody; that's fundamental. To be ignored is to be told you're nobody. You're not likely to want the message repeated by again bucking your head up against a stone wall. Indeed, analysts who wonder why low-income people who vote Republican aren't "voting their economic interests" miss this point. If you think you're somebody because you're better than somebody else (racial or ethnic minority/woman/gay/immi-grant/whomever), then voting for a candidate who reminds you that you're male and white and not "The Other" is a vote to be somebody. When you are threatened by declining economic status, you might be even more likely to respond to this kind of appeal. An appeal to economic interest that is not related to the need to be somebody is simply an appeal to an "economic man," not to the whole person.

But if you're part of a group working with an organizer, the organizer is going to challenge you. "Are you going to accept that? You pay his salary (or you buy his product or he relies on public support for his hospital). He ought to at least listen to you." That, by the way, is the role of agitation, and the question asked by those being agitated is "What can we do?"

Here's the first "win-win." The refusal to meet, if turned around, is a win. "We got the meeting with X," participants can tell their family members or housemates or a neighbors, who may have been giving them a "What are you wasting time going to meetings for?" line. And the way the meeting was gotten is the first taste of effective collective action.

There are other typical steps that follow the pattern of adversary response. In the meeting, there may be an effort to divide the group and sow confusion among the members; or the targeted person may refer you to someone else with the claim that "it's his responsibility, not mine"; or the response to the group's proposals will be vague, fuzzy, filled with what appear to be good intentions but without substance. By role-playing these possible responses in advance, the group enters the meeting prepared and ready to deal with them.

There are many ways to try to divide the group: the decision maker may accept some proposals but not others, or say that he'd like to cooperate, but there's another group that precludes the possibility (school administrators regularly blamed the teachers' union for things that were, in fact, within their scope of authority—they weren't limited by a collective bargaining agreement, though they claimed they were). He may actually meet with a rival group and make an agreement with them that he considers less costly, or propose a substitute solution that really doesn't solve the problem at all.

Your targeted decision maker has other actions in her arsenal: delay, pacifica-tion, creation of study commissions—and the list can go on. If it becomes clear that these tactics aren't working, she may decide to fight your organization—and there's a long list of weapons for this, including: infiltration and internal disruption of your organization (the FBI's COINTELPRO made widespread use of internal disruption in the civil rights movement); discrediting you in the media (as conservatives tried to do to ACORN in the 2008 election); arrests at demonstrations that will tie you up in court and cost you money; lawsuits against you; economic action (firing, eviction, credit withdrawal—all these were used against leaders in the civil rights movement); going after funding sources to cut off your money; or actually creating a "front group" to speak for your constituency (the San Francisco Redevelopment Agency tried that in the Mission Council on Redevelopment fight and failed). While we don't see it often today in the U.S., violence can be used as well and is certainly part of American history.

■ How Systems Work

Before a meeting with a decision maker, some people in the group may believe that "Once he hears our story, he's going to do something about the situation." Their implicit theory is that systems don't solve problems because they don't know about them. Or, there may be people in the group who think, "Once he hears our good proposal to solve the problem, he will adopt it." Their implicit theory is that systems don't solve problems because they're incompetent to solve them. Those holding this view think the problem is one of knowledge or training or organizational structure—and that their proposal will solve what the bureaucracy is incompetent to solve on its own. There remains a different explanation, or theory: systems don't solve problems because they have different social, political, or economic interests, or some combination of these.

Even the most dispossessed and marginalized communities include people who believe that the system doesn't know or that the system is incompetent. In these settings, the decision maker who represents the system is educating the people as to how the system really works: most of the time, when the allocation of wealth, income, status, and power are at stake the system will protect the interests of the haves, exclude the have-nots, and give just enough to the have-a-littles to keep them from aligning with the have-nots.

People who never imagined themselves taking direct action are now confronted with the choice: are we going to change this decision maker's self-interests (or change the system itself), or are we going to leave with hat in hand and return to our families, friends, and neighbors and tell them we got screwed and we're not going to do anything about it? Prior to the meeting, the organizer has likely led the group through a consideration of options available to it if it doesn't get satisfaction in the meeting.

Among the options are direct action of some kind, or perhaps alternative courses of direct action. When these options were first presented, those who thought the system didn't know or was incompetent may have looked upon them with disdain. By the end of the meeting, they will look upon them very differently.

Alinsky used to describe with relish various humorous direct action ideas he had. He was often asked why he revealed them: "If they know your tactics, aren't they going to be prepared for them?" "It doesn't matter," he'd say. "They're going to act like the Establishment." And that's the interesting thing: they do act like the Establishment. The silver lining in this cloud is that if they didn't ignore you at the outset and you got the change you wanted, people might stop coming to meetings, because their immediate concerns were satisfied. You wouldn't build an organization, because everyone would go home.

Ignoring the aspirations of marginalized people, giving them mush, dividing and conquering them, and other typical responses have worked for so long that those in positions of authority and power can't imagine they won't work again. That's why they are predictable. You too can get too predictable in your tactics. At one point in the 1960s, a major grocery chain had a "sit-in room" at their headquarters office, where they welcomed protestors, served them coffee, and let them sleep overnight!

■ "Maybe" Is Unacceptable

My favorite task in a role-playing situation was to avoid saying either "yes" or "no," responding instead with what I call "mush." Lack of clarity in response is the hallmark of unaccountable authority. Watch hearings of the United States Congress in which a representative or senator is trying to pin down a member of the executive branch or a corporate chief executive officer or a military commander who's not doing well in the field of battle. You'll see the same process at work. Those who train negotiators on the other side have a name for what they teach: "fogging." If something is foggy, you can't see through it, and if you can't see through it, you can't imagine finding a way to the other side of it.

I learned about "fogging" in a workshop I led. One of the participants, a woman from a local Lutheran church, was married to a man who worked for a chemical company. When she went home after a session in which I used "mush" and told the story to her husband, he replied, "Oh, yeah, that's what our people call 'fogging.' They go to special seminars and get trained in how to do it." "And," he added, "it's pretty outrageous." He got a big kick out of what we were doing.

After some point in a typical meeting with an adversary, if it becomes clear that a positive response is not forthcoming, the group is going to have to end the meeting. They are going to have to turn the "maybe," or mush, into a "no." Something important happens in the thirty minutes between when the meeting starts and when the group's spokesperson or someone on the negotiating team assigned to this specific task says something like, "Mr. X, we are going to assume by your lack of a clear response to us that you are saying 'no.' Thank you for your time; we are leaving."

During those first thirty minutes, the failure of the person to whom proposals are being made to respond to them in a reasonable way makes people angry. Regular people who aren't activists or militants can't believe their proposal for change is being treated in this way. But "this way" has to be made clear. If the mush ("maybe") isn't turned into a "no," it is likely that at the end of the meeting some people will think, "He's going to do something," or "We blew it, nothing's going to be done." If everyone isn't on the same page, it will be impossible to plan a next step. The organizer has to prepare the negotiating team for the possibility of mush and train them to turn it into a "no." Sometimes a caucus is needed to make sure everyone is on the same page. With a definite "no" in hand, further action is likely to be agreed upon by everyone who was in the meeting.

A Note about Tactical Research

A definite "no" requires further action. This action will be aimed at the points of vulnerability earlier defined in the discussion of "price." Finding points of vulnerability requires research—in public records and other public documents, by carefully reviewing society pages of the daily newspaper, by relying on friendly informants inside the power structure, and even sometimes by posing as a researcher conducting a phone interview and asking what appear to be innocent questions.

In 1969 MCO became the beneficiary of a full-time researcher in the person of Charles Bolton. We called him our genius in the basement—MCO's headquarters had a basement, where Bolton had his office and applied his skills. He was placed with MCO by the Robert F. Kennedy Memorial Foundation—by the time he arrived, MCO was making itself known beyond San Francisco.

But if I had to do it now, I would rather he trained people to use his skills than doing it all himself. He would probably agree. Our researcher could certainly have checked to see how the research was going. And he would have been freed up for new research projects. This was an example of my failure to fully implement the principle that our job was to assist people, not do for them.

Building People Power

in the Mission

My central role, as understood both by the nucleus of those who hired me and by me, was to assist the people of the Mission to build people power. For some with experience in community organizing, like veterans of the Community Service Organization, or clergy who had participated in Alinsky workshops, the idea was a clear one. For others it was fuzzy. The organizer's job (empathic listening, challenging/agitating, thinking through, and training) was not without difficulties.

Initial Failures

In general, in the context of taking action to build power, the Mission Coalition Organization's first-year committees failed. They became bogged down in internal conflict, served only as vehicles of communication within MCO (the confederation idea at work), or were unwilling to do more than write letters to decision makers who might do something to improve the life of the community.

For example, MCO's first Employment Committee chairman believed the committee should back whatever the member groups wanted. He saw the committee as a clearinghouse and, perhaps, a source of names of the unemployed. With few exceptions, everyone on the committee had a direct organizational interest in employment, because they were from agencies dealing with manpower grants, or they were interested in obtaining grants. The Anglo representative from the Mission Merchants Association had no such interest, but he believed that Mission District people were unemployed because they lacked motivation or training, not because employers discriminated against them, and this belief was shared by some of the other committee members. The committee rapidly got involved in the question of who was to get what grants, how jobs would be distributed among other member organizations of MCO, and what kind of motivation and training Mission residents needed. It should be understood that the committee had neither jobs to offer nor grant money, but that these issues were being discussed with the assumption that the committee could obtain them or that Model Cities would provide them.

As a source of organizational action, the committee was paralyzed because it could not get into the issues of job discrimination and job creation without immediately raising the question of how jobs and job training monies would be divided. This was accentuated by the Mission Merchants Association rep's beliefs about unemployment resulting from lack of skill or motivation—a view characterized by critics as "blaming the victim, not the system."

Given the committee's membership, probably no chairperson could have gotten it to do more. Given the discussions going on in the committee, anyone looking for a job would quickly have concluded that this discussion was no different from those going on in other community agencies.

After a year of false starts, with little action on issues except to respond to member organizations who wanted MCO support for their agendas, MCO began to find a way to use the techniques described in the previous chapter to build people power. The vehicles for this action were several of MCO's issue-based committees. Issue committees were designed for action that involved members and trained leaders. Strong committee chairs could develop strong committees that could move the organization in a new direction. In their reports to the weekly Steering Committee—the top elected body of the MCO—committee chairmen or women could present action proposals that the officers would support or find difficult to deny—especially if a large number of committee members were present, making it known that the committee chair had a lot of backing. The identification of potential committee leaders and potentially important committees was thus the first major task of the MCO leadership.

The Housing Committee: First Direct Action Results

The Housing Committee provided MCO its first actions. Father Jim Casey, a pastor regarded highly by the people of his parish, his peers, and activists in the community, agreed to accept chairmanship of the committee. At about this time, Elba Tuttle was organizing a multi-unit building in the neighborhood into the 24th Street Tenants Association. Her work was beginning to pay off; the tenants developed an association and wanted to deal with their landlord, who wanted to raise the rent but didn't want to make needed improvements in the building. The opportunity existed for a member group to enjoy the benefits of MCO membership. The landlord turned out to be a perfect target. He had a large home in wealthy Marin County; he initially refused to negotiate with his tenants.

This landlord's behavior was a perfect illustration of the principle that your opposition does most of your organizing for you. After refusing to meet with his tenants and the MCO Housing Committee, he finally came to a meeting. In the meeting, he called Father Casey a communist! It was his resistance, name-calling, and refusal to deal with legitimate tenant grievances that forced the Housing Committee to take direct action. If it failed to do so, the word would quickly get out in the community that MCO was not willing to vigorously pursue tenants' legitimate interests. The committee decided to act. And no one who knew much about the Mission District doubted that the tenants' case was legitimate if Father Casey supported it. Tenants withheld rent and deposited it in an "impound account" under Father Casey's supervision. The landlord capitulated.

Victory in the 24th Street building was celebrated by a sidewalk press conference that got the word into the media that MCO was in the landlord-tenant relations business. More people and more buildings started coming into the committee. I assigned Dave Knotts, and later bilingual VISTA volunteer Spence Limbocker, to the committee—and each of them did an excellent job. Tuttle continued to work closely with the committee too, and she was instrumental in bringing it to successful development. Finally, the committee proved that MCO could take militant action on the issues that, until then, only the Progressive Labor Party's Mission Tenant Union had been willing to handle. In fact, Progressive Labor participated in the early Housing Committee. While their role remained an "anti-leadership" one, their presence kept the committee on its toes and gave the committee a strong pro-tenant voice.

Education Committee Difficulties and Opportunities

In the Education Committee, we had mixed results. Latinos were particularly interested in curriculum content appropriate for Latino students, affirmative action hiring for Latinos, and other related issues with a Latino emphasis. Bilingual education was of particular interest to them and became a major interest of the committee. At the same time, other issues and interests that cut across racial and ethnic lines also became part of the committee's agenda. In particular, school-site parent organizations often had complaints about facilities, food services, safety, and other matters that united parents across racial and ethnic lines. At their best, Education Committee meetings were a mix of middle-class Latino and Anglo education reformers joined by working-class and poor parents who had site-specific concerns about the schools their kids attended. The added support from different constituencies gave the committee strength: especially in the Education Committee, MCO learned that it was possible to pursue the interests of a particular ethnic group while maintaining diverse composition. Further, the combined package did not dilute the strength of any particular point.

The idea that diverse constituencies and interests were sources of strength was not easily learned; indeed the organization as a whole struggled during its first year to learn how to make diversity a strength. Middle-class, moderate Anglos and Latinos were mixed with militant nationalists and lower-income people who had specific problems they wanted dealt with immediately. This was a source of tension. But when the tensions were resolved, this breadth of base was a source of power.

The Education Committee had another, more difficult problem. It was similar to that of the Jobs Committee, but compounded by the complexity of the education field and the endless grants and programs available within it. People with pet projects would come to the Education Committee for support, but they were generally uninterested in developing a base for action on school issues among public school parents. They thought the committee would have the base and that their project was the magic bullet to solve public education problems in the Mission, in San Francisco, and indeed, in the country. In effect, they were technical assistants looking for a constituency for their proposals for reform. The committee's members who were not education professionals or reformers, and who often lacked even a high school education, did not have the self-confidence to tell the proponents of these various proposals that they would not be listened to if they didn't have some constituency in the community already supporting them. MCO's Education Committee was not the Board of Education; it was still struggling to win minor concessions from the school district on issues such as food quality in the cafeteria, dirty toilets, overcrowding, and problems with specific teachers, administrators, hall guards, or other personnel. Relationships among committee members were still tenuous; the committee hadn't demonstrated any real power. For it to get into basic school reform issues was premature. Yet its agenda was constantly used in that way by well-meaning school reformers.

Mission High School

It was in the Education Committee that MCO got into its most radical issues—with "radical" this time defined by the dictionary as "associated with views, practices, and policies of extreme change." Each of them emerged from the student movement. The San Francisco State student strike has already been described. But closer to home, at Mission High School, students developed proposals for curriculum reform, including Black and ethnic studies and immigrant rights, and for facility improvements, personnel changes—particularly to get more Latino and Black faculty and administrators—revision of IQ tests, elimination of ID cards, removal of police around the campus, elimination of all truancy records, and a general end to "racist policies." They were aided by community activists with close ties to the San Francisco State student movement, and their stance was that demands were non-negotiable. In this case the MCO entered the issue with a position of its own, beyond simply urging that the administration negotiate with its students. In so doing, it risked alienating the students. However, in this case the outcome was different.

At first, Mission High's site administrators refused to meet with MCO. When they agreed to a meeting, MCO's committee included clergy and other respected neighborhood leaders. They were Latino, Black, and Anglo. The climate in the city around the issues the students raised was tense. Mission leaders were both interested in solving problems at the high school and defusing a potentially explosive situation. The school principal and two of his key staff people treated MCO's delegation in a condescending way—about the same way they treated their students, thus forcing an alliance between students and the community organization that might otherwise not have existed, or that could have been created only with great difficulty.

At the same time, conservative groups were organizing against MCO's involvement. A flyer inviting people to "Come and Hear It 'Like It Is' and Bring a Friend" asked, "Are the 'Radicals' Destroying Our S.F. Schools? And Is the M.C.O. (Mission Coalition Organization) a 'Radical' Organization?" The meeting was sponsored by the SF Fairness League, whose board of directors included neighborhood conservatives already opposed to MCO's role in the Model Cities program—the same people who had earlier opposed urban renewal but stayed out of the Mission Council on Redevelopment.

The principal's arrogance toward MCO and the students itself became an issue. (To discredit the students, he supported a new Black Student Union—something he would never have previously done.) But now, important community figures were aligned with the students. Together they mobilized a large number of community representatives, some Mission High teachers, and many students, all now fed up with the manipulations of the school's administrators, to demand that Mission High's top staff be transferred. MCO presented its demand at an April 1, 1969, school board meeting. More than two hundred students, parents, and community supporters attended the meeting. The school board heard the transfer proposal and subsequently approved it in a closed personnel session.

The campaign to move Mission High's top administrative staff was aided by the teachers' union—the American Federation of Teachers (AFT), Local 61. Early in the campaign, I called the AFT to see if its leadership would be interested in meeting with MCO leaders. AFT President Jim Ballard was. In fact, he was eager to meet. He, the local's field representative, and two Latina activist union members came to a meeting with MCO's top Education Committee and organization-wide leadership. They proposed a working relationship between the AFT and MCO. An "alliance" was formally established with a document later signed by leaders of the two organizations. The alliance demonstrated that neither the students nor the community were, as the site administrators had charged, "anti-teacher." When Mission High's principal said the teachers' union was the obstacle to MCO objectives for the school, we discovered in conversations with the union that the facts were otherwise. Ballard agreed to speak to a faculty meeting at Mission High, urging the teachers to vote to work with MCO. While a combination of the rival California Teachers Association and conservative AFT members defeated his request, the fact that he appeared cemented the alliance with MCO.

Later, when the AFT conducted a citywide teachers' strike, MCO endorsed it and was a valuable minority community ally for the union. Unlike many minority community organizations of the period, MCO did not accept the view that teachers and their unions were the primary obstacle to school reform.

■ Union-Community Alliance

The specific terms of the "Mutual Concern Alliance between Mission Coalition Organization and San Francisco Federation of Teachers, AFT Local 61, AFL-CIO" are worth detailing. The alliance ran against the grain of its times. Throughout the country, minority community groups were in battles with unions—with the building trades over employment opportunities; with the CIO industrial unions over promotion, seniority, internal representation, and political issues; and with public employee unions over the quality of the services their members delivered.

An opening preface agreed that "community organizations, teacher organizations, and student organizations must":

Be recognized as spokesmen for the people they represent, and have a clear definition of the scope of their representation [that is, that there be clarity about the areas of concern that were within their jurisdiction to speak on].

Be able to present problems, grievances, recommendations, and demands on a regular basis and in an orderly manner to the appropriate level of school administration. [A monthly meeting for this purpose must be established.]

Have a statement that Board of Education policy *requires* administrators thus approached by recognized organizations to respond to problems thus presented and to state proposed actions to resolve the problems presented.

Be assured that a failure to respond to problems properly presented by recognized organizations through orderly channels shall be cause for disciplinary action against the administrator who failed to respond.

In addition, "[p]roblems thus presented which are not resolved to the mutual satisfaction of the administration and the recognized organization may be submitted to a mutually acceptable impartial third party for fact finding, arbitration or media-tion, whichever is appropriate to the nature of the unresolved problem."

There was further agreement that "the most pressing problems facing schools in the Mission Area relate to making education available, relevant, challenging, and rewarding to all students on all levels regardless of language, cultural, racial, or ethnic distinctions."

"To accomplish the above," the Mutual Concern Alliance document continued, "there must be immediate agreement by the San Francisco Unified School District (SFUSD) to…resolve the problems at Mission High." Specifically, "No later than Feb-ruary 28 an all day student-teacher-community workshop must be held. The format of the conference will be developed by parents, teachers, students, and the MCO. A student conference must be held on March 5, 6, and 7. The format will be developed by parents, teachers, students, and the MCO."

The alliance called for employment "of Spanish speaking instructors and para-professionals in the schools…in subject matter areas other than merely Spanish," and "a larger number of minority teachers, counselors, and administrators"; and for the establishment of "a separate Ethnic Studies Department at Mission High, the chairman to be a minority teacher. This Department shall emphasize courses in the language, culture, history and current community problems of the Spanish speaking, Afro-American, Asian (Chinese, Japanese, Filipino, Samoan) and American Indian cultures" and "shall gain immediate financing."

The school district was to "Actively encourage minority group student teachers from Bay Area colleges and universities to do their student teaching in this program," and "Provide released time during the Spring semester for all Mission High teachers and administrators to attend appropriate courses in ethnic studies."

Unfortunately, the AFT-MCO agreement was not replicated elsewhere, despite its historic character. It came a year after the bitter Ocean Hill/Brownsville "com-munity control" battle in New York City, which pitted the teachers' union against a Black district administrator named Rhody McCoy, a community control board, and its community allies. That controversy and others that shared some of its features unleashed a civil war within American liberalism and the Democratic Party that turned historic allies into bitter enemies. As I write in 2008, it is the legacy of those controversies that now faces Barack Obama as he seeks to win the support of white working-class people and to bridge the divide between supporters of affirmative action and its white working-class opponents. His highly regarded Philadelphia speech on race directly addressed this legacy: "Most working- and middle-class white Americans don't feel that they have been particularly privileged by their race.…As far as they're concerned, no one's handed them anything." Resentment and anger develop "when they hear that an African-American is getting an advantage in landing a good job or a spot in a good college because of an injustice that they themselves never committed." These resentments could be "grounded in legitimate concerns." Blanket condemnation of them was "misguided." During his campaign, Obama said that his own relatively privileged girls don't deserve affirmative-action preferences, but poor minority and white students do.

Our Mission High school board campaign illustrated the principle of organization that by combining issues on the agenda of a public body's meeting, we could combine constituencies. The argument for this was a relatively easy one. If we supported each other's issues, we would be greater in number. But the argument was complicated by the fact that a number of people who wanted physical improvements at Mission High questioned the demand for the transfer of Mission High personnel. Torn by the advantage in greater numbers and hesitation on the issue, they were forced to discuss the merits of demanding the transfer; in a sense they wanted to convince themselves. Once presented the full facts of the situation by students and sympathetic teachers, they were convinced to change their own point of view. They would not have listened to the arguments had they not wanted additional support on their particular causes. Thus a more "radical" position became a reasonable position when understood. This was a dramatic instance of a teachable moment arising out of a conflict situation.

The Education Committee's action had a side effect; it was cannon fodder for some of MCO's Anglo critics. Taking a pro-administration position, they criticized MCO for entering into the situation. This issue, the "non-negotiable" position taken in the founding convention resolutions on Model Cities, the chaos at that convention, the 24th Street rent strike, and the prominence given some of the "radical" resolutions presented at the continuation convention were handles these critics used to weaken the allegiance to MCO of some of the moderate and less activist member groups. In particular, this was going on in some of the smaller, largely Anglo churches that were an important part of the MCO constituency, both because they represented people in the neighborhood and because of their ties to denominations that were supporting MCO, financially and otherwise.

▓ Strategic Balance: Keeping the Centrists and Conservatives In

Fortunately, the Planning Committee and the Community Maintenance Committee allowed the organization to deal successfully with what might be called a problem of strategic balance. "The people" remains an amorphous concept until put in concrete terms. For us, in concrete terms "the people" meant those groups in the MCO that were not the paid staffs of nonprofit community-based agencies. That is, "the people" were those who were to benefit from the existence of the MCO, the agencies, and the other services in the community. At this stage in our development, church-related groups constituted one of the major bases of "the people." Their combined memberships far outnumbered the membership of other voluntary associations in the MCO. The churches were forums in which the merits of different MCO actions were debated. While the voices of friendly clergy were important to MCO's standing in the Mission, it was also important for lay churchgoers to be heard on the subject of how membership in MCO was benefiting them. Without such allies, the church-related groups would begin to define MCO as "another radical group" and would leave it, perhaps pulling their entire church out with them. In their view, "radical" was equal to crazy. But by delivering concrete benefits to members, being rooted in justice theology and the secular democratic tradition, and having the aforementioned support of friendly clergy, MCO avoided this fate. (Note that a large church might have several groups within it that were official member organizations of MCO: a women's guild, father's club, youth group, ethnic organization, retiree association, or choir as well as a church's official lay decision-making body.)

The Community Maintenance Committee began a series of picket actions at the Crown Theater when it became part of the Pussycat Theater chain and started showing pornographic films. Catholic nuns in their habits, Protestant ministers, Latino and Anglo parents, and a few merchants marched while a couple of their number took photos (with cameras that had no film!) of people standing in line to buy tickets. A flyer distributed to the potential ticket buyers told them these photos would soon be widely publicized unless they left. The ticket line evaporated. Parent groups at a number of schools had appealed to MCO to take action on this issue, as had Frank Hunt, the president of the Mission Merchants Association. Most adults in the community opposed this kind of theater on the main shopping street of the neighborhood. The owners of the Crown finally negotiated with MCO. In exchange for agreement from MCO to promote the theater in the neighborhood, the owners agreed to return to family programming. The deal was sweetened with discounts for people who presented an MCO flyer when they bought tickets.

The Planning Committee took leadership in the fight to keep a large number of pawnshops from relocating from an urban renewal area onto the same street as the theater. The Mission Merchants Association was delighted when MCO took on the city's urban renewal agency, which wanted to get the pawnshops out of the South of Market area so it could proceed with its plans for the Yerba Buena development—plans that included a convention center. Local merchants believed that the presence of pawnshops would change the character of the Mission shopping strip; pawnshops had a reputation for being sleazy, and their presence might discourage shoppers who would otherwise come to the Mission.

Both fights were won. They were won through the use of direct action, and sometimes militant tactics—picketing and mass lobbying. Yet the issues were "conservative."

Older residents, parents, more conservative clergy, small businessmen on Mission Street, and others developed relationships with MCO leaders and younger militants who liked showing up for direct action. The more conservative elements now had a reason to be pro-MCO. The concrete activities and victories of the organization brought people into MCO membership; once there, the relationships they formed combined with other interests to keep them there. They had a stake in MCO. That meant two things: they defended it against attack and they sought to find out what was going on in issue areas that they might otherwise have viewed with hostility. Further, the action on these issues developed important leaders in MCO. Each went through the baptism of fire and emerged stronger. Leadership in mass organization develops through such tests.

▨ MCO Was Fragile

It is difficult to appreciate the utter fragility of MCO at this stage of its history. Sometimes an organization exists in the mind of the organizer alone, or the organizer and a handful of key leaders. This occurs when disillusionment reigns because of disagreements or disenchantment with what the organization is (or isn't) doing, or did (or didn't) do. If there isn't a person or core of people who believe in the organization, it can simply disappear as people vote with their feet and stop going to meetings. (That happened to me once in a subsequent, and eventually successful, organizing effort. After a successful effort by a large employer to divide the organization, literally zero people came to its next meeting. Had I not gone out to those who were expected and reassured them that this was just a temporary setback, and had ideas for what to do next, the organization would probably have died.) In MCO's case, that core group was Martinez, Tuttle, Knotts, and myself, with the staff working under my direction. Through committee activities and action, the organization was expanding the core. They were the new committed people for whom MCO meant more than a specific interest in a particular issue. Their lives and their personhood were coming to be in part identified with MCO *as an organization*.

In their participation in MCO, people formed new friendships—many of which crossed lines of religion, race, and ethnicity. They gained new skills and developed self-confidence. They also found a deeper sense of meaning. For those of religious faith, the general ideas of justice they heard in pastors' homilies or sermons, learned in Christian education classes, or read in their own Bible study gained the concrete reality of application in the daily life of their neighborhood. For others, secular democratic ideas that were part of high school civics and politicians' pronouncements took on an entirely new and different meaning. Democracy was much more than periodic voting; it was regular participation in shaping one's own community.

▨ MCO and the Media

In the beginning, we wanted to stay out of the media. That idea flies in the face of the kind of activism that is primarily aimed at getting into the media. We wanted to recruit a very broadly based array of groups to participate in shaping the Mission Coalition. The organizing logic is clear when you put on a thinking cap for organizing, not publicity.

Groups might join a federation like the MCO for several reasons, each with opportunities and problems. The Mission Coalition Organization had the mayor's recognition. Groups with an interest in Model Cities funding thought they had to be in the MCO in order to get a grant. And many groups that feared Model Cities was the San Francisco Redevelopment Agency's Trojan horse had to be in MCO to keep urban renewal out of the Mission. Groups could join MCO in order to be part of creating people power in the Mission District. This required shared core values and a shared understanding of what was possible. Having earlier beaten urban renewal, there was some confidence among Mission leaders that people power did, in fact, work. But the idea of a continuing, multi-issue organization was a new one. It created uncertainty that had to be overcome.

Activism born of the civil rights and student movements and the farmworkers' union as well as political reform in the Democratic Party was still in the air in 1968. This helped. Further, a number of the clergy in the Mission District were inspired by Saul Alinsky's workshops on community organizing. They wanted to take their faith into the world to create change. Justice and work to end poverty were meaningful calls to action. This was a big help.

Groups might join MCO because it had a track record of delivering on issues. That would come further on down the road, after a founding convention created MCO as an action organization. We simply did not have time to both effectively engage in action and organize the convention.

To engage serious commitment from community leaders required that they be invited in on the ground floor of planning the MCO. Leaders have their own identities and interests to protect. Civic organizations, in particular, saw both opportunity and threat in MCO. The threat was to their ability to speak for a constituency. Would the MCO preempt their leadership roles? The opportunity was in power that no one organization could assemble on its own. But there was an implicit admission here that a leader had to make: "We have to be part of something bigger than ourselves to be as effective in the world as we'd like to be." If leaders felt they were real co-creators of the new organization, it was less likely that they would let their fears dictate their behavior. If MCO had a media image that preceded their involvement, the implication would be that there was already a there there. A community leader might think, "Something has already been created that my organization is going to join." We wanted to get people to create the organization they would then join. That meant staying out of the media.

External recognition could be both a blessing and a curse. Recognition conferred legitimacy. On the other hand, MCO was vulnerable to the allegation that it was a "company union"—something set up by people downtown to serve their purposes. While future action would clearly demonstrate how false this charge was, it was in the present, not the future that it could be damaging.

We would later try hard to get media coverage for our activities. I thought if we carefully cultivated relationships with reporters, were accurate in what we told them, and did something newsworthy, we would get coverage. I still think that's the way an organizer should operate in relation to the news media. When we did something we thought was news, we wanted coverage for it. There were some reporters, particularly in the print media, who had pride in craft and wanted to understand what we were about. They wrote some accurate and excellent stories about us, including some lengthy feature stories. San Francisco then had a morning paper, the independently published *San Francisco Chronicle,* and the Hearst-published afteroon paper, the *San Francisco Examiner.* Gone were the Scripps-Howard *San Francisco News* and the Hearst *San Francisco Call-Bulletin.* Published three times weekly and delivered free in the city's neighborhoods was the *San Francisco Progress.* All three had reporters who were interested in what MCO was about. These reporters were willing to sit down for off-the-record briefings so they could better understand how we thought. Other reporters didn't do so well. Those that did well were often reporters with a specific urban affairs assignment.

Unfortunately, what we did best—get large numbers of people involved in disciplined action—didn't lend itself to the journalism of the spectacle that is favored by TV. Even less "newsworthy" were the results of our careful organizing process: leadership development; breaking down barriers of race, ethnicity, age, neighborhood, and gender; shifting people's sense of themselves from one of powerlessness and hopelessness to seeing the possibilities for change and themselves as agents of change. In particular, we wanted to get local people projected into the media because we were interested in creating local heroes, in developing the idea that regular, day-to-day people could make history.

If ten people engage in a crazy act, like blocking a busy downtown street at rush hour and getting arrested, they are likely to get TV coverage. But if a thousand people meet and decide to boycott a product or adopt a course of political action, that isn't as likely to make the evening news. On television, news is like the drama shows: it requires high tension and quick resolution in a specific outcome. The failure of TV news to sustain coverage of the post-Katrina disaster is a current example of the problem. TV coverage was, as is usually the case, focused on dramatic conflicts. Where there was none of that, there was no TV presence. TV sometimes covered those jobs and housing actions that involved picket lines and demonstrations. But it didn't cover a jobs-related boycott that was far more effective than the picketing, and it left a huge blank in the other areas of MCO significance.

Our tactics sought reactions from our adversaries, and we built our action on the kinds of responses we would get. At our best, we personalized "the system" in someone who could make a decision. Thus we were typically seeking meetings with political, administrative, or economic decision makers of one kind or another rather than protesting at inanimate buildings that are symbolic of something but that don't react. As one critic of the latter approach put it, "Pissing on a building won't change anyone's mind." In the tactics of most action groups of those days (and today), getting news media coverage was and is a major aim: do a demonstration, then watch it on the evening news. Our tactics were aimed at getting people to negotiate with us. As this tale demonstrates, substantive gains were made with our approach of taking action in order to obtain good-faith negotiations.

We also wanted to get our newsworthy activity covered, and we hoped reporters would get it right. MCO leaders loved seeing themselves on the evening news; their kids did too. And they enjoyed and read the written stories about their organization that appeared in daily, weekly, monthly, and occasional periodicals.

The short lesson: media coverage amplifies but doesn't build powerful, democratic organizations. Values-based relationships, action on particular and common interests, concrete benefits in the lives of everyday people, growing personal self-confidence and civic competence, real power in the real world, and the fun and sense of dignity that come from having a voice do. MCO provided these and more.

MCO and Model Cities

No single interest more defined the initial character of the Mission Coalition than Model Cities. Veterans of the earlier Mission Council on Redevelopment (MCOR) victory moved quickly to respond to what they saw as a possible sneak attack by urban renewal proponents via the new federal program. Community-based agencies responded with equal speed because Model Cities was the newly touted federal program to deal with urban problems, and that translated into grants for their agencies' programs. These two groups provided the principal leadership for TMCO and MCO in the first year. At times it was only the fact that MCO was the negotiating group recognized by the mayor for Model Cities that kept most of the better-known organizations in the coalition. The fear of losing Model Cities, the desire to control it, the fear that it was urban renewal with another name, the belief that somehow Model Cities offered a solution to all the problems of the Mission—all these, and more, played a role. But some of the MCO leadership also shared a vision of a mass-based Alinsky-tradition community organization. And it was this smaller number who were at the very center of the organization.

MCO's non-negotiable demands for control of the Model Cities program, the growing list of militant actions on other issues, and the unwillingness of MCO core leadership to back away from a multi-issue organizing agenda were cause for concern at city hall; the mayor and his staff were getting more than they had bargained for.

For MCO, the problem with Model Cities was that it defined MCO as an organization interested in running a federal program. But if Model Cities was a liability from one point of view, it had distinct assets from another. The major opportunities, given the mayor's initial recognition of the organization, were two. It tied many groups into MCO who might otherwise have departed. Further, it made it difficult for private sector business, banking, and other decision makers to dismiss MCO as "just another community group" they could ignore with impunity.

▒ Model Cities Negotiations

While MCO was developing an action agenda on issues it was also in protracted negotiations with the mayor on the rules for Model Cities governance. Already the emerging new character of MCO was beginning to stir questions among members of the mayor's staff. When MCO was involved in militant direct action, and when this action was covered in the news media, Mayor Alioto's staff would ask what MCO's priorities were, and what these activities had to do with Model Cities.

Model Cities continued to be the main interest of most of the early secondary-level Mission leadership. They would show up for key meetings with city hall staff. They took an interest in any developments that gave an appearance of either a breakthrough in the negotiations or a sellout. The non-negotiable character of the resolutions passed at the previous MCO convention reminded the negotiators that they had a limited range within which to operate. This also made it impossible for the negotiators to take advantage of certain new formulations of the relationship with city hall that might have resolved problems.

My own view is that the only thing that is non-negotiable is the question of recognition. If the organization is recognized and continues to be strong, it can deal with issues as they arise. (If it's not strong, it has to rely on courts to enforce agreements. This takes a long time; there may be no results until long after the issue is a dead letter in the life of the community; a "victory" defined by a court may not be the remedy sought by the people; going to court can be costly; and it rarely contributes to building people power, because the court is a forum for lawyers and judges, not for the action of large numbers of people.)

When the mayor's office dragged its heels in negotiations, MCO mobilizations on other issues provided leverage to move the Model Cities process along. If MCO could move significant numbers of people into action on a landlord-tenant issue, then it could do the same thing to the mayor. Internally we argued that to win Model Cities on our terms we had to show the mayor we had broad community support which was possible because of MCO's multi-issue approach.

An example of this was the closing of a street in the East Mission. Traffic ran on the block of 26th Street that went through the middle of the Bernal Dwellings Housing Project; children often ran back and forth on the street; there had been a few near-accidents and one child was hit by a car. Almost two hundred people from all over the Mission attended board of supervisors hearings on the subject of closing this one block in the East Mission. The member group immediately involved was the East Mission Action Council (EMAC), one of the groups organized by Elba Tuttle. Had this simply been framed as an issue of the people immediately affected by the street, turnout would have been limited to residents of the housing project buildings on either side of the street. Because the issue had dragged on a long time, maybe only a few of them would have participated. Perhaps a few activists would have joined them as well. But when the issue was also treated as a way to show the magnitude of MCO's support in the community to the mayor, it became possible to get more people to come to a meeting.

Another important lesson was learned in the EMAC street-closing effort. Manuel Larez was the East Mission Poverty Program's sub-area office staff person then working with EMAC. He wanted the issue to be handled as an EMAC issue, with backup support from the Poverty Program. MCO sought to project it as an EMAC issue with MCO support. Vito Saccheri, president of EMAC and an MCO executive vice president, was the man in the middle. To the casual observer, simple things like where flyers will be mimeographed seem trivial. The organizational analyst or worker knows that these are symbols indicating whose office is in the center of an activity, whose staff is working with a group, and whose central leadership is related to member or affiliated units. While the matter may at first be one of convenience, as soon as it becomes a source of tension, its organizational importance grows because it is a test of the relative strengths of two different organizing centers. When Saccheri gave his okay to the MCO-produced flyer, the question was resolved.

Larez was later to run for the presidency of MCO and to make the question of autonomy (confederation) one of his platform planks. Poverty Program leaders saw themselves playing the role of the "voice of the poor" in the Mission. After all, they were officially designated as the citizen-participation voice for the Mission in the War on Poverty.

At stake in all these questions was whether MCO could both retain the mayor's recognition as the voice of Mission residents and be a multi-issue action organization, using negotiations and direct action to win for the community things that were beyond the purview of any government program. MCO ended up doing both, despite times when this appeared to be impossible.

Recognition Won from the Health Department

The more MCO engaged in direct action outside the framework of Model Cities, the stronger became arguments by some of the mayor's staff that recognition of MCO should be reconsidered. These voices questioned whether the mayor should continue to have MCO as his negotiating partner. As a result, another strategic goal of this period was to win recognition as the voice of the Mission with some other public agency. If another city department would grant such recognition and come to an agreement with MCO, the precedent would be clear. Thus what started as a relatively inconsequential matter with the Department of Public Health—membership of a local Mental Health Advisory Board—became a major issue for the organization because victory here would establish that important precedent in relation to the mayor. This avenue had a further advantage. A loss here would not be significant for the organization because no large constituency in the community was demanding MCO control of the Mental Health Advisory Board or any specific services from the mental health center.

Accident was our major ally in the mental health issue. Accident and luck are important allies; the organizer must watch for them and use them. For reasons unknown, Dr. Ellis Sox, then head of the Department of Public Health in San Francisco, agreed to recognize MCO according to terms basically the same as those MCO was arguing for at the mayor's office—essentially a community-controlled board, two-thirds of whose members were named by MCO. The agreement was widely reported in the news media. The precedent was clear.

▦ Recognition Tested by the Mayor

In the early struggle to develop momentum for MCO, Model Cities was the only issue that could really do it. To continually use Model Cities for this purpose, however, was to pay a price. It both maintained the identification of MCO as primarily concerned with Model Cities, and it made city officials very nervous about what the mayor had gotten himself into by recognizing MCO. In January of 1969, we were hit by an aside in the press from John Anderson, the mayor's Model Cities staff person, "warning" the Mission that it ought to accept the kind of agreement worked out between the city and Bayview–Hunters Point, the other neighborhood involved in the program—or face loss of the program entirely. Bayview–Hunters Point was already slated for urban renewal, and a separate agreement—one that did not include community veto—had been worked out between the community and the Redevelopment Agency. MCO hit back the next day with a statement in the press attacking Anderson. The mayor could then step in and make peace, but MCO made it clear that we would not accept terms just because they were acceptable in some other part of the city.

Two hundred residents showing up at City Hall to support a street-closing; militant tenant organizing that included a rent strike; and the successful campaign to transfer Mission High School's top administrative staff: these were all examples of MCO's capacity to turn out large numbers of people from diverse constituencies in the Mission. MCO's leaders were explicit in conversations with the mayor's staff: if we have to, we'll turn out a lot more people on a Model Cities issue.

A new pattern began to emerge in our dealings with the mayor's office. Earlier, it had been John Anderson who was anxious to meet and work things out. Now it was difficult to get him to return MCO phone calls. Meetings weren't set or they were postponed. We concluded that city hall was stalling, perhaps because the mayor wanted out of his deal, and at least because internal discussions on how to deal with MCO were taking place.

We took care not to move precipitously into an open fight with the mayor, to allow room for maneuvering and face-saving; but a direction was established. When the course is set, it is increasingly difficult to back down. As a battle heats up, it becomes polarized. What was minor a month earlier becomes major because it is a test of strength. Our job now was to clarify (which also meant polarize) the situation so that the mayor's office would renew its recognition of MCO—not as a gift, as it had been initially, but as the outcome of a contest in which MCO demonstrated that it was a powerful and representative community organization with which the mayor must deal.

It was necessary for internal morale that we cut the issue. At the end of April 1969, MCO made a "make or break" move. A mass march on City Hall was announced. It was to be either a victory celebration or a protest march, depending on what the mayor did. The bureaucratic tactic of stalled negotiations gave the advantage to city hall, with its full-time, paid staff. The political tactic of mass action would allow us to recapture the initiative. This was our game, not theirs. With organizational letters of endorsement for our position from all major groups in the community, our bases were covered—except, that is, for one: Abel Gonzalez.

▨ Abel Gonzalez Tests MCO's Strength

Abel Gonzalez, leader of the Centro Social Obrero and its Mission Language and Vocational School, remained unconvinced of the need for a march. Indeed, he was upset by the militant activities of MCO. He understood Model Cities in much the way that some of those who feared it most understood it: as a construction program. But he was for it. It meant work for his members and new housing for people in the Mission, and he believed it could be low-priced housing that would meet the needs of present residents. Gonzalez pursued his critical view within the MCO. His disagreements with the leadership never appeared in the news media. Nor did he differ with MCO in negotiation meetings with the mayor's staff, though it was clear that he was in contact separately with the mayor's office on the issues that were being negotiated. In effect, he organized a caucus within the organization. At the heart of his position was the idea of two coalitions, one to deal with "issues" and the other to deal with Model Cities.

His approach—working within MCO—was organizationally healthy and useful. Many of his critics called him a sellout and worse. But the development of internal caucuses in a democratic organization can be a sign of its health, not of weakness. The caucus, if it does not separately negotiate with the power structure, or separately issue statements to the news media, can be a manifestation of organizational loyalty. The caucus that functions as a forum in which a particular group gathers its thoughts is different from the one that is closed to the arguments of others in the organization. In MCO, caucuses came and went, either around a hot issue or around annual elections. This nonpermanent caucusing seems to me to be a healthy internal democratic mechanism. (Permanent caucuses can be healthy too. Seymour Martin Lipset's classic study, *Union Democracy*, is about two permanent internal "political parties" within the International Typographical Workers Union.)

As staff director, I specifically made the argument for caucuses and urged those whose positions differed from those of the organization as a whole to form caucuses around their views. Since the leadership group's position was the official one adopted in the convention, they had the advantage of simply reaffirming an officially adopted position. Gonzalez was on thin ice because it was MCO's most sovereign body's position that he wanted to change.

It is in such an internal fight that the quality of organizational relationships is determined. Further, real centers of power within the organization show themselves in major internal issues. In this case, Ben Martinez took the lead, as the president, in seeing that the MCO convention position was reaffirmed. As forces developed and were tested, several things became clear. Gonzalez could split the MCO. At the same time, MCO could align with right and left groups that were against Model Cities and probably stop the program from coming into the neighborhood. While the mayor might recognize a new, Gonzalez-organized Model Cities group because of past loyalty to Gonzalez, it was not clear that he could get a majority of the votes on the board of supervisors, and it was questionable that he could win federal support for the program's coming into San Francisco in such controversial circumstances.

Just as the march on City Hall would be decisive for the Model Cities program, so the MCO Delegates Council meeting became decisive on the question of two coalitions. The outcome of that meeting was deeply influenced in Abel Gonzalez's office earlier that week. Those present were Gonzalez and Bud Johnson, a Gonzalez ally and top official in Laborers' Union Local 261; Jess Hernandez and Matt Vasquez, who were seeking to play a peacemaker role; and Ben Martinez and me. The alternatives were made clear to all participating: a unified MCO or two coalitions—one for "action," the other for Model Cities. Suggestions of "misunderstandings" allowed for changes in position and necessary saving of face. Martinez responded to Abel Gonzalez's concern that we were now moving into opposition to Mayor Alioto, making it clear that his position was only to oppose the mayor if he backed out of recognition of MCO.

A dramatic incident took place as the meeting neared conclusion. Bud Johnson went to the phone and called the mayor's office. He told the party on the other end of the line, presumably John Anderson, that all disagreements in the Mission were resolved. His apparent purpose was to stop any escalation of conflict from the mayor's end of things. Anderson evidently said he had a letter to MCO from the mayor saying there would be no MCO veto power; at least that's what we inferred from what came next: Johnson said, "Don't send the letter. I'll take full responsibility." The letter was never received, and it never came up again. Evidently Johnson's influence with the mayor was sufficient for Anderson to defer to his judgment and postpone putting the letter in the outgoing mailbox. Johnson must have felt he had enough of the mayor's confidence to, in effect, preempt the mayor himself on the issue of veto power. Johnson clearly felt that the mayor would go along with an internal MCO agreement to which Johnson and Gonzalez were parties.

■ The Mayor Reaches an Agreement with MCO

The veto-power position was central to MCO's negotiating stance with the mayor's office. Because of the fear of urban renewal, conservative homeowners became bold militants. The MCOR experience was still in many minds, and it provided an important precedent for unified community militancy. The community agencies supported veto power too. They had an additional interest. If Model Cities were run by the mayor's office, stronger institutions with a citywide base might be able to squeeze local agencies out in the competition for funds. These interests, and the power of the different groups, kept the veto-power issue central to MCO's position. Were it not for these interests, the resolutions of the convention would have been only so much paper.

The turnout for the Model Cities march was less than a success, more than failure. Between five and six hundred people participated, far fewer than the thousand or more predicted by MCO leaders. The march itself became a celebration, but then the tedious process of negotiations resumed. Now—each for different reasons—first the mayor's office, then the MCO stalled agreement on rules that would govern the relationship between city hall and the neighborhood in the development of a Model Cities plan for the Mission. Stalling on the mayor's end reflected conflicts within his staff and his desire to see things settle in the Mission. Stalling on MCO's end reflected the continuing work the Martinez leadership was doing to maintain a united front on the veto-power question. Finally, late in the year, the mayor and MCO reached an agreement. The board of supervisors later approved it by a 7-4 vote. (For: Morrison, Francois, Gonzales, Mendelsohn, Blake, Boas, (Ron) Pelosi. Against: Tamaras, Ertola, Maillard, von Beroldingen.)

In approving the agreement between the mayor and the MCO, the board of supervisors adopted what was essentially a neighborhood-controlled program. Almost all powers were vested in the newly formed Mission Model Neighborhood Corporation, two-thirds of whose members were to be from MCO. Further, while the two-thirds were formally appointed by the mayor, MCO had the power to recall them. The supervisors' approval of this structure came in a dramatic meeting attended by more than seven hundred MCO members. Spokespersons from every MCO member organization testified, appearing in alphabetical order to avoid any protocol issues; supporting statements from a number of labor, religious, and civic organizations in the city were read into the record. With two hours allocated to MCO for its presentation, well over one hundred speakers addressed the board. It had been rehearsed, and the discipline was tight. Heading the presentation and organizing it through the Planning Committee was Jack Bourne.

With this action something else of even more importance than the Model Cities victory happened. MCO asserted itself as the major organization of the Mission, with its president (at this time Ben Martinez) the informal mayor of the Mission. That had been the role of Abel Gonzalez, and part of the tension in the development of MCO surely was the implicit challenge that MCO posed.

Citywide Allies and Organizations

Once the mayor signed an agreement, MCO was in a fundamentally different position. We were now seeking allies to win approval from the board of supervisors and the U.S. Department of Housing and Urban Development (HUD); we were asking for support of the Alioto-MCO position, not for support of MCO against Alioto. Some interesting lessons in the workings of citywide labor, religious, and liberal politics were learned.

We already had church support for MCO through the efforts of Rev. Robert Davidson, director of the Joint Strategy and Action Commission (JSAC) of the Northern California Ecumenical Council—the official arm for social action for most of the mainline Protestant churches. But in heavily Catholic San Francisco, the political support of these groups was not of great significance. Our strategy was to parlay JSAC support into support from the Archdiocese of San Francisco. With the endorsements Davidson obtained, we began to seek open support from the Catholics, and we were successful. It would have almost been embarrassing for the Catholic Church not to endorse something supported by the Catholic mayor and predominantly Catholic Mission community.

Organized labor was more complex and trickier. The principles were the same. We were able to finally win across-the-board support from San Francisco unions by starting with those who supported us and playing on rivalries existing within labor, while not being a partisan in any of labor's ongoing internal struggles. And we took into account, in our own positions, labor's legitimate interest in protecting union standards for workers in San Francisco.

Labor's initial interest in Model Cities was based on its understanding that the program would provide substantial funds for construction work. In the early stages of Mission Model Cities discussion, labor representatives, including George Johns, secretary-treasurer of the AFL-CIO Central Labor Council, played an important and supportive role toward MCO. Prior to the board of supervisors' approval of the San Francisco Redevelopment Agency's request for a planning grant for the South of Market Project, Johns was a vocal critic of that project. Once the board gave its approval, the political fight—though not the legal one—was largely over. With supervisors' approval, the building trades pushed through Labor Council support for South of Market. The garment, machinist, printing, and other unions who were fighting to save jobs in the area lost their battle. Johns took a more passive support position toward MCO. The unions, we concluded, except for the Laborers and Gonzalez, must have decided to seek no more than informal veto-power status in relation to the Model Cities program and MCO, rather than be a partner in the process. In particular, given that Republican Richard Nixon was president, they didn't want Model Cities to be a vehicle for undermining labor's strength in one of the country's most pro-union cities.

Without the unions actively involved in shaping MCO, our work in the community was easier. We only needed to take labor's interests into account, not involve them in ongoing committee meetings and in thinking through what MCO was going to be. On the other hand, if one seeks a working alliance of people-power forces, including workplace as well as community organizations, then ongoing participation from unions is required. Relationships need to be formed and strengthened, shared values identified, common, particular, and conflicting interests understood—with compromises forged around the last, and trust established. These are prerequisites to creating a more powerful alliance between community and union forces, and to mitigate against the ongoing potential for divide-and-conquer tactics from the power structure.

George Johns once described his position as one necessary to allow the less organized community forces to come together. This was both a bold and risky view: bold in the sense that Johns saw the need for a community organization with which labor could ally on matters of mutual interest, risky in the sense that labor could have created a much weaker organization than MCO, had it wanted to. Johns was generally more visionary than many labor leaders, and his position on MCO was consistent with, for example, his earlier opposition to the urban renewal project in the city's downtown area.

MCO leadership consciously sought accommodation with labor on matters that might be of interest to the unions. Behind this was the idea of an ongoing labor-community alliance. The taxpayer, parent, consumer of city and private services, or purchaser of products is also the worker or unemployed person who is in or wants to be in a union. San Francisco is a union town, and union members earn wages substantially higher than those of people who are not organized. They also have a voice at the workplace to challenge unsafe or unhealthy conditions, or arbitrary and capricious treatment by supervisors. The labor-community alliance was a long-range goal, something that could only be worked on as concrete opportunities emerged. But meanwhile, opportunities to fall into situations in which the community organization was pitted against a union were many.

Almost Undone by the Building Trades Council

An example of what could have been a major difficulty came up with the Building Trades Council of the San Francisco Central Labor Council (AFL-CIO). The crafts unions making up this council are a powerful part of the AFL-CIO, but by no means dominant. In a meeting with key leaders of the building trades, we were told that "the trades" wanted one-third of the seats on the board of directors of the Mission Model Neighborhood Corporation. This was a real shift on their part from the earlier, informal veto group position taken by the full council's George Johns, who was by then retired. It may have reflected a desire on the part of the building trades to stave off strong affirmative action hiring plans that might emerge from Model Cities planning. (We learned that the national AFL-CIO Building Trades Department had sent a warning memo on affirmative action in Model Cities to its local affiliates, and feared that the memo was behind the local trades' stance.)

MCO's position was that we would sign an agreement with labor based on the following points:

Priority in employment would be given to unemployed union members residing in the Model Cities target area.

Only after such persons were no longer available would other unemployed craftsmen of the Mission be hired.

These new entrants to the workforce would join the union of their craft.

This protected union interests and was in conformity with the "resident employment plan" called for in Model Cities guidelines. It also was a de facto affirmative action plan, since it was mostly Latinos and other minorities who fit the criteria.

Faced with a fundamental challenge to our Model Cities position, we turned the game of divide and conquer to our own ends. Model Cities, it should be remembered, was not simply a construction program. With that piece of information we made contact with the two other main labor groups with whom we had relationships: the International Longshore and Warehouse Union (ILWU) and the AFL-CIO Central Labor Council, of which the Building Trades Council was the most powerful component. (There were also weaker Metal Trades, Printing Trades, Public Employee, and other subcouncils or units.) We told the ILWU and the Central Labor Council that we were calling to inform them that the building trades wanted one-third of the seats on the Model Cities board. We asked whether it would be correct for us to assume that each of their organizations would also want such representation, since Model Cities planning might take the community into areas where they had work jurisdiction. They hadn't thought about it, but once asked the question, their answer was that they did. That was three thirds. Facing the building trades with this new information, we told them that if Model Cities was to be administered by a labor union board of directors, then MCO was out of the program and would do everything in its power to stop it. We again proposed the alternative of an agreement, according to the terms already noted, between the MCO and the building trades. This time we reached agreement based on those principles.

The shift by the building trades was won in a meeting between Dan Del Carlo (unrelated to Larry and the Mission Del Carlo family), secretary-treasurer of the Building Trades Council; Joe Mazzola, president of the plumbers' union; Ben Martinez; and me. Martinez and I had agreed on a tactic: he would present MCO's point of view to them, making clear we would pull out of our agreement with the mayor and oppose Model Cities if the building trades' view prevailed; we would have some back-and-forth; if they didn't budge, I would grab Martinez's arm and say, "Come on, Ben, we aren't getting anyplace, so let's go." After about fifteen minutes, I tugged at Martinez's sleeve. We got up and started for the door. Mazzola said, "Come back here; we're going to work this thing out." They agreed to the terms we were proposing; everyone shook hands.

A rule of organization and politics is that different interests may lead to the same result. In our labor example, the rivalry between unions and the desire of each to protect their jurisdictions led them to adopt a position that resulted in our achieving the result we wanted. In examining the role played by some of the labor leaders and representatives, we learned something else.

Labor was an important avenue to Mayor Alioto, since its backing had been essential to his election. There were those in organized labor who did not want to have to relate to the Mission Latino community solely through Abel Gonzalez and the Obreros, because on some matters of concern to them, Gonzalez was politically too conservative—as, in general, were most of the building trades unions. Previously these unions thought their only way to relate to the Mission was through Gonzalez and the Centro Social Obrero. We learned that we had labor routes to the mayor other than through Abel Gonzalez. And we also learned that there were unions who wanted a route to the Mission and Latinos through us because they didn't want to be limited by Gonzalez's more conservative views.

Victory in San Francisco; Defeat in Washington, DC

With the support of labor and major churches, the Alioto-MCO proposal to the board of supervisors was assured passage. And besides these major blocs, we had substantial support from liberals in the community. The Alioto-MCO proposal now went before the board of supervisors and passed.

The irony of the whole process was that HUD, the federal agency that administered the Model Cities program, rejected the city of San Francisco's application for planning funds to develop projects in the Mission and Bayview–Hunters Point Districts. HUD's rejection of the San Francisco application included several points:

The Model Cities agency (called the City Demonstration Agency, CDA) had no clear and direct access to the mayor. In HUD planners' vision of things, the CDA director would be, in effect, a deputy mayor—influential with the mayor, perhaps his main representative on issues of poverty and race in a city. In the plan proposed by San Francisco to HUD, the CDA director was at best on a second tier of influence in relation to the mayor. Put in other terms, Model Cities was marginalized as simply another program. That was unacceptable to HUD.

If Model Cities was not close to the mayor and of importance to him, it could not provide the coordination of programs, or avoid the duplication of effort and cross-purposes, that HUD planners envisioned.

Conversely, MCO had too much power without sufficient responsibility for operation of the program. HUD did not want Model Cities to be another War on Poverty.

The proposed split of funds, almost half the total budget to each of the neighborhoods with only a caretaker staff in the CDA, was unacceptable as well, because it would not give the CDA the capacity to plan, and later evaluate and monitor, programs. Nor would the CDA have the authority to bring recalcitrant bureaucracies into coordinated efforts, because it was not clearly the "voice of the mayor"; structurally, it was just one of his voices—thus likely to become another agency to be coordinated rather than the coordinator.

▨ Technical Assistance

At the heart of HUD's rejection was the government's notion that Model Cities was a "mayor's program," not a "community program." For the Mission, this defeat offered an opportunity to reconceptualize Model Cities.

In rethinking the program, excellent technical assistance from public interest lawyer Steve Waldhorn was critical. We first encountered him at the War on Poverty's Housing and Economic Development Law Center and continued work with him when he joined the staff of the National Conference of Mayors. Technical assistance that an organization can trust is crucial in dealing with complicated programs like Model Cities.

MCO was committed to community control. In this context, "community control" meant control by a board consisting of people accountable to MCO, and administration of programs by community-based agencies. What this in fact meant was that the Mission would receive almost half of a $300,000 planning grant in order to develop a plan for the expenditure of some $7 million allotted to San Francisco by HUD, with about half of that available to the Mission (equivalent to roughly $19 million in 2009). A similar process would go on in Bayview–Hunters Point. In their analysis of Mission Area Community Action Board, Inc. (MACABI), the local arm of the Poverty Program, MCO's core leaders concluded that insufficient funds combined with "community control" guaranteed division in the community, and that issue organizing would get lost in conflicts over the division of a scarce sum of money. MCO would become the MACABI of Model Cities (which in fact it did, and this was one of the major reasons for MCO's eventual decline).

MCO core leaders recognized the community control trap and favored instead an "institutional change" approach: give Model Cities money to already existing institutions which were not necessarily community-controlled, and use people power to hold the institutions accountable (in the case of child care, for example, money might go to the school district, which already operated early childhood day-care centers, instead of a newly created agency with MCO members on the board of directors).

"But why give it to the school district?" you might ask. An institutional change approach imagined negotiating a number of things with the San Francisco Unified School District that would have wider implications for public education as a whole, including: affirmative action hiring; recognizing Latin American, Filipino, and other immigrants' teacher education credentials; incorporating child care into existing public school sites; rewriting early childhood curriculum to incorporate the lives of children of color; and creating a parallel track for newly hired paraprofessionals that could lead to AA degrees at the community college or teaching credentials at San Francisco State—and ultimately better paid and more secure jobs in the school district. MCO, through its education committee, would monitor progress on implementing such a plan and hold the school district accountable for it. A community-controlled system would not have this impact on the district. Many "models" have been created by new community-controlled organizations. Rarely do they impact more general systems. Too often they are isolated islands of positive results in seas of inadequacy.

Every time ideas about institutional change were informally presented to a wider group of MCO leaders, they were rejected. Acceptance of the MACABI-analogy analysis would have meant, on the one hand, loss of direct community control, and that was a powerful idea at the time. Further, it meant to many that MCO would give up the guarantee that Model Cities wouldn't become urban renewal, because it would no longer "control" the program. The lurking fear was that if, for example, the redevelopment agency was involved in developing scattered-site low-income housing it would somehow turn this into a bulldozer urban renewal program.

With effective technical assistance, we were able to hammer out a set of bylaws that gave us de facto veto power in the Model Cities planning process. According to HUD, the mayor's office and "delegate agencies" (other parts of city government) were supposed to operate the programs that emerged in the Model Cities plan. The process was supposed to enable the neighborhood to change the way "the City" related to the neighborhood. At the time, our own idea of what this meant was, at best, a fuzzy one. Discussions within the organization had been long and there were those who wanted to dump Model Cities because we had lost community control. In arguing that this loss was in fact a gain (because MCO would escape the MACABI-analogy problem), the core leadership received a skeptical response from other MCO leaders. It was, in large part, the confidence in which the leadership was held—not any clear understanding of what the changes would mean—that allowed the argument for "institutional change" rather than "community control" to be given a hearing.

The process of renegotiating the agreement between the city and the MCO now began. It was to be another lengthy task.

MCO pickets a landlord. Photo by Spence Limbocker

Ben Martinez, President, MCO. Photo by Spence Limbocker

Elba Tuttle, MCO 1st Executive Vice President. Photo by Spence Limbocker

Larry Del Carlo, Chair of the MCO Jobs and Employment Committee and MCO's 2nd Executive Vice President, with Segundo Lopez, Chair of the MCO phone company negotiating committee. Photo by Spence Limbocker

Ethel Kennedy visits MCO. Photo by Spence Limbocker

Mayor Joseph Alioto. Photo by Spence Limbocker

Ophelia Balderrama, Chair, MCO Community
Maintenance Committee. Photo by Spence Limbocker

MCO pickets pornographic movies at the Crown Theater, shutting the theater down; it returned to a family program format. Photo by Spence Limbocker

MCO Housing Chair Flor de Maria Crane (center). Photo by Spence Limbocker

MCO celebrates a jobs victory with a mariachi band. Photo by Spence Limbocker

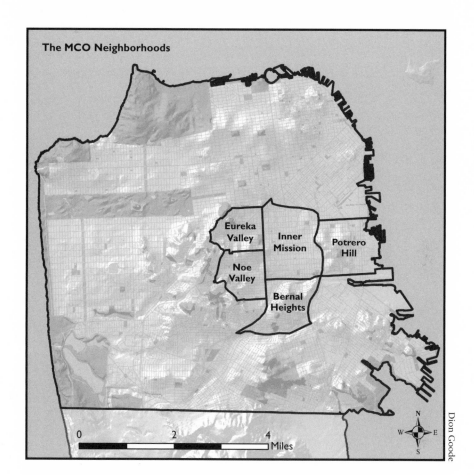

The MCO Neighborhoods

Eureka
Valley

Inner
Mission

Potrero
Hill

Noe
Valley

Bernal
Heights

0   2   4
                        Miles

N
W · E
S

Dion Goode

MCO tenant action. Photo by Spence Limbocker

Action: Tenant Organizing

and the Housing Committee

Two committees of the Mission Coalition Organization hit their stride while the next round of Model Cities negotiations took place. From its one venture into tenant organizing on 24th Street, the Housing Committee had grown to have multiple fronts for its activities. From its inauspicious beginning, when it seemed an employment committee would never get off the ground, the Jobs and Employment Committee was now huge and in regular negotiations and direct action for jobs for unemployed or underemployed people, overwhelmingly Latino plus Samoan, Filipino, Black, and some "Anglos."

Despite the loss of key people—particularly Father Jim Casey and Dave Knotts, who both left the area—and Elba Tuttle's move to an administrative position in Mission Area Community Action Board, Inc. (MACABI), the MCO Housing Committee established itself as a place where tenants could come with their troubles—and come they did. If someone came to the MCO with a housing problem, it was treated as an organizing issue. The individual was told he could handle his problem legally or with people power, though it was not put in precisely those terms. The tenant who insisted on legal help was referred to the local War on Poverty legal assistance office, which happened to be right next door. He would, by the way, usually be told by the lawyers that there wasn't much law to protect a tenant, and that the best thing to do would be to get MCO backing. (Since that time, strong pro-tenant legislation has been passed in San Francisco. But even strong laws can't defend tenants when a landlord wants to get rid of them and has the means to do so. Because the law lifts controls when a unit becomes vacant, paving the way for a higher rent to be set, unscrupulous landlords have a strong incentive to push tenants out. Many do.)

The tenant who was convinced to go the organizational route had an organizer assigned to his building and block. We asked the tenant to introduce us to anyone he knew in the building. Sometimes tenants were isolated from each other, so we were beginning from scratch. In other cases, a well-formed network of relationships already existed in the building; all the organizer had to do was put a little formality on an already existing organization.

The pattern of residency in the Mission didn't include many large apartment buildings; typically there were from six to twenty or so units. When a building was organized, 51 percent of the tenants signed a petition authorizing the MCO to serve as their bargaining agent in dealing with the landlord. Most of these tenants also attended one or more of the meetings for their building that took place prior to the first action. The organizer explained the workings of MCO; the new tenant group was prepared to go to the Housing Committee and get its building put on the committee's agenda for negotiations with the landlord.

At Housing Committee meetings, the tenants would meet others in similar situations with their landlords. Other tenant leaders would ask them if they understood that tenants in the MCO would support each other; tenants from a particular building could count on the strength of all the tenant groups together in dealing with landlords. It was not simply the pep talk, however, that got the newly organized tenant groups into the action—and into the organization. Rather, it was landlords' reactions to efforts to negotiate with them.

▥ "Notice to Landlord"

The Housing Committee developed a routine way to deal with landlords, sending out mimeographed "Notice to Landlord" forms. The first politely and in an understated manner invited the landlord to a housing negotiation; its final paragraph said, "We wish to sit down and work out this problem with you. If you could please give our office a call within the next week…" The second letter got tougher; its final paragraph said, "We have not heard from you, even though we asked you to contact us so that we could arrange a convenient hour for you to meet with our Housing Committee. If we do not hear from you by _____, more definite action will be taken." If there was still no answer, a third letter informed the landlord that the MCO would take "further appropriate action" to get the landlord to the bargaining table. At the outset, the tables were being turned, and the tenants enjoyed it. Prior to their participation in MCO, it was only the landlord who could send notices to tenants. Now they were sending notices to him.

The landlord who attended negotiations had to sit across the table from a team that including elected representatives from his building and members of the MCO Housing Committee's negotiating team, who were skilled negotiators. Sitting in the room during negotiations would be twenty to sixty tenants, depending on the number and sizes of buildings on the negotiating table. In effect, a community court existed. The landlord who refused to negotiate in good faith was dismissed, and the people present voted to take action against him. At any particular meeting it could almost be guaranteed that one of the landlords, acting in a typically paternal or abusive way, would give the meeting the spark it needed to move the people into action. Again, it was our opposition organizing for us. Once "landlord" was personalized in this way, it was not difficult for people in other buildings with different landlords to get into the action. It was finally an opportunity for the powerless to act with power and dignity. That is what the organizing was all about, and it was nowhere better illustrated than in the Housing Committee.

Personalizing the decision maker in this way could release a lot of pent-up anger at a landlord (or anyone in a position of authority and power). To reach an agreement, that anger had to become righteous anger at conditions, not hatred of a person. Indeed, some of those with whom MCO initially negotiated in an adversarial way subsequently became allies. The nonviolent spirit that I'd learned in the southern civil rights movement made me hope to convert adversaries to supporters of justice. But that wasn't essential to what we were doing.

Tactics

A battery of tactics emerged from the Housing Committee. Each tactic or set of tactics was tailored to the specifics we learned about the landlord. If he lived in a fancy neighborhood, that's where we picketed. If he went to a fancy church, that's where a large number of us would go to pray on a Sunday. If he worked in an accessible office, especially in personnel or in a professional office building, that's where a delegation of tenants and their supporters would go. If he owned a small business, it would be picketed during its busiest hours. This was action-research at its best; the information gained was immediately put to work.

In the Housing Committee's early days, the landlord who came to the negotiating table in good faith was confronted with a twelve-page, carefully worded legal document. We soon learned that one page listing rents, repairs, deadlines, and any specific miscellany was all that was needed. The issues weren't won in the courts, so we didn't need an agreement that could be enforced there. Further, even where there were legal handles, by the time the tenant could avail himself of them it was usually too late. Disgusted by lack of repairs or a big rent hike, she would just move out. It was our organizational strength that won and enforced the agreements.

In the course of tenant organizing, we learned the importance of detail. While the general rules gave guidelines as to how to proceed, we found that every case was different. The wealth and personality of the landlord affected the outcome of the struggle in almost every building. The rent strike was our final weapon, but we knew that once we were in it, a determined landlord could win. Eviction notice would be followed by court order, and finally the sheriff would arrive to put people out and take their possessions, which would be held until rent was paid or sold, with the landlord getting rent out of the proceeds.

Stories

The action generated by the Housing Committee was the source of many lively stories. In one instance, the landlord was a Russian immigrant woman whose realtor and negotiator with MCO was a real right-winger. To bypass him we got a Russian major from UC Berkeley to go to her house and assure her we were simply seeking a negotiated agreement and didn't want to take her building from her. Her response was extraordinary: "I was forced to move to China from Russia by the revolution of 1917; I was forced to move from China to San Francisco by the revolution of 1949. I was forced to move from the Western Addition (a neighborhood in San Francisco) by urban renewal. I will not be forced to do anything again." We were unable to make her budge. Her tenants stopped paying rent, accumulated their rent-strike money over a six-month period, and moved to the Outer Mission, using the accumulated funds as down payments on home purchases!

In another case, an owner we attempted to negotiate with simply abandoned his property. We knew Walter Gordon, the realtor who had sold it to him, and asked him to intervene. Gordon couldn't find the new owner either. We concluded that he had something major to hide and feared that our picketing of his home would somehow make him a public figure. The tenants remained; the property was taken over by the bank that held the mortgage and sold to yet another new owner, who kept the tenants.

In another, an outraged gay owner turned the tables on MCO. He was a hair stylist, and we picketed his salon on the relatively fancy West Portal Avenue shopping strip. With his white poodle on a leash, a few days later he picketed our headquarters, handing out his own flyer to the news media. The flyer opened with the headline "!!! LITTLE GUY vs. THE MISSION COALITION ORGANIZATION!!!" and continued, "I, James B. Short, a Mission District resident myself, am here today to protest the action of the M.C.O., a large and powerful organization with apparent recognition in this city…" We didn't know what to do when our tactics were turned against us. Only after many twists and turns, and intervention from a politician friendly to both MCO and gay political interests, were we able finally to negotiate a settlement with him.

The Housing Committee gave MCO the kind of issue and action orientation that the core leadership was seeking to build. Participants gained a sense of dignity and respect in their community, the actions were fun, and the wins were of a bread-and-butter nature. New leaders emerged in the committee, and more people were brought in to participate in the broader life of the MCO. A number of officers and secondary leaders came out of the Housing Committee, including Flor de Maria Crane, a later candidate for MCO presidency.

Problems and Opportunities

Tenant organizing was not without its problems. As suggested by the above stories, ownership patterns in the Mission were such that individual rather than corporate landlords owned most apartments. The economics of housing frequently put a squeeze on small landlords. The MCO Community Maintenance Committee had developed a longer-range strategy for working with landlords who were having trouble getting loans from banks or savings and loan associations in the Mission, or being harassed by city building inspectors, or having insurance difficulties, or being inequitably taxed, but the strategy was on paper and didn't necessarily mean that a particular landlord would be in a position to agree to what his tenants were demanding.

As the previous stories indicate, landlord responses to MCO were varied: from the extreme of deserting a building to the more common stubborn resistance to negotations. Landlords who learned of MCO's relationship with city government complained to members of the board of supervisors. They wanted to know why the city was supporting such a "radical" organization!

There were other problems as well. Tenant turnover was high in many buildings and this affected organizing efforts, even though the people who moved tended to move within the Mission. Eviction notices panicked many tenants, even though they had signed up to join their building's tenant association. Some tenants were looking on the side for a good deal, and if it came along they would leave their building in the middle of a fight with the landlord. When one moved out, others became alarmed.

At its peak, the Housing Committee could mobilize a hundred or so people on a given weekend to picket one or more landlords at their homes. And at its peak, there was a tenant organization in each of the buildings in which there were issues. These were, to be sure, very fragile organizations. But there was a network of relationships established among people who often had been strangers. And that network was available for mobilization when major actions or a convention were on the agenda.

Leaders coming out of the Housing Committee learned the workings of a mass organization; they made one of the committees work, and they developed the tenant organizations as their constituency within MCO. For them, the action and the satisfaction of participation were foremost. Their housing problems, if they had any to start with, were long behind them.

Landlords Benefit Too

On occasion, the Housing Committee represented a landlord if it was clear that a tenant was abusing his apartment, and that the landlord had legitimate grievances. Further, landlords with little money, especially resident landlords, actually had less clout than tenants armed with legal assistance from the Poverty Program. We saw the small landlord, as we saw other small businesspeople, as part of the coalition we were building. We sought structurally and in fact to represent these interests, when Housing Committee members were convinced they were just, that modest increases in rents could be negotiated if needed repairs accompanied the increases, and that the landlord was not already exploiting the tenants with high rents.

In the early organizing, except when a landlord came to MCO with real grievances about his tenants, landlord interests were expressed in MCO's Community Maintenance Committee and Planning Committee. There were two reasons for this. First, and most obvious, landlords' interests differed from those of their tenants. But it was also the case that landlords were typically more experienced in dealing with paperwork (they had to apply to banks for loans) and negotiating (with lenders, building or health inspectors, and others), whereas in some of the buildings we organized tenants who had no such experience. We wanted to create a space within MCO where civic competency could be gained by people with little or no experience in civic affairs in the U.S.

Redlining

One major success the Community Maintenance Committee had on behalf of landlords, and in fact the whole community, ended redlining in the Mission by a savings and loan association. As earlier described, "redlining" got its name from red lines actually drawn on maps around neighborhoods that lenders had labeled as "declining," giving that as a reason for charging high rates for, or denying, improvement loans and mortgages. Realtors would engage in "blockbusting," scaring homeowners and then buying their property at below-market prices. Often Black people purchased homes from these realtors at inflated prices. And the higher mortgages rates they had to get from banks and savings and loan companies gave the lenders a piece of the action. Once the first Black people moved in, "panic peddling" realtors would predict a decrease in property values and urge white homeowners to sell right away.

In fact, pent-up demand among Blacks whose incomes qualified them to buy was exploited by these realtors, just as they exploited white fears of the consequences of Blacks moving into "their" neighborhoods. Though less extensive, the same kind of exploitation took place with Latinos and Asians.

Redlining, blockbusting, and panic peddling became national issues. Two strategies were used by community organizations to counter them. One was called "greenlining." Churches and other neighborhood institutions would threaten to move their deposits or pension funds to other institutions if lenders and insurers didn't stop redlining. Where a broadly based community organization with denominational Protestant and Diocesan Catholic support existed, this was a powerful tactic, and it worked. Where local organization was weak and citywide support nominal, it didn't.

The other strategy was national legislation. It was pursued by one of the national networks that emerged in Chicago from Alinsky-tradition community organizing. Not only did legislation make redlining illegal, but subsequent legislation forced lenders and insurers to disclose by zip code where their money was going. This legislation provided for "interveners" who could, for example, challenge a bank's application to open a new branch on the basis of that bank's past redlining practices and failure to end them.

Despite both approaches, redlining persisted, though with diminished strength. As interest in inner-city investment grew, however, the issue became moot in many cities. The new problem for low-to-moderate-income residents was gentrification, not redlining and its associated practices. This was certainly the case in the Mission.

Action: Jobs and

Employment

It was around the campaign for good jobs that the Mission Coalition Organization initiated in the spring of 1970 that the greatest organizational growth emerged, and the greatest citywide resistance developed. The two are related; it was the resistance of employers and the mayor's office to our jobs program that forced us to live up to the power and independence that we claimed to have.

Summer Jobs for Youth and Youth Leadership in MCO

In the late fall of 1969, I became interested in youth groups in the Mission, hearing and finding that many groups were unknown by traditional agencies, even the so-called radical agencies in the Mission. For example, a group of teenagers hung out at Rolph Park, in the East Mission. While they didn't have a storefront or a budget, the group was real. In fact, at each of the neighborhood's parks and in other gathering places, similar groups were to be found. They weren't violent gangs, but they also weren't the kids who went home after school and did their homework.

As a result of this interest, I came into touch with Larry Del Carlo, the youth coordinator for MACABI (Mission Area Community Action Board, Inc., the Poverty Program). By this time, MACABI was hostile to MCO as a result of our growing influence in the Mission. Del Carlo shared some of the hostility but was also angered at MACABI's inability to respond to issues being raised by youth. He was, himself, still in his late teens.

As staff director of MCO, I would get "lead names" from the organizers working under my direction as well as from elected and appointed leaders in the organization. Del Carlo's was one. He and I spent several hours talking one day, and I became convinced that he was ready to leave the traditional "service" orientation in which he was working and shift to an "action" and "organizing" orientation. I set up a meeting between Del Carlo and MCO President Ben Martinez, and they had a good conversation. Martinez and I discussed the possibility that Del Carlo be asked to run for office in the coming MCO election if he brought some delegations to the community convention. Martinez moved to implement the understandings that came from these conversations.

Many younger people who, like Del Carlo, grew up in the Mission and wanted to do something for the community got absorbed in service programs. They intuitively knew that the programs weren't doing anything to deal with fundamental problems. At the same time, some of these youth were unable to identify with other, more radical-sounding groups whose analysis of the service programs was similar to MCO's but who did not offer the alternative of community organizing as practiced by MCO. For these young people, MCO had the answers that were lacking elsewhere.

In the spring, with Del Carlo now an elected officer and appointed by Martinez to head the Jobs and Employment Committee, we began developing a strategy. It paralleled that emerging from the civil rights movement and other community organizing efforts: around the country, demands were placed on an employer to develop an affirmative action hiring program. If the employer didn't sign an agreement to do so, direct action tactics like boycotts or picketing and sit-ins were used until an agreement was reached. When I started working for TMCO, this use of boycotts and direct action was fairly widespread in protests around the country.

In an effort to avoid problems with MCO member nonprofit agencies who were seeking funding for manpower training programs, we decided to postpone a campaign for full-time adult employment and make summer jobs for youth the first priority of the Jobs and Employment Committee. Since there were no funds to administer such programs, other than the War on Poverty–related Neighborhood Youth Corps, we knew that the agencies would not see the activities of the MCO Jobs committee as a threat, and they might participate because they agreed with the committee's purpose. Only after a summer youth campaign would we explore whether we had a capacity for a campaign for full-time adult employment.

We went over our strategy, did extensive role-playing on how to negotiate, examined targets for action who had a production or distribution facility in the Mission and who might be vulnerable to a direct action campaign, and decided to start with bakeries. We also decided we would not meet with community relations, personnel, or public relations staff people, "staff" being those who recommend to decision makers: we wanted to meet with company "line" management—people who had authority to make agreements with us and implement them.

▨ Summer Jobs Negotiations

MCO's jobs negotiators had a very effective ploy. In our opening statement to a top manager, we would say we wanted to see the company's EEOC report. The U.S.

Equal Economic Opportunity Commission (EEOC) didn't have very much enforce-ment power for its noble goal, but it did require that employers file reports with the commission on the racial and ethnic composition of their workforce. Employers were not required to divulge their figures publicly. However, a friendly source at the regional EEOC office was willing to tell us whether a company's record was bad. The vast majority of employers had few people of color in their ranks.

The typical response to our request for the EEOC report was "We're not required to give you that information." We had a ready reply: "We know that, but there's nothing that prevents you from doing so." Unwillingness to divulge the information suggested there was something to hide. Our negotiating team would stick with this point for several exchanges of conversation. Then, often much to the relief of the employer, we'd say something like "Okay, let's move on to another point." Some-times you could almost hear the sigh of relief! Our next question initially appeared much less threatening: "What's your turnover rate in entry-level jobs?" Sometimes a manager could give us an approximation when the question was asked; sometimes he had to get the information from a staff person. In any case, with this information in hand, we were ready to make a specific proposal regarding jobs: "We'd like X percent of your entry-level jobs for people we will refer to you." While the percent-age was negotiable, our initially high figure was based on the high percentage of unemployment in the Mission compared to overall in San Francisco.

Bakeries, dairies, and similar kinds of companies were good targets. There were several of them located right in the Mission. In the Deep South, civil rights organizations negotiated with local employers over employment opportunities for African-Americans. If an employer didn't reach an agreement with the organiza-tion, a boycott was organized. The Montgomery Bus Boycott was, of course, already internationally known. Rev. Jesse Jackson, then a rising figure in Dr. Martin Luther King's Southern Christian Leadership Conference, started Operation Breadbasket in Chicago and made this strategy nationally known. Rev. Leon Sullivan, an African-American leader in Philadelphia, pioneered the approach there with great success. On Sunday mornings, ministers would announce from their pulpits the names of companies or products to be boycotted. The program was effective and was copied elsewhere—I had copied it with success in Kansas City, Missouri, when I worked there for Alinsky.

A core of people was recruited to the MCO Jobs and Employment Committee. They were adults who either worked with youth or had an interest in youth, young adults who still identified with the problems of young people, or the high school–age summer job seekers themselves. Larry Del Carlo's mother, father, and sister all par-ticipated. This led to some humorous slogans: "Families that meet together keep together," and "Families that picket together stick it together."

Taking on a Giant

The first meeting with an employer took about a dozen of us to the personnel office of ITT Continental, baker of Wonder Bread and Hostess Cakes; the meeting got us nothing. Through our contact with Rev. Bob Davidson in the local interdenominational social action body, we made contact with the minister of an ITT vice president. Many business leaders were also leaders in their suburban churches, where they presented a different image than they did in their interactions with inner-city leaders. Churches supporting community organizing groups in the inner city could urge suburban pastors to counsel their members to negotiate. Davidson was a vigorous MCO supporter; this was another instance of his delivering for us. When we received a telegram from ITT asking us to meet with the plant superintendent, he assured us that this was not another stall. This was the man who could make the decisions, and that is what we wanted. Through Davidson's good offices, a meeting was finally arranged with Norm Steinke, the plant superintendent.

A meeting with Steinke was set on the afternoon MCO President Ben Martinez returned to San Francisco from a ten-day community organizing training session at Alinsky's Industrial Areas Foundation; the timing wasn't coincidental. We arranged to have some action cooking upon his return. Dramatizing things even further, at the last minute Steinke cancelled the meeting and refused to schedule another one. Martinez took the opportunity this stonewalling presented and ran with it. He almost literally grabbed the dozen or so of us who had been at MCO headquarters preparing for the Steinke meeting. We piled into cars and headed to ITT's bakery. Once there, we simply barged our way in and occupied Steinke's office. It was the closest MCO ever got to violence as we pushed our way in and demanded that talks resume. The situation was volatile and could have blown up in our faces. A large window separated the room we were in from the rest of the office. Employees signaled to Steinke that they would call the police if he wanted them to. He didn't. I later surmised it was because of what he'd heard from his vice president about MCO.

You could cut the tension in the room with a knife. For two hours we sat in an office that got smokier by the minute, with Martinez leading our negotiations and Steinke only sitting in his chair, refusing to acknowledge that he was under any obligation to negotiate with us.

Confronted with the fact that he had unilaterally broken negotiations, Steinke had no real response to the question of whether or not he had done the right thing. Without our action, he never would have faced the question of whether his unilateral cancellation of our meeting and refusal to schedule another one was a moral thing to do. That's what we confronted him with, not the question of jobs. And that issue got us back to the negotiating table. After two hours, Steinke finally agreed to a subsequent meeting. This time we were confident that the meeting would take place. Our action let Steinke know that if it didn't, we would not just go away.

At the same time, the militancy of our action took us onto very thin ice. Our broader constituency would not have tolerated any violence or arrests. Further, use of violence would have given anyone in city hall looking for an excuse to dump us from the Model Cities program just what he wanted.

At ITT we wanted thirty job slots for the summer. ITT started with two full-time slots. We bargained that up to eight full-time, summer-long slots, then divided the jobs into thirds, so that a young person would work only one-third of the summer. We could place twenty-four students that way. An ITT summer employee would earn as much as a Neighborhood Youth Corps worker did in the whole summer, because ITT agreed to pay union scale. News of the first agreement spread like wildfire on the youth networks in the Mission. Within two weeks, over one hundred youth were attending the Tuesday night meetings of the Jobs and Employment Committee.

Our ITT Continental negotiations established the summer pattern. We asked employers to create jobs, such as cleaning up parking lots, emptying out old basements, filling in for a vacationing regular worker if the training to do the job wouldn't take too long, or whatever else an employer could come up with. We would get a commitment of a specific number of jobs. We said the number should be 10 percent of the total workforce, but we negotiated a bit down from that. Pay would be at whatever entry level was. For the most part, these were union jobs. Finally, the employer agreed to hire young people as we sent them: there would be no exam of any kind, except if state law required a health exam.

We also covered our relationship with our labor union allies; we called the Central Labor Council and told its new secretary-treasurer, Jack Crowley, what we were doing and asked if he had any advice or any interests that he wanted to protect. He had only two concerns. First, that we not take over full-time work in the unions' jurisdictions; we agreed—we were not interested in putting adults out of their jobs. Second, he urged us to seek a two-dollar minimum wage (twelve dollars in 2009) for the students who got jobs; we were already asking for more. From that time on, any time an employer tried to tell us that he wanted to work with us but couldn't because of his union contracts, we simply said, "Call Jack Crowley at the AFL-CIO Central Labor Council." The contract issue wasn't raised again.

■ Who Gets the Jobs? The Point System

The ITT agreement led immediately to the question "Who gets the jobs?" It was discussed right after our successful negotiation with Steinke. It was an intriguing and organizationally significant discussion.

"The people who need them most" was one reply. That led to how "need" was to be determined, and by whom. I could see a new social welfare agency being created before my eyes. Soon people were talking about using application forms in which people would have to meet eligibility criteria. Since most of those in the discussion knew the youth who would apply, they also knew that applicants might stretch the truth. Would there be investigations of an applicant's claims? The energy that had been in the room when we returned from the successful negotiation quickly was lost. In its place were the implicit question "What are we creating here?" and the implicit answer "Not something we want to create."

Silence fell in the room. Then fifteen-year-old Joan Del Carlo, who hadn't spoken up to that point, quietly asked, "Why shouldn't the jobs go to the people who work for them?" A different silence was the initial response, then everyone was talking at once. According to my notes, it was Fernando Cosio who first recognized the genius of the idea. But that recognition was quickly echoed by everyone present. Given MCO's orientation toward participation and building people power, as soon as the idea was on the table, it was self-evident that it was the way to go.

From that discussion MCO's "point system" evolved. An individual got a point for each Jobs Committee activity he or she participated in, including meetings, research, negotiations, and direct action. Jobs were dispatched according to one's position on the points ladder. The person at the top of the ladder had three options when an employer called MCO to have a job opening filled: take the job; refer the job—that is, give it to someone else, such as a member of your family, club, or church (and go back to the bottom of points ladder); or pass the job on to the next person on the points list (and keep your points and position on the ladder). This system became part of the regular operating procedure of the Jobs Committee. It resolved several problems at once:

MCO was not functioning like an agency, evaluating people to see if they deserved jobs. The individual "earned" the job by participating to get it.

Jobs were not treated as patronage, but as a way to build a mass voluntary organization. Those who participated in the committee developed an allegiance to MCO because it was their organization. They were involved in its struggles and participated in winning its victories.

The system had the effect of guaranteeing that motivated people were sent to jobs. Someone who got ten points, the number later required for full-time job dispatch, demonstrated by their ongoing participation that they wanted to work.

Our approach made clear that we thought something was wrong with employers and employment patterns, not with the unemployed—who, as we quickly learned, were quite motivated when real work seemed available. We were in a fight for jobs. The stigma typically associated with unemployment was challenged by the very structure and method of the MCO Jobs Committee.

■ The Shift to Full-Time Jobs

During the summer of 1969, leaders in the Jobs Committee and in MCO discussed moving from summer jobs to adult employment. The shift was not an easy one. By the end of the summer, the committee had dropped down to its original core group plus a few others. The first adult employment negotiations took place without a constituency of the unemployed. Our assumption had been that if we proved we could win summer jobs with our approach, we would have no trouble recruiting the unemployed into the committee. The assumption was an error.

PG&E, northern California's "investor-owned public utility," was selected as MCO's first adult-employment negotiating target. The company had a plant in the Mission and a bad affirmative action hiring record. Further, it carefully cultivated an image of being a good corporate citizen. One of its vice presidents was in a number of civic leadership positions in San Francisco. Private utilities were the norm in the United States, but unlike in any other industry, 20 percent of the utility companies were owned by cities, counties, or, in the case of Nebraska, state governments. In most other places the question of switching to public ownership had been a dead letter since the end of the 1930s, but in San Francisco this was not the case. PG&E was vulnerable. Negotiations with PG&E were successful.

The PG&E negotiations led to a formula for dealing with businesses. MCO sought 20 percent of their turnover rate in entry-level jobs. This was justified on the grounds of population and poverty percentages in the Greater Mission. Further, MCO demanded that the employer take people as they were referred by MCO— there was no screening. We were developing a slogan, "The right to a job is greater than the right to an excess profit." That was our answer when an employer would try to use the cost of training as a justification for screening our referrals. Most important for MCO's growing effectiveness, the "take them as we send them" position allowed us to transfer the point system we had developed for summer jobs to our adult campaign.

After a while I noticed that leaders of the Jobs Committee were turning down the opportunity to get excellent blue-collar jobs, especially good for people whose education ranged from partway through high school to a year or two of community college. Typically, these were union jobs, offering not only good wages but also a full benefits package. In an informal meeting with committee leaders I once asked, "Why are you guys turning down these jobs?" The response was immediate. As one of them put it, "Mike, I can always take one of these jobs, but I'll never get the chance to do this for my community again." Another spoke of the recognition he was getting as a leader. Both recognized they were doing things they never imagined they might do.

The PG&E negotiations led to sixty jobs for the year. Success with PG&E was followed by success at many other firms. The Jobs Committee again grew, this time with an adult base. Our longer-range view was that as people were placed in the jobs we negotiated for, they would continue to relate to the MCO. When ten or more people were placed with a particular employer, we thought they could be organized as a new member organization of MCO. Further issues would arise on the job: discrimination, problems with supervisors, how to participate in the union if there was one (there typically was)—or how to get one organized if there wasn't. Members of these new workplace-based organizations might have difficulties on the job, or be in a dispute with a landlord, or have a child at an inadequate school. All these could become issues for MCO. The leadership and new activists were also motivated by the desire to build a base to enhance the overall organization and to continue the fights around employment.

Unemployed people working on the point system spread the word of what MCO was doing through the member organizations. If Mrs. or Mr. X got a job through the MCO and was a member of one of the churches or block clubs in the organization, the word went back to the leadership of that group: MCO membership was paying off in a concrete way for an individual member of that member organization. This created advocates for MCO within the member organizations so that if, for example, a conservative church member questioned continued participation in MCO, there was someone in the church who would say, "Wait a second, that's how I got my job." To the benefit of the MCO core leadership, there was a growing number of advocates of their positions on issues, strategies, and tactics within the member organizations.

One of the best examples of this broader organizational payoff was with Rev. Joe King and the First Samoan Congregational Church. Several of his unemployed members got good jobs through MCO's Jobs Committee. Rev. King became an outspoken advocate for MCO in his denomination and in ecumenical religious bodies. The church turned out a strong delegation to the next several MCO conventions. When Ben Martinez or I visited the church for Sunday morning services, we were treated as visiting dignitaries, almost to the point of embarrassment!

Another dimension of the committee's approach was its relationship to community manpower agencies. The "take them as we send them" position implied rejection of approaches in the manpower field that focus on alleged lack of motivation or lack of skills. But rather than bypass the agencies, MCO leaders decided that they too could be of help. When an employer said he couldn't take people who didn't speak English, for example, we had a reason to say that he could funnel people through the Mission Language and Vocational School (MLVS) who could then be hired. The same was true with other employer requirements. But such referrals had to be made with the understanding that the MCO-referred person would be hired—the point system remained intact.

Without the point system, the basic "ideology" of the MCO committee would be compromised beyond repair. Abundant evidence existed from previous experience that training programs did not lead to jobs. And our own experience indicated that the unemployed person wanted to go to work and get paid right away; delay would just undermine their confidence in the MCO program. So long as the initiative could remain in the hands of the Jobs Committee and the point system stayed intact, both the organization as a whole and the community-based agency could benefit. As we shall see, when Model Cities funds came to the Mission, HUD required that the point system be dropped.

We also learned that the point system was not without problems. After several months, we realized that one woman who was a regular participant in the committee wouldn't accept jobs; instead she referred them. When we tried to figure out to whom they were being referred, we discovered she was selling jobs to unemployed people. Technically, there was nothing to prevent her doing so, but she was expelled from the committee.

Attendance at the Tuesday night Jobs and Employment Committee meetings soon grew to three hundred or so, jamming the social hall at Mission United Presbyterian Church. The problem facing the committee now was one of generating new negotiating teams and new jobs actions so that new members would see that this organization meant business. The momentum was there. Our successes to date had replaced a feeling of defeat with one of hope.

▨ Pepsi-Cola Victory

Nothing better illustrated the interplay of militant direct action and Model Cities recognition from the mayor than MCO's Pepsi-Cola campaign. With victories at PG&E, several bakeries, and a number of other companies with production and/or distribution sites in the Mission, the Jobs Committee opened negotiations with Pepsi-Cola, whose bottling plant was in the heart of the Mission. The first negotiation ended with no progress. Dozens of committee members attended the second one—both to get points and to be part of what looked like a forthcoming battle. In particular, a number of young people attended. Instead of negotiating, the company's plant manager, Richard Campodonico, called the police department's tactical squad (an anti-riot unit) to get us out of the building. MCO leaders were angry. We decided to see if we could make the mayor an ally in this effort.

Through his Model Cities representative, we informed the mayor of the Pepsi incident. In a face-to-face meeting we asked the mayor to intercede and get Pepsi into good-faith negotiations with us. As an added touch, we asked him to provide us with police protection when we next went to Pepsi. He smiled at the suggestion, and complied with both requests. In our presence, he called Campodonico and asked him to meet with us. In the conversation, the mayor indicated he'd already heard about the Pepsi encounter—from Campodonico, who, it turned out, was an Alioto supporter. At the next meeting at Pepsi-Cola, a lone cop appeared to escort us into the building. Mr. Campodonico reached agreement with us.

A Point about Leadership

In a common pattern, a new leader fears the involvement of more new people in the organization, because they might challenge his or her newly achieved recognition and authority. Such a person can effectively kill a committee and an organization if new, and potentially rival, leaders do not assert themselves and if counterstrategies and a counterculture do not develop.

Larry Del Carlo turned out to be a leader who welcomed new participation in the Jobs Committee. Thus it was able to grow rapidly. Del Carlo recognized that new leaders would be available to be on negotiating teams; the more negotiating teams, the more action and jobs for the community; the more jobs-related action, the greater the role of the Jobs Committee in the whole organization.

Just as the Housing Committee created a new MCO base with its building-by-building development of tenant associations, so the Jobs Committee created a new base of young people within the organization. The full-time jobs campaign deepened the commitment to MCO of the many churches that were able to send under- or unemployed members to the committee in the same way they sent tenants with landlord problems to the Housing Committee.

Out of the Jobs and Employment Committee, as out of the Housing Committee, a number of talented leaders were to emerge. The full flowering of the committee's possibilities did not begin to be realized until it got into adult employment. But the creation of the committee's first core of leaders took place in the summer jobs campaign.

A Closer Look at

MCO's Political Makeup

Much of what we have discussed as "politics" in the Mission Coalition Organization has been the "who gets what, when, why, and how"—the emphasis of the behaviorist approach to political science and the kind of thing media cover in American electoral politics. But behind this aspect of politics are values and points of view, and these were also important to shaping the internal struggles that took place in the MCO. In what follows, I have divided the conflicts in the MCO according to a number of ideological points of view and the social base most associated with each of them. This conceptual clarity is useful in one sense, but there is an associated risk to be considered as well: reality can be artificially made to seem clearer than in fact it is. Leaders were often ambivalent in their views and sometimes shifted from one position to another. Positions taken were sometimes filled with ambiguity and internal contradiction. Personal relationships of trust and loyalty were sometimes more important than arguments. But whether implicit or explicit, clear or fuzzy, it was the basic views discussed here that often guided the actions of major and minor actors in the MCO drama.

For some groups, the idea of a broadly based people-power organization was itself of value. They shared in a consensus on this value and were willing to compromise on specific formulations of their ideas in order that others with whom they wanted to be in an ongoing relationship could work together with them. At the other end of the spectrum were groups whose view of MCO was strictly instrumental. They were ambivalent, or even antagonistic, to the idea of a permanent people-power organization but recognized that they had to be part of it if their views were to be heard in constituencies they wanted to influence. The populist, small-d democrats, the pluralists, some elements of the Anglo left, and some of the nationalists viewed MCO as a value in itself. They saw it as a forum within which to pursue their particular points of view. Others, particularly among the organized Anglo left, the conservative populists, and the Latino nationalists, had a more instrumental view of MCO. They were in it because they thought they had to be: to keep it from selling out; to recruit; to avoid being isolated from groups with whom they wanted a relationship.

▓ Overview

Briefly stated, I identify the ideological views behind MCO's internal struggles, and the base associated with each of them, as follows:

Radical populist, small-d democrats. This point of view characterized the leadership of the organization for the period covered in this tale. For religious participants, the view was elaborated and rooted in their understanding of the Bible's mandate for social and economic justice. Saul Alinsky's thinking was important to this group, as were the ideas of the southern civil rights movement. Alinsky used "radical" in the titles of two of his important books: *Reveille for Radicals* and *Rules for Radicals*. In the former, a widely read description of his early organizing work, he defined "radical" as going to the root. He considered powerlessness of large numbers of people, on the one hand, and concentration of power in the hands of a small corporate elite, on the other, the root evil and Achilles' heel of American democracy.

Conservative populists. This group was never really inside MCO but their views were taken into account because of the responsive chord they struck with older Anglo homeowners in the community, some of whom were important in MCO member churches—a constituency MCO's core leadership wanted to reach.

Traditional pluralists, who thought the American political and economic system worked fairly well for those who were organized to negotiate within it, but failed for those who were unorganized. In this view, the task of community organizing was to bring the marginalized and excluded to the decision-making tables, where they would become another bloc whose interests would be counted when policy was made.

Political centrists. Often Anglo, this group, though not central in MCO's early development, was particularly important in the early politics of Model Cities: had they quit MCO and denounced it to the mayor, he might have terminated his recognition of MCO.

The organized Anglo left. Generally Marxist, this group was disproportionately influential because its members were deeply committed and spent a lot of time on their commitment. The Progressive Labor Party was the major organized left organization with a public presence in MCO, via its influence in the Mission Tenant Union and two other member groups, but individual Spartacists, Communists, socialists, and independent leftists were active as well.

Nationalism. This view, pro-Latino but not separatist or anti-white, was widely present among activists, some radical, some liberal. They shared the idea that it was ethnicity or nationality, in this case Latino, that should be MCO's central theme and provide its guiding principles. By the late sixties, nationalism was a major influence in African-American and Latino communities. (Conservative Latino organizations didn't join MCO.)

The relationship between self-interest and ideology is critical to understanding the politics of the Mission.

▩ Populist Democrats and the "Issues Orientation"

The Martinez leadership was based on an issue orientation, with the issues being those which derived from a radical populist democratic perspective. It was no accident that the organization was most at home negotiating for jobs and dealing with the problems of low-income tenants in relation to their landlords; low-income immigrants in relation to *notarios publicos* and some lawyers who charged exorbitant fees for simple, English-language paperwork; homeowners in relation to public services; and homeowners and small landlords in relation to banks, savings and loan companies, and insurers.

Actions coming from these constituencies were in tune with the majority of the membership of the organization. They could be formulated into immediate demands. They were directed at dominant corporate or political institutions or middle-class professionals who exploited their own people. They could be defended against critics by pointing to the real discriminatory practices of employers, or the lifestyle of absentee landlords who sought to milk slum buildings and exploited their tenants in the process, or the politicians who considered their poorer constituents to be second-class citizens. Public service inadequacies were examples of the political powerlessness of the poor and of politicians who didn't consider them to be first-class citizens.

Underlying the approach of organizing people around concrete economic interests and public service issues were a number of sometimes implicit assumptions. One was that people can be legitimately organized around their immediate self-interests. Once so organized, they will join with others in alliances so that their interests can be maximized. Out of the series of trades—"you scratch my back and I'll scratch yours"—and alliances, a people's program can emerge.

Another underlying assumption was that the purpose of a mass-based organization is to confront unresponsive power. The organization demands the right to sit at the negotiating table and be treated on a basis of respect and equality. Negotiated settlements with specific improvements and financial benefits were sought from the private sector. Improved services and greater accountability were goals in the public and nonprofit sectors. In whatever arena, MCO people power would make decision makers negotiate.

The basic mode of operation was as a pressure group using the strategy and tactics of independent mass action. To avoid being a narrow or selfish pressure group, broad constituencies were organized and the organization was multi-issue in its approach.

In this view, democratic citizenship is itself a value. As Barack Obama has said, "Real change comes from the bottom up, not the top down." Participation is important both as a humanizing end in and of itself and because it is the basis of the power that brings concrete benefits to the community. People were assumed to be social in character, and if given the opportunity, desirous of having a voice that counted in public affairs. Having acquired such a voice, people would behave with the decency that would result in a better society for all.

MCO organizers actively cultivated the rewards of active citizenship. People learned skills and gained a new sense of themselves. They were recognized in a variety of ways for the contributions they made. They were treated as serious human beings with a capacity for self-governance.

Developing leadership in people who lacked organizational experience, especially in an organization that engaged with the powers that be, required patience. The leaders of the MCO frequently doubted their own equality to people with whom they had to negotiate. A most memorable illustration of this occurred when we left negotiations for jobs with an executive of the phone company. The leader of the MCO negotiating team said of the executive, both in satisfaction and in some amazement, "He called me 'Mister.'" No example could better summarize the internalized oppression that arises when class, racial, ethnic, or gender stereotypes are internalized. The results of this internalized oppression are what the organizer must constantly work with and overcome.

The primary alliance in the MCO supporting the radical populist democratic leadership was made up of block clubs, tenant organizations, churches, church-related groups, and other grassroots groups. Leaders of some community-based agencies (including the Mission Language and Vocational School, led by Abel Gonzalez, and OBECA/Arriba Juntos, led by Lee Soto and Herman Gallegos) and labor unions with delegations in MCO (there were three) supported the leadership's "issues orientation," though not necessarily the broader ideological position behind it.

It should be noted that populism has a complex history in the United States. The original populists were small farmers, both black and white, who fought against banks, railroads, and intermediaries to whom they sold their products, and who sought to pay low prices for what the farmers grew. They were small-d democrats. But they abandoned racial unity for explicit racism. Their influence declined by the end of the nineteenth century. Modern populism has alternated between these two variants. Alinsky represented the former; Alabama governor and presidential candidate George Wallace the latter.

Left, Liberal, and Centrist Traditional Pluralists

A number of church, neighborhood and labor leaders were pluralists. While some pluralists thought American society was for the most part fair and just, requiring only minor tinkering at the edges, and that major social groups were already players in the decision-making game, a growing number doubted this. They had come to conclude that significant numbers of people were left out, and it would take more than tinkering at the edges to get them included. By the mid- to late 1950s, the civil rights movement was making exclusion of Blacks a key issue. Other racial and ethnic minorities soon were identified as among the excluded.

The Student Nonviolent Coordinating Committee's use of "Black Power" as a slogan was initially nothing more than a militant assertion of traditional American pluralism. Stokely Carmichael and Charles Hamilton's book *Black Power*, published in 1967, elaborated a pluralist view. Blacks, the book argued, had to act like other U.S. minorities: organize themselves and use their strength as a power bloc to build their own institutions, and use collective economic buying power in the marketplace and voting power in politics to further their interests. While the slogan stirred a media fury and frightened church, labor, and liberal allies, there was really nothing very radical about it.

The Mostly Anglo Liberals and Centrists

The Anglo liberals and centrists were generally antagonistic to the language of power, mass organization, self-interest, and conflict that characterized the MCO leadership. They thought problems were solved by reasonable people discussing them. They obtained access to politicians by working on election campaigns or in civic associations of various kinds in the city and in the neighborhood. In their view, social problems emerge as a result of lack of communication. For example, if communication occurred between racial minorities and the majority society, discrimination would begin to disappear. Conflicts of real or perceived self-interests are not the heart of the problem; rather it is a lack of mutual understanding, which could be achieved if people sat down and talked with one another in a realistic and problem-solving way.

The centrists were hostile to the central organizing concepts of MCO. They sometimes acknowledged their necessity, but with great reluctance, and they generally abstained from participation in direct action. It was in the nature of their position to seek to bring reason and moderation to the MCO. But MCO was the political ball game in the Mission, and they were playing in MCO's park. In this sense, they were elements of the loyal opposition within the organization that made it a vital force. Their political expertise was helpful, and they were frequently the mediators of internal conflicts that might otherwise have torn MCO apart.

The base of the centrists tended to be in the clergy, older lay leaders, and the older civic associations of the neighborhood. They tended to be Anglos. Civic associations were formed with broader missions than those of the homeowners' associations, who protected their members' narrowly defined interests in home and neighborhood. As liberal counterparts of the homeowners' associations, the civic associations drew neighborhood liberals and centrists, while the homeowners' organizations tended to draw conservatives.

Many of the liberal activists were community-oriented teachers who preferred to participate in MCO through block clubs and other associations, rather than through the teachers' union. They were also mostly Anglos, though this was not entirely the case. Like the centrists, they tended to avoid thinking in power terms. They believed that ideas carried important weight independent of the power of their advocates. They sought access to and influence upon decision makers, not the power to bring about negotiations with them. Many Anglo liberals and centrists who lived in the Mission were active in other citywide organizations and viewed the Mission simply as the place where they went to bed at night.

Socialists of Different Traditions

At the left of the political spectrum was the Mission Tenant Union (MTU), led by the Progressive Labor Party (PL). PL was a "revolutionary" organization in the tradition of Chairman Mao Zedong and the Chinese Communists. It split from the "reformist" U.S. Communist Party, which remained in the camp of the Soviet Union. The MTU was the only organization in the Mission attempting to deal with the steady increase in rents and the deterioration of maintenance and services that was going on in many of the neighborhood's rental units, especially the older ones. As a result, MTU came in contact with many people who were having problems with landlords. As a matter of fact, priests and ministers of the district often referred people with rent problems to the MTU. They advised them not to accept the PL ideology; at the same time, they felt obliged to tell the renters that this was the place to go if you were having problems with your landlord. PL also expressed interest in and support for small landlords in the district.

PL's Mission District leader, John Ross, was the guiding influence in MTU. He was an energetic and forceful figure in later Mission developments, and his participation in the district was to be noted in the debates on the War on Poverty that took place in Congress. Conservatives pointed to Ross's membership on the Mission Area Community Action Board, Inc. (MACABI) as evidence of the subversive character of the Office of Economic Opportunity, which administered the Poverty Program.

The Maoists were the loudest of the Marxist groupings in the Mission. Their work with tenants earned them a grudging respect; their ideological rigidities kept their numbers smaller than they might otherwise have been. PL was suspicious of MCO's leaders while viewing MCO as an arena within which to recruit and provide leadership. As earlier described, their ideas were sometimes adopted and became part of the program of the populist democrats. Red-baiting conservatives in the Mission District and the city as a whole latched onto the visible presence of Marxists in MCO to try to stir up fear. They were unsuccessful. The organization was too broad and had too many defenders to be susceptible to these efforts to isolate it.

Other leftists were present in MCO, but not as organized party representatives. To the extent they played a role in MCO, they framed their ideas either in the language of pluralism or democratic populism.

The New Left

The New Left was not organized in the Mission, but its ideas were in the Bay Area air. New Left thinking connected with both the San Francisco State student strike and Mission High School, and with Los Siete de la Raza, seven Latino youth accused of shooting to death a San Francisco policeman. Marjorie Heins, in articles and her book *Strictly Ghetto Property*—primarily a report on the case of Los Siete—voiced New Left ambivalence toward MCO. Here she writes about MCO in 1970, in *Hard Times*, a short-lived weekly whose editors included Andrew Kopkind, James Ridgeway, and Ralph Nader:

> When it became known in 1966 that urban renewal was planned for the Mission, the Mission Council on Redevelopment was formed. Its purpose was to make sure any renewal would be done with the advice and consent of Mission residents. The Council soon became the Mission Coalition Organization (MCO), a multi-issue group with committees on housing, education, welfare, employment, etc. But its purpose remained to gain control over any Model Cities program. Finally, in December, after much bad-mouthing from the left ("just a tool of the Mayor"; to which one MCO organizer [namely me, making an analogy to the United Farm Workers and a liquor company they had signed a collective bargaining contract with] replied, "Is Chavez a tool of Schenley?"); and from the right ("just a paper organization"); and from dead center (the City Attorney said MCO's demands for control would be illegal); and after

producing over 700 earnest, well-behaved citizens to jam a Supervisors' meeting, MCO won: it will appoint 14 people to the Model Cities Planning Board and the Mayor will appoint the other seven.

Here, Heins's account is ambivalent toward MCO, rather than hostile. She continues:

MCO may not be able to stop…plans to make the Mission a middle class residential area and adjunct of downtown finance; but it's encouraging that MCO exists at all, and has forged a workable alliance among a great diversity of groups…The Mission won't be destroyed without a fight…At the moment, though, MCO occupies the middle of the road in community politics. At its infinitely well-organized convention in October, the 800 MCO delegates passed a gutless resolution condemning the media's orgy in the Los Siete incident but not really supporting the brothers. Two resolutions supporting the S.F. State strikers then on trial were not passed. The MCO came out in support of the New Mobe, draft alternatives ("rights of conscience"), and the grape boycott. The greatest debate at the convention raged over a resolution passed requesting more "police protection," with a limp emphasis on recruiting minority cops…The police are the clearest reminder of the Mission's colonial status, and they are thoroughly detested, especially by the brothers who fought them at the college strikes last year.

Within the year, Heins's ambivalence changed to sharp criticism. From *Ramparts*:

Just before the [Los Siete] trial ended, the Mission Coalition, which Mayor Alioto had made unofficial spokesman for the district, held its third annual convention. The Coalition had just helped appoint an acquiescent "Model Cities Planning Board," and massive urban renewal could be expected to begin in another year. Los Siete's newspaper, *Basta Ya*, described how renewal would raise property values so high that brown people would be forced out of the Mission, and the district would become, as planners hoped, a center for middle-class high-rises and for tourism. By the time the convention arrived, the Los Siete organization had convinced many community leaders that the Coalition was useless. When the leadership of the Coalition began to push through its agenda with a distinct lack of finesse—cutting off floor microphones when opponents began to speak—about a third of the delegates walked out shouting, "Vendido!" ("Sellout"), "Oportunista" and, most tellingly, "Mafioso." With that sense of liberation which comes from rejecting untenable and compromising situations, the rebels resolved to form a new grass roots organization that would not sell out. This was only one sign of the Mission's new confidence and desire to guide its own destiny. "Something in the community is different now," says Oscar Rios, one of José's brothers [José Rios was one of the seven] and a founder of Los Siete.

In content and tone, Heins is illustrative of the mood of the dominant voice of the New Left in that period: American society was hopelessly corrupt, corporate power concentrated beyond democratic accountability, and hope for anything better only to be found in Third World revolutions. As the phrase of the times went, "We live in the belly of the beast." No doubt a stratum of Mission youth and activists shared this view. But from everything I saw, heard, and understood, and from all the evidence of votes inside MCO, this was the view of a very distinct minority whose voices were amplified in the Bay Area far beyond their actual constituency or community influence by upper middle class, largely Anglo, political leftists, by the student movement, and by TV coverage that treated news as a spectacle.

▦ Populist Conservatives

At the right of the Mission political spectrum was Jack Bartalini, perhaps a classic right-wing populist. He supported George Wallace for president, he later told me, but became disillusioned when he found out that Wallace had a lot of corporate backers and wasn't really serious about helping the little guy. Bartalini and Mary Hall, both independent businesspeople, led the conservative voices of the Mission in opposition to the War on Poverty and later to Model Cities. In their view, both programs were examples of creeping socialism. But worst of all to them was urban renewal, which they fought and hated with a passion. While Bartalini's politics went too far for many of the homeowners and merchants of the district, his was seen as a voice for their interests. Bartalini once told me he was a misunderstood man, and cited as an example his support for universal publicly funded medical care.

On housing-related issues, the conservatives in the Mission had vocal spokespersons in Jack Bartalini and Mary Hall. A parallel group of Anglo conservatives, joined by a few Latinos, participated in the Mission High School dispute and sided with the site administrators. The conservatives resented the new minority militancy. They were for "equal opportunity," they said, but wanted people to be "qualified." They were against welfare, public housing, special minority programs in the schools, and especially affirmative action hiring. Federal programs like urban renewal and public housing were, to them, forms of socialism. But they didn't oppose all government efforts for the public welfare—they weren't free marketers. From their perspective, government programs' chief beneficiaries were the government bureaucracies that grew through them and the banks and big developers who profited from them. They saw Model Cities as a scheme to benefit those who were organized: big business, big labor, the politicians, and the minority blocs. Left out of this picture was the conservatives' constituency—the small businesses and older residents, particularly homeowners, of the Mission.

For many older homeowners and tenants, most of them from ethnic groups that had long been in the Mission—Irish, Italian, German, and Russian—these arguments made some sense. For many of the smaller merchants, owners of the mom-and-pop stores of the Mission, this was also true. It was these groups that gave the conservatives most of their base in the Mission.

Conservatives were frequently active in Catholic parish organizations and, to a lesser extent, in the Protestant congregations. An active member of Catholic St. Peter's Church, for example, with whom Joe Del Carlo and Jack Bourne regularly argued about MCO, was a leader of the Bartalini/Hall grouping. The battle for the minds of church leadership was a sharp one, because the churches were so important to MCO success.

Both ideologically and in practical action, the MCO challenged these conservatives. Ideologically, in the resolutions of its convention, the MCO called for tax reform, demanding that the burden of taxes for public services be shifted from homeowners to big corporations. Practically, the MCO's Community Maintenance Committee served as the vehicle through which negotiations with local banks and savings and loan associations took place; actions on pawn shops, city services, pornographic movies, and other in-the-neighborhood issues were expressed through this committee as well. All these were important to the base of the populist conservatives.

Challenging the conservatives was particularly difficult because of the generational, ethnic/racial, style, and ideological differences between the "white ethnics" and the minority base of MCO. In addition, the mass media suggested that minorities were receiving huge government benefits in special programs designed for them. These were the government programs established in response to the civil rights movement and the riots of the mid-sixties. The retired person living on a fixed income, the older "ethnic" homeowner, and the small businessman who had been in the Mission for more than twenty years saw themselves as the people squeezed in the middle. Their taxes went up, but the benefits seemed always to be for someone else. It mattered little that the imagined benefits for the poor and minorities were far greater than the reality.

Nationalism

The emphasis on one's identity as a member of a racial or ethnic group, discussed here under the heading of "nationalism," was at the height of its influence among activists in the days of the Mission Coalition Organization. It was particularly strong on college and university campuses, but its influence was by no means limited thereto.

Centrist and Liberal Nationalists

The broadest-ranging expression of this nationalism was from groups that ran from centrist to liberal. Their major critique of American society was that it was prejudiced in its attitudes toward Latinos, excluded them, and was racist in its policies—such as curriculum design in public education. Mass-based direct action was not a major strategy of this group, though it was not averse to the picket line. Its central strategy, however, was to win funds and leadership positions for Latinos. The development of Latino leadership was of primary importance, and this included breaking down all employment barriers, in both the private and public sector, but particularly in administrative and decision-making positions. The creation of Latino-run organizations, whether businesses or nonprofit community-based agencies, was also important, because it created a community infrastructure. On occasion this group could engage in militant tactics, but these were not directed toward building an independent mass action organization.

The leaders of this point of view tended to operate in organizations like the League of United Latin American Citizens (LULAC), the Mexican-American Political Association (MAPA), and other explicitly Latino organizations. They saw gaining control over the distribution of services as the means by which they could develop a base and political clout. By providing the channels through which "outside" institutions had to travel in order to deal with the barrio, they would become the political brokers for the community. In this dimension of their thinking, they were in the traditional American pluralist view.

The primary base of this group was in the just-mentioned Latino organizations, some of the community-based agencies, and, more generally, the Latino middle class. Teachers and administrators in various Latino school-related organizations were in this group. On the other hand, Latino teachers whose main identification was with the teachers' union followed the Ben Martinez leadership.

These centrist and liberal nationalists tended to operate outside of the framework of the MCO, though on particular issues there was a joining together—particularly when the former needed the mass base provided by MCO. Generally, however, the relationship was a tenuous and at times tense one.

Without the participation of the middle-class activists who were more likely to be found in MAPA, LULAC, and similar groups, MCO lost access to organizational skills. The price was probably a necessary one to pay, because their participation would have meant a very different kind of organization. Instead, MCO found these skills in professionals who broke away from their own social group, experienced trade unionists who became active in the community, and church members who developed organizational skills within the churches. Equally important, people learned organizational skills by participating in the MCO committees.

The committee as a training ground for developing leadership was therefore essential to the internal growth of the organization as well as to its external effectiveness on particular issues. Indeed, the two cannot be separated.

Radical Nationalists

The radical nationalists were another group within the Mission. They presented their views as the ideology of liberation. Borrowing from a wide range of historical materials, most especially from their reading of Latin American nationalist revolutionaries, they placed at the heart of their position the slogan "Community Control." By this they meant not only the administration of local programs, as their centrist and liberal middle-class counterparts would have it, but the transformation and control of local institutions operating in the barrio.

The leadership for this view primarily came from the La Raza political groups based on the campuses around the area, or led by former student movement activists. Most of their base in the Mission was young. Unlike the centrists and liberals, they operated as, in effect, a left caucus within the MCO. As such they at times played an important role in both building the organization and in defending it against some of its critics. A key figure in this group was Jim Queen, who walked the organizational tightrope of participation with forces that he considered to his right and of continued leadership among the radicals. As with others who played a role in MCO, it was the fact of MCO's grassroots base that drew them to the coalition.

It was in their interest to participate if they wanted to see a strong community. MCO provided a forum for their ideas. While the nationalists would criticize MCO leadership "from the left" on issues having to do with education (at San Francisco State and at public schools), they could not on issues of jobs and landlord-tenant relations. Since the radical nationalists were interested in the constituency that MCO was successfully organizing through its Jobs and Housing Committees, they had an interest in playing by MCO's democratic rules.

The style of the radical nationalists alienated many people in whose name and interests they believed they spoke. Working-class immigrants, church members who were poor and working-class, and informal youth groups that hung around Mission street corners and parks were among the groups in MCO who reacted negatively to what observers called gesture politics, or symbolic confrontation.

▧ Nationalist Issues and "Community Control"

The slogan "Community Control" appeared to unite centrist, liberal, and radical nationalists. But each gave it different meanings. The former two simply meant the administration of programs by Latino-run agencies. Since the power of city hall in what was then a relatively patronage-free city was limited, and since the federal government was the source of funding for the agencies in question, for these nationalists, control of federal programs was one of two major vehicles for community development. The other was economic development, the development of locally owned business. Both offered the minority community an opportunity to develop its middle class—which these nationalists saw as the major agency of progress. As an educated middle class develops, the argument went, so will opportunities for the community as a whole. The Latino-run agency would hire Latinos, as would the Latino-owned business. Programs administered by Latinos would be more sensitive to the needs of Latinos, including the poor. Out of a Latino middle class would emerge Latino politicians to protect the interests of the community.

The radicals were less interested in the development of a middle class than in the transformation of institutions. By "institutions," they meant either newly created agencies, or facilities and programs of major institutions, like school sites, district health departments, and police precincts. They saw the control of institutions as a means by which new programs could be established. Their vision included participation by the beneficiaries of the programs in their governance. Through this participation a political base would be organized in the community.

Each group of nationalists responded more to some issues than to others. Police brutality or harassment, bilingual programs, funding for community-run agencies, and the hiring of Latino personnel in social service and administrative positions were among their priorities. As these were areas of great interest for nationalists, so were they areas of less interest to the leadership of the MCO. It was not that populist democrats opposed action in these areas; rather the nationalist formulation of the issues was difficult for MCO's top leadership to work with—for two reasons. First, most of the Latino working class and poor, both in the organization and in the community, did not support either the style or program of the nationalists—whatever their political stance—particularly when it took on separatist hues. Second, MCO's constituency was not limited to Latinos or racial minorities.

The Mission's nationalists reflected a dilemma that recurs in the history of minority struggles in the United States: how to vigorously pursue your interests in a country in which you are, by definition, a minority, and in which you need majority support. A good example of the conflict came around school issues, and this was reflected in MCO. The populist democrats found common ground with the nationalists on issues of affirmative action hiring and promotion as well as curriculum reform, bilingual education, and other education-related concerns. They also supported teachers' interests, as represented by the American Federation of Teachers, Local 61 (AFT), and they formulated minority issues in ways that a progressive union could support. This approach was important to MCO, which did not want to rupture its alliance with the AFT. However, nationalists did not always agree and, in fact, frequently defined the union as a primary obstacle to the realization of education reform.

This came to a head when MCO was asked to support an AFT-led strike. In addition to teacher bread-and-butter issues and classroom size, the union included demands for paraprofessionals, many of whom were from the Mission District. This directly connected the union with the community. An overwhelming majority of the MCO Steering Committee voted to endorse the strike; the nationalists within the organization either opposed endorsement or remained neutral on the question. Their constituency within the school district was mainly composed of minority administrators, some of them anti-union, and minority teachers, some of them critical of the primarily Anglo leadership of the AFT.

Another, though quite different, type of situation occurred around incidents of police harassment and brutality, usually aimed at youth in the community. The nationalists' formulation of the issue included vigorous and general attacks on the San Francisco Police Department. (This was a period when the Black Panthers made cops "pigs," calling for "offing the pigs" in some of their most militant rhetoric.) The MCO had, in its convention, adopted a position condemning such police behavior, but also called for more effective police protection in the community.

At the height of their antagonism toward the police, militant youth groups simply would not support a demand for more police protection. At the same time, the overwhelming majority of people in MCO and in the community would not support blanket indictments of the police. Stepping outside the coalition, youth groups, in this case with the radical nationalists, would attack the police department. In policy terms, they gained nothing, and they would attack the MCO for failing to support them. The impatience of militants turned off centrist adults, who might have been persuaded by radical patience, to look seriously at how the cops treated Mission youth. In fact, when youth and seniors did sit down to talk about these things, they worked out platform language for the second MCO convention that included respectful treatment for youth, disciplining cops who abused young people, *and* increased police protection in the neighborhood.

Nationalists were very sensitive to evidence of discrimination. This included the centrist nationalists as well, who on occasion were more responsive to youth demands than was the leadership of the MCO. This apparent contradiction becomes understandable when one looks at the base of the MCO. The older people in the organization, whether Latino or Anglo, did not understand the militant style of many nationalists. (Note: I use "militant" to refer to tactics and style, and "radical" to refer to program ideas or content.) Furthermore, they were being ripped off by burglaries and purse snatchings and did, in fact, want more police protection. This was rarely the case with younger people and radical nationalists, or even middle-class centrist and liberal nationalists who either lived outside of the highest crime areas or could afford some of the simple protections that make a house less vulnerable to being broken into. It is low- and moderate-income people who most experience robberies and street attacks.

While MCO's leadership wanted to respond to these issues, it could not find the handle with which to do so. An organization that wants to do more than issue pronouncements must have handles on issues. The handle is the tactical means that allow you to grab onto an issue and work on it practically. It allows you, rather than your adversary, to define it. It gives you ways to "move" on the issue—that is, specific decision makers that the organization can identify and proposals to be made to them.

A further irony in the police situation was that lower-class youth sometimes were more cautious in dealing with the police than the Latino middle class. The latter, with economic security, access to lawyers and politicians, and some faith in the courts, would explode when an instance of police brutality took place. Some of the youth, equally antagonistic to the police, were more careful about expressing this sentiment publicly. Understanding their powerlessness in the system, they feared the retribution they might suffer at the hands of local precinct cops.

The radical nationalists didn't have a base in the Mission community as a whole. They did have a base among the youth and some support in other sectors of the community. They played a role much greater than their numbers would suggest, because many of them devoted a great deal of time to their activity. While their formulations of issues frequently posed problems for MCO leadership, their presence was generally an asset to that leadership and to the community. Whenever any question about giving up on basic demands around Model Cities emerged, or whenever there was a threat to the MCO leadership on questions of tenant and jobs actions, the radicals within the organization were allies. And outside the organization, the existence of the radicals allowed the leadership to say simply, "Either we act on these issues or the people will have no alternative but to go to groups like the Progressive Labor Party and the La Raza organizations"—most of the latter were not members of MCO.

I am particularly interested in addressing those to whom radical claims appeal. No radical change can take place within this country without mass organization, and large numbers of people will not respond to radical slogans unless these slogans relate to their experience, values, and self-interests. I think MCO engaged in radical action—given the limits to the power that can be achieved in one multi-neighborhood district that at most includes 15 percent of the city's population. Basic city hall, private employer, private financial institution, and landlord prerogatives were challenged on issues of significance to the people of the community. And MCO often won. People aren't mobilized for action unless there is hope for victory. Thus, radicals must not only be "correct" in some abstract analysis of reality; they must also involve the people who are the base for building social change. That implies an openness to broader ideas, and an understanding that ideological correctness is not the litmus test for radicalism. It was because action on them was irrelevant to the lives of Mission people that MCO did not adopt more "radical" policies; symbolic action or gesture politics aren't of great interest to people who struggle day to day to make ends meet.

Indeed, as the Student Nonviolent Coordinating Committee (SNCC) vividly demonstrated in the Deep South during this very period, the more militant its rhetoric, the more isolated the organization grew from its mass base of southern, poor Blacks. Ideology replaced the slow, democratic practice of actual on-the-ground organizing. The more SNCC articulated its Black Power slogan, the more it was isolated in the local communities that had once welcomed SNCC field secretaries into their hearts and homes.

In Mississippi, for example, from 1962 to 1964, SNCC built the Council of Federated Organizations, sponsored the Mississippi Summer Project, organized the Mississippi Freedom Democratic Party—the political expression of dozens of local town and county voter leagues, civic associations, NAACP branches, and other grassroots groups—and gripped the nation with the 1964 Democratic Party

National Convention challenge to the seating of Mississippi's racist Democrats. Going from almost nothing to national prominence in three years was an expression of the reality of Black power.

The southern civil rights movement's recognition and power didn't come from community control of anything other than the churches and local civic associations that African-Americans created and paid for with their own money in collection plates, dues, chicken fries, and the like. Rather, its source of power was the organizing and mobilizing engaged in by Black people as they confronted institutional racism.

National agitation around the idea of "Black Power" was accompanied by abandonment of the actuality of building it! SNCC's organizational decline began in fall 1964. By the SNCC national staff meeting at the end of 1966, the organization was a shadow of itself. About the vote to expel the few remaining whites on the staff, the legendary Fanny Lou Hamer cried. She came up to me and said, "Mike, I just don't understand what's going on with them."

In San Francisco, there weren't other neighborhood organizations with their own mass base with which MCO might have made alliances. Such alliances could have addressed problems that required deeper policy changes because they would have had a larger people-power base. Militant rhetoric isn't a substitute for organizing. Nor are the occasional mass mobilizations that can turn significant numbers of people out for a single demonstration but are unable to engage them in continuing action.

▧ The Myth of Community Control

It was on the issue of community control that the radical nationalists were most critical of MCO. MCO did not take an explicit position for community control of health, education, police, and other institutions that were supposed to serve the community. Rather, it sought negotiated agreements with dominant political and economic institutions.

The radical nationalists who advocated community control could not answer this question: "Why would the very government you have so critically analyzed turn institutions over to the community that the community would then use for its own transformation?" The centrist and liberal nationalists simply wanted their piece of the pie, with modifications to reflect their particular concerns—and the system, under pressure, could respond to that. The radical nationalists wanted not only to have a modified fair share of the pie, but to determine the ingredients that made it up, who the baker would be, and how the baker, the bakery workers, and the consumers of the pie would bake, cut, and eat it. For example, in a locally run health center, this might include rules under which doctors and other medical workers would receive equal or near-equal pay; patients, doctors, and medical workers would jointly administer the center; no means tests would be imposed on patients; and paperwork for potential beneficiaries would be minimal. How can one imagine public funding for such a program without a tremendous base of power to overcome that of the San Francisco Department of Public Health, U.S. Department of Health, Education and Welfare, San Francisco Medical Society, American Medical Association, for-profit insurers, private and large nonprofit hospitals, and all the other interests organized around the health industry?

Government policy and the "free market" can be influenced by the collective action of large numbers of people lobbying, voting, negotiating, boycotting, striking, disrupting, or otherwise using tools available to them to affect policy. For a brief period, the Mission exercised the people power generated by MCO, using most of these tools to defend and advance the values and interests of the neighborhood's low-income people. But "community control" was not one of those tools.

The alternative to community control, MCO's "institutional change" approach, would make demands on institutions and seek political power that might later lead to more substantial institutional change. Implicit in the MCO approach is the notion that political power must precede administrative reform or community control.

It is a tragedy of MCO's development that the energies and talents of young radical nationalists, and other radicals, were only sporadically available. The radicals who did participate in MCO leadership were not in the mainstream of radical sentiment of the period. What possibilities might have emerged from an organization with the participation of the radicals around the strategy of institutional change as opposed to the strategy of community control must simply remain a question of speculation.

Perhaps something can be learned, however, by contrasting their behavior with that of their counterparts in the Great Depression of the 1930s. Young radicals of the thirties were central players in building the industrial union movement. Every major industrial union hired them as organizers; and they played leadership roles in many of these unions as well. John L. Lewis, president of both the United Mine Workers and the then newly formed Congress of Industrial Organizations (CIO) was, at least for his first two terms, a supporter of Franklin Delano Roosevelt, president of the United States; he was not a leftist by any stretch of the imagination. But he was devoted to increasing the power of, and improving the working and living conditions of, working people. Lewis hired Communists who made no attempt to hide their politics, because he knew they were talented and committed organizers interested in building broadly based people power in non-discriminatory unions.

The radicals of the thirties understood how to avoid style and slogans that would isolate them from the very "masses" in whose interest they sought to work and for whom they hoped to speak. Perhaps this is because many of them were themselves working in the factories they sought to organize. There is a big difference between the radicalism that flows from a shared daily experience with people struggling to make a living and one that is born and raised in an academic atmosphere.

Some of the radicals in the Mission were curiously elitist in their politics. They used the idea of being in the vanguard to justify isolation from the people. A parallel development took place among some clergy and lay activists. In the name of "prophetic ministry," itself central to Christian beliefs and action on social and economic justice, they engaged in activities that isolated them from the majority of the people in the pews. The prophet as moral witness calls us to be our best, and may stand alone in her calling. The prophet as institutional leader moves us toward our best, and is failing if she can't bring us along. The two shouldn't be confused. Both are important.

While discussion of the religious right is far beyond the purview of this orga-nizer's tale, I know from my continuing work (over a forty-year period) with religious groups that the growth of the religious right at least owes a piece of its success to the isolation of mainline Protestant denominational leadership from the people in their pews. (When I did a workshop for one of the country's mainline Protes-tant denominations, one-third of the headquarters offices were vacant because of cutbacks in budget. The people in the pews were not only shrinking in number; those who remained were not giving money to the national offices. Nonetheless, the staff people at the workshop insisted that the isolation they were experiencing was a necessary part of their prophetic stance. They were unwilling to critically examine the question of whether there were ways to both be prophetic and bring along the people in the pews.

If they are isolated from the people, militants and radicals tend to have contempt for them. They justify their isolation by arguing that the people don't participate in radical politics because they are brainwashed. A kind of colonial view emerges that is not too different from the ideology of all colonialists who claim to lift the colonized from their state of ignorance. From this perspective, the task of radicals is to engage in consciousness raising that will liberate the masses from their backward ways of thinking. By the end of the twentieth century, university-educated radicals of all kinds, imbued with deconstructionist thinking and an entire new language of social thought, were in near-total isolation from the vast majority of the American people.

In the period discussed in this book, many campus radicals knew more about Che Guevera or Mao Zedong than they did about John L. Lewis or Eugene V. Debs, and more about the Long March or the Sierra Maestras than the CIO or the New Deal. They could quote the Little Red Book more readily than the Declaration of Independence or the Bill of Rights. Indeed, many believed that the U.S., the "belly of the beast," would only be changed by external pressure from revolutions in the Third World, not by anything that could be done from within this country.

Like others, the radical organizations have interests of their own. Their discipline and dedication may make them more tenacious in the pursuit of their aims than others within a mass organization. They may at times be tremendously divisive in a broadly based organization that is seeking to build a lowest significant common denominator. My own conclusion in the Mission experience was that it was worth trying to keep them in, at least those who were willing to recognize that the very grassroots people for whom they sought to speak and act were in fact active in MCO and supporting its populist democrat leadership.

The country badly needs an effective left, like the one that participated in industrial unions in the 1930s and the one that played an important role in the early stages of the Deep South civil rights movement. Human rights and economic justice in the U.S. move forward when there is a center-left political alliance. The left pushes "from the bottom up"—that is, it engages large numbers of people in action to defend justice. It also agitates for a program whose ideas go to the core sources of economic and political inequality. But this left cannot act successfully if it is isolated. Left leaders who recognize this push as hard as they can and argue as forcefully as they can, but in the face of a coming election or a strike showdown, they reach an accommodation with the center, so that a popular front can defeat the political right or entrenched economic power.

▨ Core Ideas

Underlying my work are some core ideas that have become clearer and more sharply defined over the years, though they were implicit in my MCO work. Here I'd like to make them explicit.

▨ Lowest Significant Common Denominator

MCO's organizing strategy was to develop a platform of ideas that could unite most groups and build a majority coalition in the Greater Mission. This "lowest significant common denominator" gave voice to the values and interests of the predominantly low-to-moderate-income people of the district, the small and medium-sized enterprises they did business with, and the local institutions that served them and gave meaning to their lives. It drew common themes of justice and democratic participation from the religious and secular perspectives of those comprising the Mission. This was the basis upon which program, strategy, and tactics could be developed to challenge the conservatives and radicals who were outside MCO, as well as the non-participating agencies that were threatened by MCO. As a result of its approach, MCO won the active participation of some of the older Anglos and, equally important, neutralized the conservatives' attack on it.

Lowest significant common denominator united large numbers of Mission District residents from churches and other existing organizations and newly formed groups like tenant associations and youth clubs in a powerful voice. A slogan that was occasionally used at the time summed that voice up: "Self-determination through Community Power."

The majority coalition strategy made an issue like tearing down a burned-out house important, not only because it was something around which a block club could be organized, but also because it was something around which Latinos, other minorities, and Anglos could unite. This was true of a number of other issues on which MCO worked. At the neighborhood level, issues could be found that cut across the racial and class antagonisms reflected in Richard Nixon's landslide election in 1972 and which were—and are—reflected in the backlash that is common in cities across the country. Out of the experiences of the Mission, it was possible for people to begin to rethink who their adversaries were and who their friends and allies were, and might be. This was done in the context of issues that the people themselves cared about and around which they wanted to organize. The lowest significant common denominator approach also made it possible for Anglos to rally behind what might otherwise have been solely "minority group" issues—like bilingual education and affirmative action hiring.

By the end of 1970, to many Mission District conservatives, particularly in the churches, MCO was not "that radical group" but the community organization. To a significant number of radicals, MCO was a forum in which they could participate, sometimes in support of the populist democrat leadership, at other times a loyal opposition. Regardless of whether one agreed with or liked everything it did, MCO was the organization that represented the Mission.

Unity in Diversity

MCO celebrated unity in diversity. This theme was expressed in all the forms of recognition that every group in MCO received in the organization as a whole. These ranged from the representation, in top offices of the organization, of all the racial and ethnic groups in the Mission to the more symbolic roles of giving an invocation or benediction at an annual convention or other event. Rather than ignoring, submerging, or seeking to homogenize distinctions, MCO encouraged people to get to know each others' backgrounds and the unique circumstances of their life stories.

American ecumenicism had already established this idea among mainline Protestants and, to a large extent, among Catholics and Jews. In the Mission, Evangelicals and Pentecostals were part of it as well.

Self-identified radicals, liberals, centrists, and conservatives all participated in MCO because the people-power idea, and the lowest significant common denominator platform and action that flowed from it, made sense to them. Within the organization they tried to persuade others to their larger agendas, but they had to do so with respect if they wanted an audience.

Recognition by Decision Makers

With the exception of the education establishment, including the San Francisco Unified School District and the federally funded Far West Laboratory, MCO was the organization recognized by the major public institutions of the city. While some of them sought to go around MCO, and succeeded on occasion, they did so with the fear that MCO might come after them. Insider MCO allies would give us information about these end runs. They were always a source of amusement, and sometimes a source of concern. MCO's idea was to negotiate changes, build its power, then negotiate for more substantive changes that got deeper into the social and economic problems facing the people of the Mission.

Recognition implies negotiation. Negotiation implies collaboration between parties who have different interests. Reaching and living by agreements means an orderly way of changing things, even if disruptive direct action is part of the order. In a next round of negotiations, more can be sought, fought for, and agreed upon—if your people-power base deepens and expands; if not, you will have to accept less.

Only where there was a locally based agency that could serve as an alternative to the MCO could a major institution bypass us on a program of major impact. As the Model Cities experience finally demonstrated, MCO never did learn how to deal with the community-based agencies within its own membership.

■ "Educating" the People of the Mission

Leftists often criticized MCO and the broader Alinsky tradition for "not having an ideology," and for "not taking positions on" the public policy issues of the day. These criticisms persist. From the left, the implication is that community organizing is reformist rather than revolutionary, or that it is not anticapitalist or explicitly socialist. From liberals, it tends to mean that community organizers do not take the kinds of policy positions that are typically debated by candidates for public office or developed in policy think tanks.

Almost everyone in MCO, including the student movement, the Progressive Labor Party, some of MCO's moderates and liberals, some of its clergy and lay leaders, and the Mission Merchants Association, had the idea that MCO's organizing staff, and the organization as a whole, were obliged to educate the people of the Mission. The content of this education varied according to the interests, values, or ideology to be furthered.

MCO's centrists and some of its liberals wanted MCO to educate people about the necessity for compromise—even before a battle was waged or people power demonstrated that the issue was important to significant numbers of people. Teachers' union President Jim Ballard called this "negotiating with yourself."

Some of MCO's merchants and businesspeople wanted MCO to educate people about how development would benefit the Mission. Somehow this was to be accomplished with people who would be dislocated by development. The executive director of the merchants' association, rather than assuming the unemployed wanted to work but couldn't find jobs, wanted MCO to educate the unemployed so they'd be motivated to seek work.

Some of MCO's radicals wanted MCO to educate people about how capitalism or "the system" worked against their interests and about the necessity for a fundamentally new system.

While each disagreed with the others on content, they all shared some common assumptions about how education was to be accomplished: it would be dispensed to members by those who knew why something was the way it was, and what had to be done to change it. This wasn't much different from what is assumed in most school curriculums: a teacher who knows more about the subject tells students what to think.

A corollary to this approach to education is leadership that views itself as acting on behalf of others, rather than engaging others to act on their own. In the case of the former, leaders want to "educate" members of their organization to accept and agree to what they, the leaders, think is possible. In the case of the latter, members evaluate the experience they are having and draw their own conclusions, with the assistance of leaders who have more experience and, in some cases, better understanding than they do. The difference is subtle but crucial.

The student movement and groups on the political left often associated education with brainwashing and false consciousness. According to their view, the majority of Americans were brainwashed by the mass media and capitalist culture. That's what made them consumerist, racist, sexist, ageist, and classist—to name a few of the false views which Americans were supposed to have uncritically adopted.

Young activists, particularly those at San Francisco State University, wanted MCO to educate the community about the validity of its program for change at the university, as well as defend and explain the student movement's tactics. Their counterparts at the local high school wanted a similar kind of community education. In particular, they wanted MCO to educate Anglos about the depths of racism in the United States and its consequences, particularly in the area of education.

Some leading groups of the student movement believed the American people were hopelessly corrupted by their materialism and co-opted by the crumbs fed to them by imperialists exploiting the Third World. In this view, the role of the left in the United States was to bore from within "the system." For some who despaired of bringing about constructive change by the nonviolent use of constitutional means, a radical and militant minority could disrupt business as usual, undermining the system. For others, the hope was to create liberated enclaves within the system, where different values might demonstrate how a more just society could operate. Either way, it was understood to be unlikely, if not inconceivable, that the majority of Americans might be involved anytime soon in bringing about greater social and economic justice at home and in the world. In this context, and from the point of view of these groups, the job of organizers and leaders was to inform people of how the ideas they now held were really not in their own interests. To that end, different educational methods were proposed, including media, seminars, participatory workshops, popular education, lectures, panels, films, and other educational tools.

A Different Understanding of "Education"

Millions of dollars have been spent by churches, foundations, and labor, civic, and other organizations to educate against the "isms" of race, gender, age, sexual orientation, class, nationality, and other ways of looking at The Other. While each of the individual programs may have some merit, it is hard to deny that by and large they either preach to the choir or fall on deaf ears—they don't reach those who need most to be reached.

When people from diverse backgrounds support each other in their particular concerns, they create the reciprocity of a "you scratch my back and I'll scratch yours" deal. When they work on a common problem that is too large for any one group to tackle alone and achieve victory against the power structure, they see the power of unity. In both cases, and especially when this work is framed by shared core values of justice and democracy, they come to see each other as persons. In the course of struggle they share experiences and hear each other's life stories. Stereotypes of The Other don't fit the concrete experience of being in a relationship with another human being.

Begin Where People Are

Beginning "where people are" allows an organizer to draw people into experiences they wouldn't otherwise have. Community organizers throughout the country can tell stories of people coming into an organization because of an immediate concern in their lives, getting to know people of different racial or ethnic groups in that organization, and discovering that their stereotypes don't match their experience of people different from themselves—a phenomenon that social psychologists call "cognitive dissonance." Men who never thought they would accept women's equality found themselves accepting women in key leadership roles. Traditionalist straights found themselves in organizations with gay men and lesbian women. These situations of cognitive dissonance are teachable moments for an organizational leadership that is committed to democratic values. When a participant (or "learner") is perplexed that his or her direct experience isn't in sync with previously held beliefs, the "isms" can be challenged. There was no explicit litmus test on these diversity issues for entry into MCO. But once in, people stayed because they liked the experience. And their horizons broadened as they met and engaged with people different from themselves.

Multi-constituency community organizations offer opportunities in which people of diverse backgrounds get to know one another as individuals. People share stories of pain, hope, excitement, victory, and defeat. They work together in common efforts and support one another in their respective particular efforts. As they learn to respect each other, they also are open to looking at the most fundamental question to be asked in America today: Whose interests are best served by the vast majority of the people being divided from one another by the various "isms"? A small-d democratic answer is clear: the worst parts of the status quo are served. And my experience is that regular, everyday people quickly grasp this fact. However, for this rejection of stereotypes to last, action toward particular and common ends—and the experiences and relationships that accompany it—must continue, with positive results. Thus the permanent, broadly based, multi-constituency, multi-issue organization, explicitly committed to a program of action and democratic education, is the best school against the "isms."

▉ MCO Lacked a Strong Internal Education Program

Unfortunately, the community organizing tradition is relatively weak when it comes to implementing a full educational program that makes use of teachable moments to challenge stereotypes of class, status, and power. This failure is doubly to be damned because so many opportunities for true education arise in this work. A corrective is to be found in the tradition pioneered in this country by Myles Horton and the Highlander Center and paralleled internationally in the work of Paulo Freire.

Horton's work was based in the South, where, in the 1930s, he worked with industrial unions and helped the CIO challenge racism. During the civil rights movement, Highlander pioneered adult citizenship classes. Dr. Martin Luther King and Rosa Parks both participated in Highlander activities. The Student Nonviolent Coordinating Committee's leadership was influenced by Horton's thinking. Horton was a friendly critic of Saul Alinsky on the question of education, though at times he acknowledged that Alinsky was educating people in the course of organizing them.

Freire was an adult educator among the poorest people in one of Brazil's poorest regions, the northeast. He discovered that some of the people with whom he worked didn't understand themselves to be fully human. His educational approach used the daily work and experience of poor landless workers to help them see themselves as fully human. Freire's *Pedagogy of the Oppressed* was influential in the development of Latin America's liberation theology and base Christian communities, and was standard reading for U.S. community organizers.

One further observation: a cousin of the prejudiced personality is the authoritarian personality. Indeed, they usually coexist in the same person. In a world of uncertainty, with no avenue for the expression of pain or to seek constructive solutions to problems, people blame scapegoats and turn to "great men" to solve their problems. Having turned their judgment over to the maximum leader, they then follow his dictates, exchanging their own capacity to reason and make judgments for the certainty that comes from following orders. An organizing approach that begins with the life experiences of people and urges them to engage democratically in problem solving with people of diverse backgrounds will challenge this tendency. But experience without reflection is insufficient. The art of democratic education is to use, or create, situations in which education can take place. While the multi-issue and multi-constituency organization creates those situations, the educational result is not automatic. It needs to be cultivated.

Community organizations have experimented with "educationals": separate meetings whose purpose is to step back from immediate action and learn from it; the education is closely related to what the organization was doing in the world, but no decisions are on the agenda. Such sessions allow participants to engage in deeper exploration of the history of, for example, racism and to begin to answer the question "Whose interests does racism serve?" Some education directors in the industrial unions of the thirties did this; Myles Horton did it too. But it should be understood that the action framework of such an organization must continue...and continue successfully. Most people don't participate in a community organization unless it is dealing with problems that face them in their daily lives. (In Appendix A, I've elaborated on how such education can be done.)

Education alone will not sustain such an organization, nor will it change many deeply held attitudes or points of view. It is one of the pillars on which to build strong organizations. In the late 1880s the Populist Party, in the period of its expansion and growth, opposed racism, but in its decline it succumbed to it. Some members of the CIO who built unions with Black and Latino workers supported George Wallace in 1972 and by 1980 had become "Reagan Democrats." The fragile alliances that brought Blacks, Latinos, whites, and in fewer cases Asians or Native Americans together were torn asunder when whites were persuaded that special privileges based on race were more important to them than interracial unity.

The New Deal itself, and postwar programs such as FHA lending, were built on premises that excluded Blacks from being their full beneficiaries. Yet during the War on Poverty, white workers who weren't in continuing relationships with Black workers often thought Blacks were "getting everything." Surveys at the time indicated vast misperceptions of the benefits to the Black community of the War on Poverty. George Wallace and others played to white resentments.

Beyond "Blame the Victim" versus "Blame the System"

Community organizing assumes the possibility of agency on the part of most people, including the most oppressed people. People need not remain victims; they can be actors in the process of creating their own futures. This encompasses individual self-help (the emphasis of conservatives), mutual aid or community development (conservative unless it involves changing systems), and collective action to change institutions (the emphasis of liberals, progressives, and radicals).

Community organizing assumes that there are situations, structures, and systems that must be changed if values of justice, equality, freedom, security, community, and democracy are to be realized. Agency here is expressed by participating in a community organization that seeks to change these circumstances by changing the systems that are responsible for them.

Thus community organizing theory transcends the "blame the victim/blame the system" debate. That's the sense in which it goes beyond usual definitions of conservative and radical.

Consciousness, Consciousness Raising, and Experience in MCO

My organizing emphasis was to move people into new experiences in which their present consciousness could be challenged. The typical community resident becomes involved in action because of a perceived self-interest. Learning politics becomes part of the experience of organizational participation. The basic organizing problem is one of getting people involved, and that means convincing people that their action can lead to some results. The college-educated political reformer or revolutionary and the religiously motivated prophet frequently, and mistakenly, assume that others will learn and define positions as they have—through debate, discourse, reading. On the contrary, ideas become real through experience.

Perhaps the capacity for people to change their attitudes, beliefs, and behavior is greater than elite education and coffeehouse radicalism would suggest. Most people have a sense of justice and fairness. I think it's part of human nature—we are social in character, not isolated individuals who rationally enter into a contract because of selfish interests.

The idea that people should be treated justly or fairly contradicts the sense that "The Other doesn't deserve what I have." To hold the two ideas at the same time requires thinking of The Other as less deserving because he is lazy, shiftless, criminally inclined, or some other negative characterization that doesn't stand up in the circumstance of a relationship. Justice and fairness prevail when we encounter The Other as a human being, one with whom we share experiences, like raising children, and values—like justice and fairness. People will come into these encounters when it is in their interest to do so—specifically, when they have problems of day-to-day living that can be resolved through the power of a broadly based community organization.

The first step toward creating a situation in which mutually respectful relationships can be encouraged and developed is to ensure that the boundary lines that define an organization's membership are drawn very broadly. In the case of the Mission District, this was not difficult. The diversity of the Greater Mission's population couldn't have been greater: Anglos, white ethnics, Blacks, Latinos, Samoans, Filipinos, Native Americans; gay and straight; Roman Catholic, mainline Protestant, Evangelical, and Pentecostal; low-, moderate-, middle-, and even a few upper-income households.

MCO was conceived with ideas of the relationship between organizing and education in mind. The geographic boundaries proposed to MCO's founding convention were broad. The preconvention Platform and Resolutions and Nominations Committees brought diverse people together in the process of creating a new organization. Within the MCO action committees, people engaged in problem solving, then went out into the community in common struggle. Education took place in the course of issue campaigns. Reflection on basic values took place as we connected the abstract idea of justice to specific situations—and talked about it informally in coffee shops, pre-action briefings, and post-action debriefings.

Ten years after I first encountered St. John the Evangelist Episcopal Church in MCO, the church was much more open about its gay membership, who had become a larger percentage of the parish. In the San Francisco Organizing Project (SFOP), the issue of AIDS treatment at San Francisco General Hospital became very important to St. John's. White ethnic (Italian and Irish) Catholics worked with Episcopalian gays to develop a campaign to increase funding for AIDS care and education. From that campaign new friendships and relationships of mutual respect were forged. Such stories of transformational opportunities are part of every good organizer's experience. They are not uncommon; quite the contrary!

MCO's broad boundary lines served another purpose: the base was large enough to have political weight in San Francisco. MCO's "turf" included well over 10 percent of the city's population—a number capable of making a difference in election outcomes and a critical mass for boycotts or nonviolent disruptive direct action. A problem in many anti–urban renewal fights was that the boundaries of the constituency were the same as the urban renewal site. The population in these sites was typically too small to be politically significant in local politics. City council members, particularly if elected "at large," could ignore a small constituency. While this constituency might influence the vote of a councilperson elected in a district, it wasn't powerful enough to make him or her treat the issues as significant. A member could vote "no" on an urban renewal proposal but not press other members to also vote "no."

▓ Summing Up

My understanding of how change comes about begins with core values—like freedom, community, equality, justice, security, democratic participation. These are the standards against which any ideological conclusion or policy formulation needs to be measured: does it bring us closer to or take us farther away from these core values? The next question is about how to build the people power that will bring us closer to realizing those values. What alliances, in what form of organization, with what relationship to a broad constituency of people, are required to hold those in power accountable? Further, what will it take to transform dominant relations of power in which a relatively small group of people holding great wealth or key political positions defines the parameters of how the people live—what kinds of jobs they have, at what pay; what kind of housing they live in, at what cost; what kind of health care they receive, paid by whom; what kind of education their children experience, serving whom; what kind of environment we live in, at what price to whom?

This way of thinking can be applied to national politics just as it applied to a community organizing effort in a Latino community, or it can be applied to a women's organization or the organization of any other constituency. In addition to the broad values we articulate, this question can be asked: "What more specific vision of a better future can unite large numbers of people to struggle together for a better world?" In this framework, policy options—and these include public ownership—are viewed from the perspective of whether they unite or divide the social groupings needed to democratically bring about changes that bring us closer to our core values. I might think public ownership of gas and electricity is a good idea, or that a single-payer health plan is the best way to provide quality care for all Americans. But if only a minority of the people who are meant to benefit from these ideas agree with them, a broadly based community organization will not adopt them. Some people may advocate for them, trying to convince majorities of their merit, but these are not the ideas that will build people power. Lowest significant common denominator ideas—ideas around which majorities can coalesce—build people power. These same majorities, through their community organizations, can evaluate the implementation of such ideas if they become public policy. They can continue, modify, discard, or otherwise amend those that don't work. If they are engaged, and if policy X (let's say single-payer health care) is what will work most effectively, efficiently, and appropriately for the greatest number of people, then they will arrive at that conclusion themselves, because they have tested other approaches and they don't work.

Here's the central point: within the context of organizing, ideas must be assessed with two measures—first, their merit, and second, their capacity to unite the broad and diverse base that is required to build effective constituencies for change. For the most part, intellectuals focus on the former to the exclusion of the latter. It is like a group of friends debating the merits of a safari in Africa versus a trek in Nepal versus visiting the Arctic, when among them they only have the money to take a bus across town to the zoo.

▧ An Aside to Marx

Marx's oft-quoted (out of context) "opium of the people" statement on religious belief is, "Religious suffering is, at one and the same time, the expression of real suffering and a protest against real suffering. Religion is the sigh of the oppressed creature, the heart of a heartless world, and the soul of soulless conditions" [or] "…the spirit of a spiritless situation. It is the opium of the people. The abolition of religion as the *illusory* happiness of the people is [required] for their *real* happiness. To call on them to give up their illusions about their condition is to call on them to give up a condition that requires illusions."

In fact, Marx was wrong about religion: it is the impulse for a great deal of positive change. But he was right about a danger in religion: it can be used to rationalize the status quo. Similarly, today's activist intellectuals who spend their time debating the nuances of positions—whether they be positions on revolution or on public policy options—harbor the illusion that if only they can get the ideas correctly formulated, they will then be able to persuade people, and change will come about.

The fundamental problem in the United States has two parts: the concentration of wealth and power in the hands of a relatively small group of people, and the lack of a democratic, people-power social movement to effectively challenge the status quo. In the absence of the latter, the former will continue and get worse.

MCO and Model Cities,

Round Two

By the time serious Model Cities negotiations resumed with the mayor's office, the Mission Coalition Organization had resolved some of its earlier identity problems and was in vigorous action on the jobs and housing fronts. As a result of these activities, the mayor's office and members of the Board of Supervisors were beginning to express deeper doubt over MCO's role in Model Cities. MCO was now regularly using its official recognition in Model Cities as one of its levers in negotiations with employers, landlords, and public agencies. In effect, our argument went, "If we're good enough for the mayor, why not you?" This was an invitation to them to raise hell with the mayor's office for recognizing such an organization—and this they did.

As earlier noted, even in 1969 MCO was acting in controversial or militant ways: organizing the rent strike on 24th Street, effecting the transfer of Mission High's top administrative staff, closing the block of 26th Street that went through Bernal Dwellings Housing Project, partially supporting striking students at San Francisco State, and opposing pawn shops and pornographic theaters on Mission Street being examples. But these were only a taste of what MCO was to become.

During the summer of 1970, these problems in our relationship with city government came to a head. Michael McCone, newly appointed by Mayor Alioto to handle the Model Cities program (he took John Anderson's place), was personally contacting leaders of MCO member organizations, trying to cool our summer jobs and housing actions. He argued, and may well have been right, that the MCO activities were jeopardizing our Board of Supervisors majority. MCO's response was of both a legal and a political nature.

MCO Wanted Both Model Cities and Action on Issues

MCO insisted that its independent activities had nothing to do with Model Cities and didn't violate either the law or U.S. Dept. of Housing and Urban Development (HUD) regulations. On political grounds, it was impossible for us to withdraw from those activities. We had argued within the organization that the way to defeat urban renewal was to have a powerful organization. Without power, legal guarantees in Model Cities bylaws would be meaningless; with it, we could win an urban renewal fight at the Board of Supervisors or with HUD and we wouldn't need detailed legal guarantees. To build such an organization, we had to have a multi-issue thrust, one that took us outside the framework of Model Cities. Further, our own analysis of the inadequacies of Model Cities, combined with the threat that MCO's leaders generally acknowledged that Model Cities posed to MCO's action orientation, required that we develop a strong, issue-oriented base. Our argument with the mayor's office was that our membership would not tolerate abandoning direct action on issues. The organization's 1969 convention was a major success. Almost a thousand delegates and alternates, and many new organizations, participated. No serious "two coalitions" argument was put forth this time around. A confident leadership stood firm in relation to city hall.

Divide and Conquer: From the Bottom Up

As this second-round fight began to heat up, MCO played on an important division inside the Democratic Party. San Francisco's Democratic Party was and is less an organization than a collection of star figures or constellations. Two bright stars in San Francisco in this period were Congressman Phillip Burton and Mayor Joseph Alioto. At that time, most Democratic politicians were in one or another of their orbits. If not, they were quietly biding their time to assert their own independence. As negotiations with Alioto became more difficult, MCO began to deal with "Burton forces," especially Assemblymen John Burton, Phil's younger brother, and Willie Brown, then a rising young African-American liberal politician. (He became more centrist later, as speaker of the California State Assembly, a position in which he was second only to the governor in the political power he wielded in California.) Brown and the Burtons were accessible, had no direct stake in the conflict, "ideologically" supported community-control arguments, and welcomed opportunities to make Alioto look bad. Our next strategy in the Model Cities fight was based on this division and these rivalries.

In order to neutralize MCO's influence, Michael McCone visited key member groups and tried to get them to pull out of the organization. His efforts failed. The Mission Merchants Association's Frank Hunt later told me that McCone asked him to pull the merchants' association out of MCO. Hunt, though a Republican, was a big Alioto supporter, but he told McCone, "I may not agree with everything they're doing now, but when I needed help with the girlie movies and pawn shops it was

MCO, not the merchants' association, who won the battle. I'm not abandoning them now."

The Frank Hunt experience illustrates an important lesson that good community organizers know. Beyond being a conservative and a Republican, Hunt was other things more important to him than ideology and politics. When I first met him, he told me a story about racial prejudice that he saw as a young man growing up in Oklahoma. "I told myself then, Mike, that I'd fight that kind of thing wherever I found it." He loved being a small businessman in the diverse Mission District. When an Anglo member of the merchants' association asked him what he was going to do "when the Mexicans take over the Mission," he replied, "Sell them donuts." He donated donuts to any nonprofit that wanted to sell them. They charged his retail price and kept the entire proceeds.

Hunt thought small business was important. Many small businessmen get caught up in "free market" ideology and are locked into political conservatism because of it. But if you push past the politics and ideology, there's often much more there: pride in product, the desire to sustain something you've built, service to a community, loyalty to employees and customers—all good things to work with when building people power. There's also self-interest. Most small retail businesses rely on customer loyalty, and in the Mission their customers typically came from a very circumscribed neighborhood. Move the business not-too-many blocks as a result of urban renewal, and it's likely to fail.

McCone met a similar fate with Father Jim Casey at St. Peter's. Casey knew from his own experience of having been called a communist that many people had inaccurately labeled MCO. He wasn't going to let red-baiting dissuade him from his social justice commitments. These value commitments were one part of Casey's allegiance to MCO.

Father Casey also valued the role he was playing on the Housing Committee, because of the people he was meeting, working with, and getting to know, and he made the cause of people in MCO-related tenant associations his own. Personal relationships born of struggle are strong! And this is the mother of broader ideas of solidarity.

On July 13, 1970, Michael McCone told us that we would have to choose between our direct action housing and employment activities and Model Cities. Allies in the mayor's office and on the Board of Supervisors informed us that the mayor's staff had drafted new Model Cities legislation that excluded MCO. Friendly members of the Board of Supervisors told us that we did not have the magic six votes, a bare majority, needed to win our position with the supervisors. It was our view, and is necessarily the view of an organizer and organization in this kind of situation, that a counterattack was being mounted. And it was necessary that we respond. This response took two forms, one "inside," and the other "outside."

The inside strategy asked people who were both allies of ours and of the mayor to express concern to the mayor's office over reports that he was "reneging" on the agreement with MCO. No accusation was made; only concern was expressed.

The outside strategy called for MCO to use divisions between politicians to bring Alioto around to renewing an agreement with us. The implementation of this strategy began when Michael McCone told us that we had to choose: we said we would no longer talk with him and wanted a meeting with the mayor. Given the history of his relationship with us, the mayor could not reject such a meeting. Further, while we necessarily assumed that a counterattack was being mounted on us, we also assumed that war had not yet been declared. The meeting was a lively one, and we almost blew it.

■ The Mayor and His Rivals

On a warm Friday afternoon, the mayor cordially welcomed us into his office. We swiftly moved to the point. The mayor said, and the words are so clear in my memory that I can hear him saying them, "It seems to me that there is an incompatibility between the conciliatory role called for in Model Cities and the adversary role you play in your other activities." Our reply was that "Model Cities says that we must be representative of the community, not 'conciliatory.'" As we went into this meeting, we knew that our inside strategy was having an impact: the mayor's office was telling those who inquired that "no final decision has been made on MCO; the mayor is committed to working with MCO." The line between mounting a counterattack and declaring war clearly was maintained. But in the course of our presentation to the mayor, one of our major negotiators accused the mayor of "reneging" on his agreement with us. We declared war; the mayor could have responded with his own declaration. He chose not to and gave us a way out of the position in which we had placed ourselves. Such are some of the delicacies of negotiations.

It was our otherwise cautious Planning Committee chairman, Jack Bourne, who made the accusation of reneging. An Anglo leader in St. Peter's parish, Bourne was not a participant in any of MCO's militant direct action activities. When he made his accusation, there was stunned silence on the part of the other twenty or so MCO leaders in the room. Ben Martinez asked the mayor if we could caucus. The mayor asked where, and in a moment of humor, Martinez asked him if he would mind leaving his own office. The mayor did. When he came back, a composed negotiating team withdrew its charge and instead asked the mayor—as we had initially planned—to be our guest and take a tour of the Mission District. A politician is in a difficult position when a major organization invites him to visit its community. After some jockeying on the point of the tour, a date was arranged and the mayor agreed to attend.

When we left the meeting, we immediately called the Burton camp, first inviting, then confirming their participation in the tour. Later that afternoon—and MCO's president predicted this would happen—we received a call from the mayor's office asking for a postponement of the tour. We responded that too much was already underway; the tour was on. We hoped that the mayor would be there. I called Dave Jenkins, an activist from the longshoremen's union who was a liaison to labor from the mayor's office, and who I knew personally because his daughter Becky had been active in Friends of SNCC, and said to him, "Dave, the mayor's making a big mistake." He grumbled; I knew from his response that he agreed but had been defeated internally by others on the mayor's staff.

How should this drama be understood? The mayor, we knew, was under cross-pressures. Inside his office and among his close supporters, and in the city as a whole, there were conflicting voices as to how he should deal with the Mission situation. As a politician interested in the balance of political forces, he must weigh carefully a situation in which there were conflicting views even among his own close supporters. An anti-MCO decision would be an invitation to a long, drawn-out battle with a minority community organization and its allies in the city. It would also push MCO into the Burton camp. A pro-MCO decision would invite attacks for dealing with a group of "irresponsible radicals."

The mayor had to test the situation. In allowing his staff to follow their own positions while remaining neutral himself, he was able to test the strength of MCO, its flexibility in negotiations, and its ability to sustain itself over time. Where a question of recognition is in doubt, and the organization seeking recognition is weak, it will not be long before rivals emerge within the community, calling themselves the "voice of the people" or at least challenging the claim that is made by another. No such rival emerged within the Mission. When Michael McCone posed the question as an either-or choice for MCO—Model Cities or direct action—no substantial Mission organization publicly challenged the official MCO stand that we would do both. Groups who had earlier disagreements with MCO checked with our headquarters and leadership before responding to McCone's question—including the earlier described Mission Rebels, who the year before had called MCO a "sellout" organization. There were no weak links, either to the left or right, in the unity that had been forged by MCO leadership around the Model Cities position and the direct action activities of the organization.

The tour of the Mission came off as a great success. Assemblymen Brown and Burton participated, as did several supervisors, Congressman Burton's field rep Doris Thomas, and a representative from the Republican lieutenant governor's Model Cities coordination office, Tom Duffy. (To "buy" support from governors, HUD created in each governor's office a "Model Cities coordinator." In this case, we were suddenly dealing with then-Governor Reagan's administration, specifically with Lt. Gov. Reinecke.) It turned out that Duffy was a "Mission boy," having grown up in St. Peter's parish, and this worked to our advantage. Mayor Alioto didn't show. The tour took its participants to many of the sites of MCO activities. At each site, dozens of MCO members from all ethnic backgrounds, homeowners and tenants, young, middle-aged, and old, parents and singles, greeted the visitors. That we were representative was clear. Indeed, no other organization like MCO existed in the city at the time. We gave the press an off-the-record interpretation of the mayor's absence. A good newspaper reporter did the rest. The Sunday major daily headline, running over eight columns, declared, "Top Reagan Aide Impressed by MCO." A large picture showed Assemblymen Brown and Burton shaking hands with a small child in a schoolyard. The story gave a full description of the day's itinerary and said that well-informed sources speculated that the mayor's absence was due to the controversy stirred by MCO in the city.

By the middle of the next week, the answer was in. The mayor met with MCO President Ben Martinez and said that MCO had demonstrated that it was the organization with the capacity to handle the Model Cities program. The struggle for a renewed agreement was won. And, it was won by MCO through its own orga-nizational effort. We had asserted our right to determine our own course. It was a peak in organizational development, particularly because of its relationship to the activities of the Housing and Employment Committees. Note finally that MCO was never "pro" or "anti" any of the politicians. We were pro-Mission and judged the politicians accordingly. It made no sense for MCO to try to further Mission people's interests while being in the camp of any particular politician. Allies were to be supported, but no permanent relationships were made.

On Playing the Mayor

After one of our meetings with Mayor Alioto, and I'm not sure which one it was, I noticed a certain coolness towards me as our group was leaving City Hall. "What's the matter?" I asked, "Do I have bad breath today?" Of course everyone laughed. Then the question came: "Mike, did you talk with the mayor before we met with him?" That puzzled me. "No, why do you ask?" "Because he said some of the same things you said when we role-played," was the reply. This time I laughed. After a while, you learn that the people with whom you meet have some standard responses to things you say. It strengthened people's confidence in me as an organizer when I predicted them.

Urban Planning

Because San Francisco is a forty-nine-square-mile peninsula, land is scarce and in high demand, and urban planning is especially important to the character of the city. The Mission Coalition Organization got deeply involved in aspects of urban planning.

Housing and Land-Use Questions

Underlying much of MCO's politics was the long-standing fear of urban renewal. As Bay Area Rapid Transit (BART) neared its fall 1972 completion, MCO leadership increasingly was concerned that a new move to introduce urban renewal in the Mission would somehow sneak in with Model Cities. A definite pride characterized MCO leaders who had earlier been involved in defeating urban renewal. They, and the newer leaders brought up in that tradition, watched land-use issues in the Mission with some wariness.

By early 1970, MCO had developed a rather sophisticated overview and elaborate strategy for dealing with housing and land-use questions. First, and it was almost self-evident by that time, no urban renewal could happen *without* MCO having veto power—it was the Mission's equivalent of "no taxation without representation." At the same time, the potential of joint planning with the urban renewal agency began to develop. It was essential for MCO to have veto power with regard to Model Cities, because it would be through Model Cities that urban renewal funds would come into the Mission District. The presence of an "advocate-planner," who would assist MCO to develop its own capacity for thinking and planning for the future of the neighborhood, helped to make a positive relationship with the urban renewal agency seem possible to MCO.

It is worth noting a difference in scale between Model Cities and urban renewal. The Model Cities *implementation* money that the Mission finally received from combined federal sources for child care, education, housing, and employment programs was a little over $3 million (more than $16 million in 2009 dollars).

The *planning* grant (note: this did not cover implementation) that the San Francisco Redevelopment Agency (SFRA) wanted for its urban renewal project—the one defeated by the Mission Council on Redevelopment—as noted in the December 5, 1966, minutes of the Board of Supervisors, was $2,160,155 (more than $14 million in 2009 dollars). It was for good reason that MCO's leaders gave careful thought to whether they could turn urban renewal to their own ends. It is also indicative of federal priorities that an urban renewal *planning* grant was over two-thirds of the federal Model Cities *implementation* grant.

A Different Vision

MCO first became aware of the idea of an advocate-planner when the Presbyterian Church's Department of Urban Work brought a Milwaukee-based architect and planner by the name of Leonard Styche to visit the Mission. Styche had worked in Chicago with The Woodlawn Organization (TWO), an Alinsky- formed group in the largely African-American community east of the University of Chicago. The university was interested in a slum-clearance approach to Woodlawn in order to create a middle-class buffer area around the campus. The Black community had different ideas.

As was the case wherever the urban renewal bulldozer threatened a low-income neighborhood, local people were accused of defending slums, being parochial, and not caring about the big-picture good of the city. Leonard Styche was paid by the Presbyterian Church to help TWO come up with an alternative to the university's plan, one that would eliminate slum conditions but wouldn't eliminate the people forced to live in them, or their local institutions and businesses. Now, several years later, the Presbyterians offered Styche's services to MCO's Planning Committee. His visit provided the Planning Committee and MCO top-level leadership with a different view of the city. A couple of dozen people heard Styche present a vision of a Mission District renewed for the people living and working in it. MCO leaders now became at least willing to consider using urban renewal's authority and power—eminent domain, land-cost write-downs to developers, subsidies to make housing afford-able, and clout with city and federal officials—to serve the interests of the people in the Mission.

Simply blocking urban renewal would not be sufficient. Without some kind of program for revitalizing the neighborhood, it would either continue to deteriorate, perhaps facing more aggressive redlining from financial institutions, or code enforce-ment and gentrification would eliminate affordable housing and small business storefronts. In either case, the result would be to drive working-class and poor people out of the district. MCO needed a proactive strategy that would shape the district's future and make use of all possible planning tools available to the community.

To preserve and improve the Mission for its residents, institutions, and businesses, MCO had to be able to positively affect public and private sector activity through negotiations and powerful direct action. An aggressive MCO could create long delays in any construction project that was initiated in the Mission without its approval. I was told by a conservative, wealthy, Republican mayoral appointee to the Mission Model Neighborhood Corporation board that MCO was "creating an atmosphere inhospitable to investment." His comment was intended as an instructive and friendly criticism. He distrusted urban renewal, had been lied to by SFRA director Justin Herman, and thought the market could best serve the people of the Mission. For me as an organizer, his comment was about the best compliment I could receive. MCO's ability to create that atmosphere was one of the organization's most effective tools for preserving the Mission for those who lived and worked there. "Development" is not an end in itself. The question that must be asked is "Development for whom, and at what price?"

As its proposal, MCO wanted to see development take place in the largely abandoned northeast industrial portion of the neighborhood. Advocate-planner Styche provided a vision of how urban renewal could strengthen rather than destroy a neighborhood. His ideas were shared by a relatively small group of planners who became technical assistants to low-income neighborhoods faced with urban renewal. Key elements of his concept for the Mission were:

> Build affordable housing on vacant sites that were close to housing that had to be torn down; make these units available to people who had to be relocated; after relocation, rebuild or rehabilitate on the vacated site; offer relocatees an option of returning to their old site, but in their initial move, house them in a place acceptable to them.

> Use rehabilitation rather than demolition wherever possible.

> Strengthen local businesses and institutions by a combination of grants, loans, training, marketing assistance, and other programs to stabilize and enhance a local economy and local social, religious, and cultural centers.

> Create job opportunities that could be filled by Mission residents on sites in the largely vacant or abandoned northeast Mission area.

> Build neighborhood-based services, such as health-care and child-care centers, close to public transportation sites so that working people could readily access them.

> Use the talents of local building tradespeople, artists, and others in the process of renewing the neighborhood.

Together, these ideas gave voice to a different vision of the Mission District—an implicit one that was just beneath the surface of the alleged parochialism of its residents, small businesses, and local institutions. But this vision went against the grain of the postwar corporate power that was reflected in Bay Area metropolitan planning. Urban renewal, interstate highways, and the routing of BART (bringing suburbanites into downtown San Francisco's financial and shopping districts) all were part of a planning design to specialize the parts of the Bay Area (light—and some heavy—industry to Alameda and Contra Costa Counties; the container port to Oakland; finance and tourism in San Francisco; high tech—Silicon Valley and genetic research and development—in San Mateo and Santa Clara Counties; warehouses to the outer ring of the Bay Area and even Nevada; the middle class to remain in San Francisco and inner-ring suburbs; working class and poorer people to Oakland, elsewhere in Alameda County, and outer-ring suburban areas). SFRA's Justin Herman even said, "San Francisco is not a city for Negroes." Urban renewal agencies and other metropolitan planning agencies were, in fact, the public-authority expression of corporate power.

Contrast this corporate agenda with a view emphasizing the value of neighborhoods that were more than places where one slept: neighborhoods that accommodated walking or taking local public transit to work, small and medium-sized business, and diverse social and cultural resources. In sum, this was a different vision of what cities should look like, one that planners in Europe still appreciate and advocate-planners in the U.S. voiced. Styche gave a language to what was implicit in MCO thinking—as did people like Jane Jacobs nationally.

▉ MCO's Planning Committee

City planning issues were the purview of MCO's Planning Committee. It did not cause the stir that the Housing and Jobs Committees did, but its impact was long lasting. In 1971 and 1972, seeking ways to secure the gains made when urban renewal was defeated in 1966-67, MCO continued the land-use fight into zoning disputes, including height and bulk limitations for buildings. It led mass testimony at a city Planning Commission hearing on the uses of the Bay Area Rapid Transit corridor and major BART corners at 16th and 24th Streets and Mission. MCO was able to win major victories here: a height limit of forty feet at the BART corners and along Mission Street. Restrictions on high-rise development meant speculators wouldn't be able to bulldoze affordable housing units located near BART stations.

Dean Macris, then director of the city's Planning Commission, was an ally in this fight. (Macris and SFRA's Justin Herman often viewed development in San Francisco differently. Macris was often an ally of the neighborhoods and a more human scale of urban development, but the city's Planning Commission was bypassed by the urban renewal efforts of SFRA, which in effect did its own planning within areas designated for urban renewal.)

From 1969 to 1971, the MCO Planning Committee was also looking at the lack of recreation facilities in the Mission. Their solution was to seek funds to develop new open space and rehabilitate existing buildings for recreational uses. These funds were to be directed not only to the Mission, but to other high-needs neighborhoods as well, including Bayview–Hunters Point. Farmworker leader Cesar Chavez was the keynote speaker at a rally at Folsom Park to kick off the campaign, and it was because of MCO's relationship with him that he came. The campaign succeeded in getting an initiative, Proposition C, on the ballot. It narrowly failed. The next year, it was tried again, as Proposition J, with a broader, citywide focus and coalition and with larger involvement of the Park and Recreation Department. This time it passed. The first expenditures included rehabilitation of a major Harrison Street site to recreational use as well as other mini-park and park sites. The principle guiding the MCO Planning Committee was that if you have a problem, you need an implementation scheme. The members were interested in long-term solutions and worked hard to design them.

An MCO-produced paper on the Inner Mission/northeast industrial area offered ideas about how industrial and residential areas could coexist rather than be antagonists. Despite the relatively high density of the Mission, there were vacant lots and abandoned industrial buildings in the northeast area. Some of these came to be artists' live-work space.

In 1972, as MCO began its decline, the nucleus of the Planning Committee formed a new organization called Mission Planning Council (MPC) and continued work on these issues. MPC won a major zoning fight on the narrow, mostly residential streets just east and west of Mission, thereby limiting what developers might do in the Mission.

Toby Levine and Judy Bowman were co-chairs of the Planning Committee. The presence of each of them testified to another benefit of MCO as a multi-issue organization. Levine's participation in MCO came initially because she was a teacher in the Mission District and a member of the teachers' union. Bowman's participation came initially because she was a public housing tenant in Holly Courts, and MCO had done organizing work there with the tenants on public housing issues.

MCO action was consistently centered around maintaining the neighborhood as one in which low- and moderate-income people could comfortably live, small businesses could thrive, and local institutions could be preserved and enhanced.

The Question

of Allies

The Mission Coalition Organization was limited in what it could accomplish for the people it represented. There were various ways in which it could have expanded those limits and broadened its people power.

Politics involve questions of "with whom" and "for what." Furthermore, as political scientists John Scharr and Wilson Carey McWilliams once wrote, it involves these questions in precisely that order. Questions of relationships, constituency, and allies were always central to the populist democrat strategy in the Mission. Having grown to a certain size and composition within the geographic area it defined as its area of operations, MCO faced several alternatives:

Deepen its roots within the area of its "turf"; this is primarily a job of organizing more groups in the district and deepening connections among members of existing organizations (particularly the churches)—seeking to change "consumer members" into "participant" or "co-creator members." It was a common complaint of church leaders that too few of their members did too much of the work and provided too much of the leadership. MCO training did contribute to leadership development in some of the churches, but it was not an intentional focus of the organization.

Seek allies citywide or further, both for the purpose of pursuing immediate ends and for the purpose of developing broader solutions to problems which could not be solved from a neighborhood base alone.

Encourage the development of organizations that would function for other parts of the city the way MCO did for the Mission. Such organizations would be natural allies because of their commitments to shared values, the possibility of common agendas, and their willingness to engage in mass action. These alliances would be deeper than the instrumental relationships typically forged in citywide coalitions, which come and go depending on the issue.

Remain at its current level of organization and power and shift to a strategy of stabilizing what was already organized—a pursuit which flies in the face of the dictum "organize or die." That dictum suggests that organizations are never stable unless they are stagnant. In the absence of new challenges, leaders begin to protect turf rather than expand it; to see new leadership as potential rivals, rather than a source of additional people power; and to be threatened by new voices and points of view, rather than embrace them as part of the music of democracy.

To deepen roots in the community meant a continued allocation of staff time to new organizing and internal organizing. This was done for a time, but as Model Cities came closer, staff was less and less available for organizing.

There were many external pressures for MCO to move citywide. We were viewed as a powerful organization, and others wanted to make use of that power to pursue their interests. For example, the Alioto campaign sought and finally received substantial assistance in the Mission from MCO activists. This came after MCO victory in the Model Cities fight. Many of the same activists supported the liberal Richard Hongisto in his successful campaign to become sheriff, but the Alioto campaign was more important to MCO as a means of comparing its strength with that of the Centro Social Obrero in relation to city hall. That jockeying for formal and informal recognition still went on. While the Obreros were in the Martinez camp in MCO's internal politics, Abel Gonzalez was not about to concede that MCO, either formally or informally, spoke for the Mission on matters of electoral political alliances. MCO's precinct work proved it could deliver in the Mission, but Gonzalez continued to show that he could deliver as well; his electoral work was independent of MCO's.

Difficulties

The question of allies was a difficult one. In the absence of independent mass organizations in other neighborhoods, MCO's relationships began to move toward the more progressive labor unions in the city, which included a number of unions with a large minority group membership. Some of these unions participated in MCO, sending delegations to the annual conventions; some participated more actively, assigning members to play roles in MCO committees. The American Federation of Teachers, Local 61, was particularly active. Their involvement was an excellent example of how new voices stretched leaders: parents, teachers, and community leaders all grew in the relationship with the AFT. The union offered parents and community leaders a different perspective on education reform. The participation of parents opened teachers to new relationships with them and opened the union to a wider agenda in San Francisco.

Other unions gave support to MCO during its fight with the mayor. Most of them were firmly in the Alioto camp, not that of the more liberal Jack Morrison, in the 1971 city election. A key figure in putting together this progressive alignment in the Alioto coalition was the International Longshore and Warehouse Union's Dave Jenkins, an early ally of MCO in the internal fight in the mayor's office. The ILWU was one of the left-wing unions expelled from the CIO during the McCarthy era. Based in San Francisco, it was a relatively strong political force in the city, but usually in the background. With the Alioto campaign, the ILWU became a public player in city politics: even this historically left-wing union with a large minority membership was in Alioto's camp.

Alioto's strong majority vote in low-income and minority districts, as well as his big majority in the city as a whole, confirmed something else that had guided MCO in building alliances. The militants of the Black community who did not support Alioto could not deliver majorities in Black precincts. Rather, it was the alliance of Black churches and labor that provided Alioto with substantial majorities in the Black community. He defeated Jack Morrison, who had the support of the militants. Although this confirmed the utility of MCO's alliances, there was a negative as well: between elections, the organizations that backed Alioto tended to be those least engaged in direct action on unemployment, housing, education, and other issues that characterized MCO's between-election activities. Thus MCO's most likely allies for citywide direct action were its least likely allies when it came to electoral politics.

Most important, MCO developed a commitment to Alioto because of the new relationship in the Model Cities program. The battle was over; the peace had been signed; the agreement was being honored. MCO now was showing it could continue to deliver and was protecting the relationship it had established with the mayor. How that relationship was transformed by the Model Cities "process" will be reviewed when we resume the Model Cities story. Suffice it to say here that the protection of that relationship was at the center of the MCO's commitment to Alioto.

MCO's principal leaders backed Alioto for mayor against his liberal opponent but backed liberal Richard Hongisto for sheriff and the Burtons in the offices they held. None of this was done officially, since the organization had a no-endorsement policy: at this point in the Alinsky tradition of community organizing, there was an almost inviolable rule that the organization did not formally back political candidates. At the same time, top leaders did informally support politicians with whom their organization had hammered out a relationship of mutual respect. This approach allowed the organization to continue its official nonpartisanship while at the same time "rewarding friends and punishing enemies." The practice also had weaknesses. Because it was informal, it meant that within the organization there wasn't a deep discussion of electoral politics or how a powerful grassroots organization might relate to them.

In later years, Alinsky-tradition organizations developed more sophisticated approaches to electoral politics. In my judgment, the best of these was to bring candidates before very large public assemblies and ask them to endorse the organization's key issues. This approach turned the table on politics-as-usual. Candidates endorsed the platform of a people's organization, rather than the organization endorsing the candidate. Post-assembly meetings would then inform the organization's constituency on "where the politicians stand on the people's issues." In some cities this approach turned out to be decisive in key electoral contests, including the 1972 governor's race in Illinois. In New Orleans, a community organization's window and yard signs outnumbered those of all the candidates for office in a citywide election. This approach could be called "partisan nonpartisanship" or "nonpartisan partisanship." A flyer might be headed "XYZ (the name of the community organization) Urges You to Vote." A next headline might read, "Where They Stand on the People's Issues." Then there would be two columns: "For the People" and "Against the People." Candidates' names would be listed in the appropriate columns. The community organization's name would again appear at the bottom of the flyer, along with its address and contact number. This flyer would be used at rallies and as part of a voter education, registration, and get-out-the-vote drive.

MCO's alliance with the churches continued. The ecumenical Joint Strategy and Action Commission, headed by Rev. Robert Davidson, kept up Protestant support for the organization. Growing MCO influence in Catholic parishes in the Mission finally led Archbishop McGucken to write a letter to parishes asking them to consider participation in MCO. That was as far as the archbishop would go; but it was, in effect, an endorsement of MCO. The Second Vatican Council had concluded only a few years earlier, and the winds of change, including greater participation of the laity, were felt in San Francisco. Catholic clergy and laity were calling for the church to take a more socially active role, which led to a desire to participate in MCO. Our primary focus was not on the already existing liberal Catholic organizations, like the Commission on Social Justice or the Catholic Interracial Council. However much any one of us might have agreed with their views, they generally couldn't deliver the people in the pews. Rather, we focused on institutional leaders like pastors, parish school principals, and the leaders of voluntary groupings within each parish, ranging from parish councils to nationality groups to parent groups. Within this context, the organizing process also developed new leaders within these churches.

Liberal and Minority Community Critics

As MCO made its allies and determined its course, it came under increasing criticism from liberals and minority activists. These groups frequently were in citywide coalitions themselves, and these coalitions frequently requested MCO endorsement of their activities. By late 1969, the corresponding secretary's report to MCO's Steering

Committee was a single-spaced, letter-size (sometimes legal-size!) piece of paper mimeographed on two sides that for the most part listed requests for MCO endorsement. Initial ideas about courtesy led Steering Committee leaders to spend time on each request, until they discovered that almost half of their two-hour meeting was being taken up with these discussions. At that time, the leadership decided it would simply adopt a report that showed it had received the communication. In their view, these were coalitions that could not deliver in their own constituencies. They suffered from the formula "zero + zero still = zero." The question of whether or not to align with them was first a question of who they represented, then of whether or not there was a basis for agreement on the position for which they were seeking endorsement. (On the other hand, had there been serious, broadly based, especially multi-issue organizations in other constituencies, MCO might well have entered into a partnership with them to accomplish something on a citywide, regional, or even statewide basis.)

MCO leadership sometimes agreed with the issues being raised by citywide coalitions or groups in other neighborhoods but could not accept the terms of the proposed alliances. In some of the manpower (employment opportunity) organizations, unions were named as the worst enemies—a position MCO didn't accept. In some education situations, MCO was to be given one vote, the same as an organization with just a handful of members. MCO would not accept that inequality in voting strength.

The problem of alliances never had to be seriously addressed in MCO because during the period of its peak activity as an action organization, there wasn't an organization similar to MCO at work in another part of San Francisco. Only later did counterpart possibilities come into existence. By then MCO was no longer engaged in much action other than that related to Model Cities.

Community organizing elsewhere during this period didn't successfully address the question of alliances either. Chicago, for example, had numerous effective organizations, each capable of speaking for its own constituency—that is, each could "deliver." But these organizations only sporadically came together. Alinsky attributed the failure to organizer ego: organizers were unwilling to give up the autonomy of a specific organization for the sake of greater power in a larger arena. No doubt the influence of organizers on this question was major, but there was a bigger problem as well. The very design of these organizations mitigated against the broader view: by the end of the 1970s, community organizers were targeting larger constituencies, framing their work in the context of a single organization, rather than (as MCO had done) organizing a series of local groups, each powerful in its own right, and then trying to bring them together under a common citywide or metropolitan-area umbrella.

▥ Redefining "Radical"

I earlier said that in my use, "radical" means going to the root of things, and that the roots of our social problems are to be found in the powerlessness of the majority of the people, on the one hand, and on the other, the concentration of wealth and power in the hands of relatively few. With knowledge of the Mission Coalition Organization's experience in building and exercising people power, we can now come to a more precise understanding of one meaning of "radical," and I use it here in a positive sense.

▥ Negotiated versus Unilateral Relationships

Ideas that bring large numbers of powerless people together to act in their own behalf are themselves radical. Thus the very idea of a mass-based, multi-issue, multi-constituency, highly participatory, small-d democratic community (or labor) organization is itself radical—even though the membership includes "radicals," liberals, centrists, and conservatives. It is radical because it shifts power, enabling people who didn't have an effective voice in the past to now have one.

Ideas that lead to a change in status, so that a supplicant voice (whatever the Constitution and civics textbooks say about "rights") becomes an effective voice, change the relations of power. The broader the scope of the matters made negotiable, the more radical the proposal. And these negotiations usually lead to formal recognition of the community (or labor) organization. When the members of a tenant association gain recognition from their landlord as the group with whom he will negotiate on matters of rent, repairs, maintenance, and treatment of tenants, that is radical because it alters the power relationship between those tenants and their landlord. Their next time around in negotiations, the tenants might propose that this recognition become part of any sales agreement between the present landlord and future owners of the property. They might seek inclusion in planning for improvements and setting priorities for building repairs and maintenance. The tenants' interest in the property as home now gains status in relation to the landlord's interest in the property as investment. In the give-and-take, a landlord might respond with the idea that only after X number of years of tenancy should the tenant be part of the deliberations on major new investments in the building. Why shouldn't tenants gain an equity stake in a property, when their rent pays the mortgage?

In labor-management negotiations, givebacks often reflect a loss of power by the union, not a change in the "objective economic circumstances" of the company. Or the company may have participated in creating the new "objective circumstances"—for example, by supporting tax incentives to locate production offshore and then telling a union, "We're moving, unless..." Why shouldn't workers gain an equity stake in a job, so that if capital decides to move the job, the worker has to be compensated?

At a broader policy level, what would happen if realtors' commissions were paid not just when a sale was made, but according to how long a buyer remained in a home? And could tax breaks or other incentives reward stability instead of turnover?

When the mayor considered withdrawing recognition from MCO, he couldn't, because MCO's people power was too great—he didn't want to pay the price. But had MCO not kept its base together, the mayor might well have said, "You're not the organization you once were, so I'm changing the terms of our relationship."

MCOR (the Mission Council on Redevelopment, MCO's predecessor) wanted veto power over urban renewal for two major reasons. For one, it knew that with a $2 million planning grant in hand, the San Francisco Redevelopment Agency might well be able to divide and conquer MCOR by making side deals with loosely affiliated member organizations, getting them to withdraw from the neighborhood coalition in exchange for a private benefit—for example, a parking lot next to a church, or church sponsorship of some nonprofit housing. MCOR also knew it could not count on a liberal majority of the Board of Supervisors to defend the Mission District. The liberal supervisor Leo McCarthy (later an assemblyman, speaker of the assembly, and lieutenant governor of California) voted against the urban renewal planning grant. The supervisors' official summary minutes explain why: "[H]e questioned whether this legislation [with its protective language for the Mission] would be binding on future Boards and whether the Board and the Redevelopment Agency are in a position to make good on its promises with respect to housing supply and the relocation of persons and businesses."

In the case of Model Cities, the mayor gave MCO his recognition without a struggle. Had he changed his mind, in the absence of a powerful organization there was little the community could have done. In demanding veto power, both MCOR and MCO asserted the continuing right of those most directly affected by government programs, particularly urban renewal, to not only have a voice, but to stop any program they thought was detrimental to their values and interests. Veto power went a step beyond negotiating differences.

▓ Who Is Qualified?

After a Jobs and Employment Committee campaign, employers came around to the idea that MCO should send them "qualified applicants." But they wanted to determine who was qualified. MCO said, "We negotiated for entry-level positions, and we will send you 'qualifiable applicants'; our point system (based on participation) will determine who they are." The point system shifted determination of who an employer would hire from the employer to the community—just as union hiring halls took away the prerogative of employers to use a "shape-up" or other screening mechanism to filter out those they thought were pro-union, to hire a friend's son, to pick someone who gave them a kickback for the job, or simply to hire who they wanted to hire because they owned the company.

▓ Power Is a Continuous Struggle over Prerogatives

When the relations of power change between landlords and tenants, matters that were heretofore the sole prerogative of owners and managers now become matters for negotiation with tenants and a community organization. They may even turn into matters for a whole new set of decision makers—as when housing becomes cooperatively or condominium-owned, or in the workplace, when workers gain ownership of an enterprise.

Similarly, in the public or nonprofit sector, elected officials, boards of directors, administrators, and others who recognized or accepted MCO's power engaged in negotiations with the organization on matters of policy. In relation to elected officials, this was often a difficult idea for some MCO supporters to accept. After all, wasn't it at public hearings that elected politicians were supposed to hear the facts, consult with their staffs, then make up their minds? In fact, that's not how their decisions are typically made. Those organized enough to get the ears, before the hearings, of elected officials establish what they want and obtain commitments of support for it. And they make clear the price an elected official will pay if she or he doesn't arrive at something mutually acceptable. Rarely are there occasions when a hearing changes a vote.

While I was working at MCO, I had a couple of highly instructive conversations with a veteran leader of a major union. In one of them he said, "Our union is in a continuous struggle over prerogatives with the employer." To place this discussion in a broader perspective, it seems to me that unions should become vehicles for broader issues. In particular, members of public employee unions should have a say on issues having to do with the quality, effectiveness, appropriateness, and efficiency of the services they deliver. Why, for example, should we assume that administrators who are appointed by a school superintendent or school board are more deeply interested in the quality of education than the rank-and-file teachers? Any particular question having to do with the quality of education might be equally or better answered by site-elected faculty or by a teachers' union—assuming the union was willing to address these questions.

Or think about this in the light of what the wizards of the financial world did with the mortgages and investments of millions of Americans: why shouldn't government have a decision-making voice on the boards of lending and insuring institutions? And why shouldn't organizations of borrowers have a voice as well? And what about the communities that are devastated by widespread foreclosures and industrial abandonment? Shouldn't broadly representative organizations in these communities have a voice? Lenders, investors, suppliers, and buyers have representation on typical corporate boards. Employees, consumers, neighbors, and government don't. Some businesspeople will refer to all of them as "stakeholders," but in the allocation of votes, some stakeholders have far bigger stakes than others. These ideas are now beyond the pale of political discourse among most Americans. They shouldn't be.

MCO Loses

Momentum

Toward the end of 1970, discussions were taking place within the Mission Coalition Organization about key changes in personnel. I was phasing out of the role of staff director; I thought it was time for the outside agitator/organizer to leave, and a local person to take over. The understanding I had at the time was that Ben Martinez would become staff director and Larry Del Carlo would run for the presidency.

Also at this time, our attention was again forced to Model Cities. Having reached a second agreement with the mayor, we now awaited Board of Supervisors approval. There, with some revisions that again almost blew the agreement sky-high, the basic terms of MCO recognition were adopted. Finally, the federal Department of Housing and Urban Development (HUD) approved the San Francisco Model Cities planning grant application, which included the Mission and Bayview–Hunters Point. We now had to address ourselves to a Model Cities strategy.

MCO core leadership's view was that Model Cities projects were, as much as possible, to be run by existing nonprofit or public institutions, with Model Cities funding to entice change, along with MCO influence and pressure from the outside. For example, if MCO wanted a new bilingual program in the schools to enhance educational opportunities for children raised in monolingual Spanish-speaking homes, it could negotiate for the creation of a bilingual "corridor" which would allow these children to enter any grade level and find an appropriate bilingual class. If the school district agreed to the program, MCO would be in a position to say funding from Model Cities was available to help implement the agreement. As discussed earlier, this approach was called the "institutional change model," to be distinguished from the "community control model," in which funding would go to existing or newly created community-based nonprofit organizations.

Now, we thought, in addition to our power of negotiation and, when required, confrontation, we would have federal dollars and recognition with which to enhance our bargaining position. The relationship we had to the Model Cities program was such that any institution or agency wishing to administer Model Cities–funded projects would have to be acceptable to us!

These various understandings began to break down prior to MCO's 1970 convention. One of the most important of them was who would be the new president of MCO.

From the beginnings to the peak of its development, the leadership of MCO went through dramatic change. In any growing organization, the beginning leaders will not necessarily be in power two years later. The change is a natural one. Some people do not like to function in a large organization, or do not learn how to; they prefer the intimacy of a small group. Or they are unprepared to engage in the internal struggles and external confrontations that characterize a mass organization. Others tire, burn out, move, or lose interest. Further, existing community leaders who take a wait-and-see attitude during the beginning trials of the organization soon want to become involved in it because there is a serious game to be played. The organization has met their tests of seriousness, and they want a role commensurate with their standing in the community. To the extent that they have a following, they have to be involved, or they will become enemies that the organization cannot afford. Also, new leaders arise in the course of campaigns undertaken by the organization. The organization becomes a meaningful part of their lives, above and beyond any specific concern or issue that first brought them into it.

▨ The Changing Character of MCO Leadership

Between 1968, when Mayor Alioto announced his interest in making the Mission District part of San Francisco's Model Cities program, and 1970, when MCO held its third convention, a number of leadership changes took place in MCO. First, agency people were less prominent in leadership as the organization grew. Because of perceived threats to the interests of their agencies (or, contradictorily, because they realized that MCO wasn't a threat to their interests—it varied from one agency to the next), or because of the increased demands MCO made on its core leadership's time, or because emerging forces within the MCO pushed them aside, they shifted from active to passive roles. A major and important exception was the Centro Social Obrero, whose members began to play an active role in the now successful Jobs and Employment Committee. For them, self-interest dictated that they get active. Their agency "job development" approach could not deliver jobs in the way that MCO's mass action could. Yet for continued success for their program, they needed placements. It was an example of how an independent mass action approach could strengthen local agencies.

The early preponderance of Mexican-American leaders shifted to a balance among all the Latino groups in the Mission. Further, at MCO's second convention, Italian-Americans and Irish-Americans demanded that vice presidencies be created for them, similar to those of the different Latino groups. "We're not 'Anglos,'" they said, and we should have our own vice presidencies." Some of them joked, "I know we all look alike…" The white ethnics of the Mission were clearly not the middle-class Anglos who were the majority of the liberals and centrists in MCO.

By and large, new leadership increasingly came up through the committee structure of MCO: leadership training was an ongoing function of committees and of staff work. Early reliance on people with middle-class skill backgrounds was balanced by an internal process that identified potential leaders and developed them.

As new leaders were taking over the organization and making it theirs, they were also beginning to show some of the "we-they" symptoms of a leadership that is not in continuous contact with its own rank and file. Their growing confidence in their own power was a healthy development from an organizational point of view; at the same time, it was accompanied by a forgetfulness of how that power was achieved. Indeed, in some ways a serious defeat at this point might have been helpful to the organization so long as it was not a disaster.

The possibility of a real collective leadership now existed. The commitment on the part of a large number of people to MCO as "their thing" was deep. The common experiences emerging from mass action gave everyone a common language of action. MCO had a style and character of its own. The name meant something in the neighborhood. People wore their MCO buttons on their lapels with pride. Yet at the very time this leadership was developing, the question of presidential succession was becoming a problem.

Meanwhile, the core leadership, if it wanted to maintain control of the organization, had to accomplish three things as it moved a populist democrat agenda forward. First, it had to maintain and deepen its support in the churches. Second, it had to keep at least one, and ideally both of these organizations in its support group: Arriba Juntos/OBECA and the Centro Social Obrero/Mission Language and Vocational School. (Each had a constituency broader than its stated purpose would suggest; each was widely respected in the community; each was relatively stable in its funding base, thus not dependent on Model Cities for its future.) Third, core leaders had to continue to expand MCO's grassroots base by organizing new groups among the "unaffiliated"—unemployed people, parents of public school students, tenants, block groups, and others.

▨ The Top Leadership Team

In its initial stages, MCO could not have developed without a president like Ben Martinez. A strong figure, he devoted almost all his working hours, and his nonwork time as well, to the organization—his employer, OBECA, was generally supportive but sometimes ambivalent about his role. He was everywhere in the development of MCO: visiting member organizations, sometimes sorting out difficulties between them, playing a role in committee development, sitting in on staff meetings, heading up negotiations, and serving as media spokesman. This kind of leadership may well be essential to the beginning of an organization like MCO. Martinez had the will to build MCO when many did not believe it was possible. The fields were fertile in the Mission, but they had to be plowed, and Martinez was willing to do the plowing. However, this kind of leadership begins to be counterproductive when new leaders arise in an organization, seeking an important role in a growing team "at the top." An existing core leader or leadership group will test newly emerging leaders to see whether they are in for the long haul or just shooting stars that fade after a quick burst of energy. If the core wants to build the organization, it will incorporate in a central decision-making body these new leaders. The inner core does not appear on an organization chart, but it is the heart of the organization. It eats, sleeps, and breathes the organization, and hammers out options and recommendations on critical issues that must be decided upon in formal decision-making bodies.

In this situation, an organizer who is building a mass organization is in a precarious position. During much of the first year, I was involved in building the office of the presidency, in establishing the idea that the people can elect and hold accountable a person who is chief spokesperson for the community. At the same time, and to a growing extent, as the organization grew, secondary leadership needed to learn how to hold the president accountable and how to be team members with him. The emergence of a team or collective leadership is central to the success of the mass organization. The organizer, then, must train additional leaders in the development of accountability. The philosophy of mass organization, the ways in which strategies, tactics, and policies affect the character of the organization, and many other topics are on the agenda for discussion as the organization develops. This means that when questions initially discussed between staff director and president come up, other leaders in the organization are now included. In the MCO, this shift only partially took place.

▨ The Core Leadership Splits

A breakup of the developing leadership team occurred in the summer of 1970. At the time, from among those active in MCO's internal life, three candidates were emerging for the office of president. They were Elba Tuttle, Larry Del Carlo, and Ron

Gomez. Gomez was something of a dark horse, being a newcomer in MCO. Yet he was devoting considerable time to the organization, had demonstrated leadership in numerous actions, and for a while was a real contender. Elba Tuttle was one of MCO's founders, served as an executive vice president for two years, and was acting president when Martinez was in Chicago for training, a job she handled well. Larry Del Carlo was developing the Jobs and Employment Committee. Each of the candidates had strengths and weaknesses.

Martinez chose an interesting approach in this situation. He neither declared himself for one of the candidates, nor did he throw the question into a larger arena in which core leaders who supported direct action and the institutional change approach could, in a caucus, decide whom they would support. Instead, he called a meeting of the three and asked them to agree on who would be the candidate that each of the other two would support. A deadlock emerged; no one of the three was acceptable to the other two.

Had Martinez clearly made a decision, the other two candidates might well have supported the individual he endorsed. In any case, that person would have to mount a campaign and act like a candidate for president. The members of the organization could watch the campaign, test the candidate, raise issues, and decide for themselves whether they liked Martinez's choice or not. This process might not lend itself to the broadening of the core leadership, but it would clearly allow a new leader to emerge.

The other option, opening the question to a broader group, would have placed something of central importance to the future of the organization in the hands of those most actively working in it. Nothing would more clearly develop the concept of a team of leaders. Such a caucus could test the various alternatives, but at some point a decision would be made. One possibility would be to support the nomination of more than one of the candidates, with an agreement that if no one got a majority, the winner in the first round of voting would be supported by the caucus in a runoff. (MCO's constitution required that officers be elected by a majority, not a plurality, of the convention's delegates.)

In the absence of decision, there was a stalemate. As the days went on, concern started spreading among the core leaders and activists as to who their candidate for president would be. From among this group, perhaps spontaneously, perhaps not, a move to draft Martinez for a third term emerged. Martinez accepted the draft move. In order for him to run for a third term, a constitution and bylaws change would have to be approved at the convention, since the constitution provided for a maximum of two one-year terms for the same office.

No internal decision in the formative years of MCO was more important than this one. The position of staff director, now informally beginning to be filled by

Martinez as I was phasing out of that responsibility, and that of president would be occupied by the same person. In addition, in the preconvention activities Martinez served as chairman of the Constitution and Bylaws Committee—the body that made the proposal to the convention to change the constitution to allow him to run for a third term.

■ An Opposition Jells

At the base of the organization, polarization was developing. The Latino middle class, grouped around Manuel Larez in the third convention race for presidency, joined with some Mission Latino agencies and began to form a cohesive opposition bloc within MCO.

MCO leadership managed to retain most of its original base. The churches, block clubs, tenant organizations, unemployed groups, significant Latino organizations, and other grassroots organizations supported it. So did most of the non-Latino groups, the unions, and the small businesses.

Still supporting the leadership, but more actively developing its own coalitions within the MCO, was the Centro Social Obrero. The Obreros sent delegations to MCO conventions; they acted as a caucus within the Laborers' Union. They also sponsored the Mission Language and Vocational School; it was funded by the Poverty Program and other grants. The students at the school were organized as a student body that also sent delegations to the MCO convention. Together, the Obreros and the language school student body constituted the largest bloc of delegates of any single organization at any of the MCO conventions. While some believed their leader, Abel Gonzalez, to be nothing more than a cacique (a traditional boss in Mexican politics), I came to think of him as much more complex than that. His staff and leadership included exiles from Salvador Allende's Chile and near-illiterate, undocumented Mexican farmworkers trying to earn money to send home and in some cases hoping to bring their families to the U.S. Gonzalez was not unfriendly to MCO's larger vision. At the same time, he was a very cautious man politically.

Youth groups by and large still supported MCO's core leadership, especially those that grew from the MCO Jobs and Employment campaigns, but also those that worked with Jim Queen, who headed the youth-serving agency Real Alternatives Program (RAP). However, some of the agency-related youth shifted into the coalition of the Latino middle class and the Latino agencies.

On a Saturday morning in late fall of 1970, MCO's third annual convention was called to order. A brief news story, buried in the back pages of the usually thin Saturday papers, announced the names of Mayor Alioto's twenty-one appointees to the Mission Model Neighborhood Corporation (MMNC), the officially designated "citizen-participation component" of San Francisco's Mission District Model Cities program. MMNC would initiate all plans for Model Cities programs in the Mission. This went even beyond veto power for MCO, which would nominate two-thirds of MMNC's members and could also recall them by vote. MCO had achieved its goal of community control of the planning process.

The news hardly affected a convention that was rocked by the effort of the Martinez caucus to amend the constitution and bylaws to allow him to serve a third term. Almost all the internal life of the organization had been directed at this issue since late summer. With important exceptions, the nationalist forces gathered around the candidacy of Manuel Larez from LULAC. Some of the moderate Anglos, some church people, and some of the grassroots groups gathered around the Elba Tuttle campaign. About twelve hundred delegates and alternates attended. MCO was now a serious organization and, as such, its elections were taken seriously.

The emerging core leadership now began to break apart. Del Carlo dropped out as a contender for the presidency, Tuttle became a vigorous opponent of the third term and continued to run for the presidency, and Gomez dropped out of the organization. The convention began with credential challenges and a dramatic fight on the proposed change to the constitution and bylaws. Tuttle flyers called Martinez "King Ben." Larez forces spoke of dictatorship and likened Martinez's efforts to those of South American dictators. The rhetoric flowed on all sides. When the votes were counted, a bare two-thirds majority supported amending the constitution and bylaws. Martinez was elected to the third term, but a steep price was paid: a decline in the populist democrat forces that had controlled MCO's operation from its inception. Tuttle dropped out of MCO. The Larez and Tuttle core forces, probably no more than a hundred people, walked out of the convention and held an impromptu press conference. They threatened to form a new coalition in the Mission. Their group held several meetings at the Mission Neighborhood Health Center, but nothing materialized—in part because there was nothing to hold these two camps together, other than their dislike of the Martinez third term.

This dramatic shake-up occurred at the very time that Model Cities funding was coming around the corner and MCO had to give serious consideration to how that program would be handled. MCO lacked the depth of leadership to handle the internal crisis of leadership succession and also give serious direction to the Model Cities program. What emerged was a situation of drift. Leadership talents were absorbed in the internal life of the organization; external forces began making plans for what they thought MCO should be and do in relation to Model Cities.

Internal Democracy Erodes

After the convention, a change in mentality took place; it is best illustrated by the way in which the newly elected leadership handled the post-convention challenge. Whatever the political consequences of what Martinez had done, it was agreed to by two-thirds of the convention, thus meeting MCO's constitutional requirements. Clearly Martinez held the allegiance of a large majority of the people active in the growing MCO.

The leadership faced two alternatives in dealing with the challenge to its legitimacy. It could have taken the issue to MCO's rank and file, letting them defend the legitimacy of their convention. For example, the newly elected leaders could have circulated a petition reading something like the following: "We, the undersigned delegates to the third annual convention of the MCO, and members of MCO member organizations, support the changes in the constitution and the newly elected officers of our organization. We demand that so-called 'reform' leaders in the Mission cease their attack on an organization in which they lost a democratic vote." The wording is illustrative; the concept is to let the people speak on the issue.

The alternative was to use the organizational apparatus (for example, by excluding an item of discussion from a Steering Committee agenda) to effectively prevent the opposition from raising these post-convention "reform" questions within the MCO. The leadership chose this latter "bureaucratic" method. They argued that in this way they would get back to the issues of the community and reestablish whatever legitimacy MCO had lost. However, for several months after the convention, top leadership time was still devoted to handling various thrusts made by the opposition; and the thrusts were being parried by the same bureaucratic means, which gave the opposition the appearance of being the true spokesmen for democracy in the Mission. While MCO's leaders were winning the battle within the organization, a more important war was being lost. The leadership had lost its confidence in the rank and file of its own organization and became unwilling to clearly pose to that rank and file what it saw as the issues and ask for support. And this erosion of internal democracy was directly related to an increased preoccupation with Model Cities.

The leadership wanted to secure control of the boards of directors of Model Cities–created agencies in order to make sure that loyal people were placed in positions of authority. The fear was that if not so controlled, the Model Cites program would provide the base for the opposition to MCO to further its own position within the Mission. Rather than control from below, MCO leaders were seeking to control from above. Control from below requires confidence in one's relationship to the rank and file, continued involvement of that rank and file in decision-making processes, deepening the relationship of the organization to its base by involving more and more people in the democratic workings of the organization. It also means organizing new groups from scratch, getting existing organizations to join, and getting member organizations to make MCO's discussions a deeper part of their own internal discussions. This was the kind of organizing that encouraged secondary and third levels of leadership to emerge in MCO's second year. The continuous expansion of this approach could have created new fronts in the community. To take a simple example: the more negotiators trained, the more job negotiating committees can be created; the more negotiating committees created, the more possibilities to obtain jobs.

The favors that Model Cities had to bestow should not have competed with the development of a strong and independent mass action organization. Further, the programs could not deliver the things that they seemed to promise. Those who administered them might gain some patronage for their supporters. But they would be stuck with the inadequacies of the programs.

In Victory

Lies Defeat

Shortly after the third convention, Martinez became acting staff director and president of the Mission Coalition Organization. He asked me to become acting director of the Mission Model Neighborhood Corporation (MMNC), to insure that a plan consistent with MCO's interests emerged from the Mission. But what were MCO's interests? That was the question with which the leadership wrestled in the five-month planning period for Model Cities.

The fundamental question MCO faced in planning Model Cities was what its relationship was to be to the operation of programs in the community. The "community control" and "institutional change" models have already been discussed, but they need to be revisited. (While "models" was and is commonly used to discuss organization structures and processes, it should be used with caution. Drawn from mathematics and physics, where culture, history, and personality are absent, the term doesn't fit very well in politics and social life.)

Institutional Change versus Community Control

To take a step back, here are the alternatives that MCO leaders were discussing, though I don't think they were as clear then as I hope to make them here. MCO and the mayor were to jointly create the MMNC. In MCO's view, shared by almost all groups in the organization, two-thirds of the MMNC members were to come from MCO, and one-third were to be at-large mayoral appointees. This body would use its share of the citywide planning grant (the rest would go to central administration and Bayview–Hunters Point) to identify programs that would improve the quality of life of the people of the Mission.

It is at this point that the debate over community control versus institutional change arose. To whom would the task of implementing MMNC-approved programs be assigned? Would it be to community-based nonprofit organizations (the community control approach), or would it be to mainline public, nonprofit, and even private organizations with whom MMNC would negotiate agreements on program content, and to whom funds would then be appropriated to contribute to implementation of the agreed-upon program? Should, for example, a department within city government depart from the initial agreement, MCO's people power would enforce the agreement by taking public action that made the department honor it.

In some cases, there was no existing institution to which MMNC could assign program responsibility. This was particularly true in housing. To fill this gap, MMNC created a nonprofit corporation, the Mission Housing Development Corporation (MHDC), whose purpose was to build new, low- to moderate-income housing and to rehabilitate existing housing while keeping it affordable. Housing development corporations (HDCs) were invented at this time—a new kind of organization to meet a need that was not met by existing institutions. The question of how the Mission HDC would be governed quickly arose.

Just as a decent union monitors a contract, so an ongoing community organization is necessary to monitor agreements reached with agencies and institutions. In the institutional change approach, MCO would play this role. Model Cites just gave us some money to sweeten the pot, and the recognition added to our legitimacy. Now we had not only our own strength to win victories, but money we could promise to an agency or institution that agreed to implement a program we wanted in our community. MMNC might agree with a recipient of Model Cities funding to jointly design a program, jointly hire a program director, make sure there was an affirmative action hiring policy, and otherwise be a partner in determining what a program was to accomplish, but neither it nor MCO would administer the program, either directly or indirectly.

Those who favored the institutional change approach envisaged MHDC's board being made up of builders and representatives of financial institutions, building trades unions, and various governmental agencies that had something to do with housing. A national search would find a highly skilled executive director who would be hired jointly by the MHDC board and the MMNC. The executive director would train an associate director—a person with roots in the community—to become the executive director of the corporation in three to five years. Similar, parallel positions would be created for other jobs, so that neighborhood people could be trained to staff executive-level positions. The HDC would have a specific and clear mandate for the kind of housing it was to create; this mandate would be accompanied by specific goals and timetables for creating affordable housing. Should the agreement not be honored, MCO would enforce it with people-power negotiating and action.

Critics argued that such a body would become the Trojan horse for urban renewal. Instead, they wanted two-thirds of the members of the MHDC board to be from the community. This was the community control approach. Further, they wanted a person from the community to be MHDC's executive director from its inception. Only in this way, they argued, would the neighborhood be assured that the HDC wouldn't become a front for a bulldozer urban renewal program that would destroy the neighborhood.

The community control approach—and this is what was generally meant by the term at that time—called for the distribution of Model Cities funds to community-based agencies that were part of the MCO. MCO would not itself administer programs, but through the MMNC—the citizen-participation component of Model Cities—it would monitor and evaluate programs and withhold funds when necessary. Further, where no community-based agency existed to administer a needed program, MCO would establish one, either directly or indirectly selecting two-thirds of the members of its board of directors.

Proponents of the institutional change model responded that if the community control approach were taken, the MHDC would lack the clout to do what the community wanted it to do: instead, it would become a buffer between the community and those who did have the clout to create the kind of housing needed in the Mission. That clout existed "downtown," not in the Mission. If they worked through institutions, not community-based agencies, MCO and the MMNC, now in an alliance with the mayor, could pressure banks, builders, and the building trades to be part of such an enterprise. The mayor could make various city departments participate as well.

Generally, I was not a party to political discussions and debates that took place inside MCO. But when something arose that seemed to me to threaten the character of MCO as a people-power organization, I did speak up. This was one of those times; I thought "community control" would kill MCO's organizing and action thrust. One of my most vivid conversations was with Joe Del Carlo, with whom I had an excellent relationship—he trusted me a lot. But on this point he simply shook his head in wonderment, telling me, "Mike, that's just an invitation to downtown to take over the Mission."

While Ben Martinez and other respected leaders favored the institutional change approach, their voices were a distinct minority. Community control won the day. Aside from philosophies and principles, there was another reason for this victory as well. The populist democrat majority in MCO was in disarray as a result of the fight over the Martinez third term. Some of its key leaders quit the MCO; others were disheartened and spent less time in the organization than they had earlier; still others became employees of Model Cities–funded agencies, and their attention shifted from civic action to program administration. Perhaps even under ideal circumstances, the MCO would have been too young an organization to withstand the sudden influx of $3 million (more than $16 million in 2009 dollars) into the community. And the circumstances were far from ideal.

Model Cities Transforms the Jobs and Employment Committee

The transformation of MCO's point system provides one example of the inadequacies of the Model Cities programs. For various technical reasons and to make it politically acceptable, MCO's job distribution system was funded as the Mission Hiring Hall, now to be a community agency distinct from MCO's Jobs Committee. Some of the key Jobs Committee leaders went to work in the Mission Hiring Hall or became members of its board of directors. But notwithstanding the best of intentions and militant leadership, the Hiring Hall became just another agency. The Jobs Committee had been growing and developing momentum—hundreds of people were coming into the MCO to get jobs. But now, the committee could no longer involve them in action. Instead of training new negotiating teams, leadership was spending its time on the administration of the Mission Hiring Hall, and the organizing staff no longer had a sense of direction. Soon participation withered. Volunteer teams of members negotiating with employers, with people-power clout behind them if they needed it, were replaced by "job developers"—full-time, paid employees of the Hiring Hall who sought jobs for Mission people but had no clout to back up their search. The result was that Mission people translated antagonism they once felt for the Department of Employment to the MCO/Model Cities program.

HUD required MCO to eliminate the point system, under which participation in the Jobs Committee led to job referrals. HUD's rationale was that jobs for the unemployed should be made available according to need and on a first-come, first-served basis. From the point of view of social welfare planners, HUD's was no doubt a defensible and appropriate position. But from the point of view of building people power to change the way hiring was done for minority and unemployed people in the Mission, the point system was indispensable. The point system had other benefits as well: people who participated in negotiations and action to get jobs were clearly motivated to go to work. The concept behind the point system went beyond the heated "blame the victim" versus "blame the system" debate that was current at the time and continues today. The system had to be changed, and people had to participate—they couldn't simply complain or be victims.

MCO Overwhelmed

As if the divisive MCO election, the remaining leadership's increasingly bureaucratic responses to their challengers, and the federal legislative, administrative, and inadequate appropriations to fund programs weren't enough, MCO was now overwhelmed by the sheer number of agencies that, seeking Model Cities dollars, wanted to bring their programs into the Model Cities planning process. MCO leadership developed a number of tactical and bureaucratic means to prevent agencies it didn't like from getting funded, but the means used were such that the effective decision-making core of MCO was shrinking, rather than expanding. This is a natural consequence of bureaucratization of an organization that, unable to solve problems democratically, tightens its internal controls.

At the same time, the MCO delegates to the MMNC board of directors and the MCO convention-elected leadership in the Steering Committee were beginning to divide. A clear majority of the MMNC board was from the Martinez caucus. It was ably led by Luisa Ezquerro, who had come into the MCO via the teachers' union, and ably staffed by MMNC's director, Ramon Barbieri, who succeeded me there. Luisa Ezquerro's experience in union politics made her a natural to develop a caucus of MCO members on the MMNC board and to hold that caucus accountable to positions MCO had adopted in its convention. But the MCO Steering Committee began to shift from its commitment not to operate Model Cities programs to greater involvement in the day-to-day administration of Model Cities and to a concern for placing "its people" in Model Cities–funded jobs. Actually, there was no change in official position; but MCO's key leaders were increasingly active in the politics of who got what grant and who got what job. It was on this point that the MMNC board began to take issue with MCO leadership. MMNC members said, in effect, "This is not what the convention decided, and this is not what MCO is supposed to be doing." Whether they were right or not is immaterial here. They legally controlled the Model Cities apparatus, and the MCO leadership was, because it had abandoned control from below, unwilling to take the issue to the larger Delegates Council, where it could, for example, censure or even recall its MMNC appointees (something the mayor, Board of Supervisors, and HUD had given MCO the authority to do!).

To make things more difficult, the San Francisco Board of Supervisors and HUD were watching, very closely, the relationship of MCO to the Model Cities program. The agencies antagonistic to MCO leadership went to these governmental bodies with their complaints, and there were those in the governmental bodies who still viewed MCO as a radical organization and didn't want to see it in control of Model Cities.

Once on this track, irony followed irony. As MCO became embroiled in Model Cities, it lost its radical character: mass action could not be sustained in the framework of federally funded or other government programs. And the more MCO tried to bureaucratically control Model Cities, the more Model Cities controlled MCO. By the end of the program's first year, members of committees who had previously supported each other in actions on the picket line, in resolutions in the organization's conventions, and in defending the mass action orientation that characterized MCO's jobs and housing campaigns now were rivals on boards of directors in competition for the limited funds available in Model Cities. They were now playing a zero-sum game, while earlier, when the rivalry was over who could organize the most people, they were playing a positive-sum game. Who got what paid job in what program and who got what amount of Model Cities funds appropriated for their program became the major MCO questions.

The history of both labor and minority communities in this country suggests that the only institutions they control are those they create, maintain, fund, and administer themselves. Thus, labor unions, credit unions, cooperatives, burial societies, union-run education programs, self-help programs of various kinds that are paid for by their members, and churches with voluntarily constituted membership paying their own way are all examples of the kinds of independent institutions that have existed in minority and working-class communities. But this is not what Model Cities was all about. Model Cities was created by Congress and administered by HUD in conjunction with mayors of cities across the country. Funds were appropriated by the same Congress and administered in the same way. To expect that radical programs could operate under these auspices was to believe what experience did not and would not confirm. Further, Model Cities funds were to be linked to existing "categorical grant" programs of the main agencies of the federal government—Labor, Health, Education and Welfare, Commerce, and others. (These grants were for already defined and more narrow programs, as distinct from the broader federal block grants that left discretion for their use to cities, counties, and other local jurisdictions.)

Into this morass the MCO marched, and marched with amazing integrity. It is a fact that the MCO-led Model Cities program did as good a job as most Model Cities programs across the country. Further, there was little of the "ripping off" that was common in many OEO and Model Cities programs elsewhere. Administrators in the community-based programs did not receive very high salaries. Staffs tended to be competent. Program services tended to be fairly good. But this was limited by the general inadequacy of the programs to meet proclaimed goals. As MCO became increasingly absorbed in the administration of the Model Cites program, it lost its people-power capacity to struggle for those things Model Cities programs did not and could not provide.

Ironically, the shift toward community control was also inconsistent with national Republican aims for the Model Cities program. The Nixon administration's position was that the program should be a mayors' program, increasing the competence of city governments to deal with the issues and problems of poor neighborhoods. Whatever the politics behind this position, it might have been helpful to the MCO had it been vigorously enforced in San Francisco. It was Mayor Alioto's consistent view that the program should be a neighborhood program, and in this his views were not very different from those who wanted a community control approach: the effect was for city hall to make community organizations take the responsibility for government. Indeed, the mayor took remarkably few immediate patronage positions in the Model Cities program. (He no doubt knew that the whole program would tend to become a patronage apparatus.) Rather, the program was treated as basically a program in which the neighborhoods could develop their patronage; rather than getting involved with who got what job, the mayor left that to the neighborhood, knowing that the program as a whole was a patronage operation for him because of his relationship with MCO.

The "pie" that was being distributed was roughly $3 million per year for the Mission (more than $16 million 2009 dollars). Of this, about $800,000 ($4.4 million 2009 dollars) each went into jobs, housing, and education programs. Another $200,000 went into child care, with a three-to-one match in funds from the U.S. Department of Health, Education and Welfare bringing its total also to $800,000. The remainder was spent in administration of the central office and in the MMNC citizen-participation component.

The newly created Mission Housing Development Corporation—the grantee for Model Cities affordable housing funding—further illustrated the inadequacy of the Model Cities program. HUD said it wanted HDCs to create or maintain affordable, decent, safe, and sanitary housing, but then HUD also rejected most of the MHDC applications for grants to build or rehabilitate such housing: every application MHDC made during its first three years was rejected because the proposed project was close to a freeway, the price of the land was too high, or for some other reason. Only a short time earlier in MCO's history, such rejection would have been cause for mass action. The inadequacy here was not with MHDC, but with the federal guidelines. But in the absence of mass action, which would have included real education for residents on the limitations of federal programs, few members of the MCO or residents of the neighborhood understood the struggle with HUD for the release of funds.

Completing the irony, Model Cities–funded agencies ended up organizing their program beneficiaries against the MCO for its perceived intrusion in the operation of their programs. MCO was now city hall, and the community-based agencies were the advocates of "the people." The bureaucratization of MCO led inevitably to this situation. So began the end of the MCO as the Mission's people-power organization.

History Repeats Itself: MCO's Fourth, Fifth, and Sixth Conventions

MCO's fourth annual convention, held in late fall of 1971, was well attended. The Model Cities planning year was over, and funds were beginning to come into the Mission. Eduardo Sandoval took up the challenge to incumbent MCO leadership.

Carlos Carrillo became the victorious compromise candidate for the forces that had supported Ben Martinez, as Martinez completed the shift to the position of staff director. Carrillo proved to be a weak leader but was able to survive a threat to his presidency a year later, in the fifth convention, when the Obreros finally gave their support to him as part of a new alliance that shaped up in the MCO.

The credibility of the fifth convention was suspect: challengers claimed, with some validity (so I was told by admittedly biased observers), that people who were simply program beneficiaries and not members of member organizations were told to come to the convention and vote as instructed, or the services they valued would be defunded. The election was close; now the cry of illegitimacy was taken up by Carrillo's challengers, namely the supporters of David Aldape and Flor De Maria Crane. In a runoff election in which hundreds of votes were cast, Crane was defeated by a few dozen. The fifth convention's peak attendance was near two thousand nominal delegates and alternates, but it was a final display of chaos preceding decline.

The Crane supporters were a majority of the MMNC, and they began to use their position in control of that Model Cities planning agency to play in the internal politics of MCO, taking the same stance toward mass organization that the other agencies had. But MCO's leaders could not complain, because they had, in more than a year of playing the Model City game, lost their relationship to mass action and to the MCO rank-and-file membership.

By its sixth convention, in late 1973, MCO was a shadow of its former self. About five hundred delegates and alternates participated. The Obreros had gone through their own internal struggles, with Abel Gonzalez defeated in an internal union battle and sent by the Laborers' International Union to Texas. Gonzalez's supporters retained control of the language school and continued to send a number of delegations to the MCO conventions. They supported the newly elected president, Mario Herrera, but it was abundantly clear in the sixth convention that there was no more unified people-power voice for the Mission, nor was there either the will or capacity for mass action on justice issues outside the framework of Model Cities.

Given the assumptions concerning community control that were current at the time, the fears of urban renewal, the desire to control Model Cities, the leadership's growing lack of faith in the rank and file of the organization, and the inherent inadequacies of the federal program, any other ending is difficult to imagine. Each assumption is part of an overall politics of the time that established the framework for debate, the terms of discussion, and the reference points for action. Because of this, it would have taken a superhuman effort for MCO to survive as a mass organization, and the people of the Mission were no more superhuman than the people of any other community. Nor should that be expected of them. This is what

I call the tragedy of MCO's history. Even if one assumes that each of the drama's major players had the best of intentions, no other end to the story is possible—the essence of tragedy.

The farce is what happened to the Mission in the course of MCO's decline as a mass organization. People who once led picket lines in front of landlords and large corporations and who negotiated with the mayor and corporate vice presidents now fought with one another over who would get a particular job. The final farce was that the contenders always justified their claims with reference to their roles in the days of mass action—much as revolutionaries corrupted by power hearken back to the days when they overthrew leaders who acted as they do now. Yet these same former activists and leaders retained a personal integrity; with a handful of exceptions, they weren't pocketing funds or simply seeking status. Again: the appropriate view of what happened is that it was a tragedy.

The "Crippled

Programs Syndrome"

By 1969 I was regularly getting calls from faculty and others asking me to talk with them and their students about community organizing. I thought it was an excellent opportunity for Mission Coalition Organization leaders to practice articulating what they were doing. The last Friday of the month (with occasional variation) was scheduled as an MCO public briefing, usually held at Mission United Presbyterian Church. Anyone interested in MCO could come, and some of our leaders would talk with them. I handled questions about the Alinsky tradition and the theory of community organizing.

Stanford University Becomes an MCO Partner

In 1969 a group of Stanford University students came to one of MCO's public briefings accompanied by two professors: Joe Sneed, a philosopher, and Bruce Lusignan, an engineer. They were running a program designed to orient students to social and urban problems. Visiting MCO was one of a number of visits to San Francisco in which the students learned about social problems and what was being done to confront them. Sneed and Lusignan concluded that MCO was the most effective community organization they'd seen in San Francisco, and they asked me about a possible relationship between Stanford and MCO.

At this time I was concerned about how Mission residents might gain access to independent expertise in the fields of health, education, welfare, employment, and others that might become part of Model Cities or of other program planning and negotiations. The Stanford visit suggested an idea. I wrote a half-page memo to Sneed and Lusignan suggesting that they organize a panel of Stanford-based academics, researchers, and others who would be supportive of MCO's values and interests and who could provide independent expertise for MCO's leaders and committees when they dealt with various government agencies, or others, and their in-house experts.

Both were interested. They took the memo and turned its core idea into a proposal to the National Science Foundation. Gladys Handy, then a program officer at the foundation, became an advocate for the Stanford proposal. It received a substantial grant, including funds for MCO to hire a liaison staff person who would relate Mission interests to Stanford capabilities.

Stanford hired Steve Waldhorn as director for the Stanford-MCO project. Waldhorn had previously worked for the League of Cities/Conference of Mayors as their Washington, DC, representative for Model Cities and, earlier, as a lawyer at the National Housing and Economic Development Law Center. In both positions he provided invaluable technical assistance to MCO on affordable housing and Model Cities issues.

The Stanford project created a de facto parallel body of expertise to that offered by government agencies or the private and nonprofit sectors. It provided critical intellectuals an opportunity to connect their ideas with people power—a welcome option for many who had in the past either simply spoken their truth to power—testifying before legislative bodies or writing research reports for public bodies—and seen it ignored or distorted in implementation, or were limited to writing to each other in left-of-center academic journals or to an interested "progressive" audience who read general-interest magazines like *The Progressive, The Nation, Dissent,* or *The New Republic.* The faculty participants in the Stanford project included people well regarded in their respective fields. Sneed became deeply committed to it; many years later a Stanford colleague of his told me he failed to gain tenure at the university because of his involvement in the project.

A number of papers were written by Stanford faculty on matters of interest to MCO and Mission residents. For reasons unimportant to this discussion, the program was ultimately lodged in the Stanford Research Institute, which by that time had no formal relationship with the university. (Later the name was changed to "SRI International.") While at SRI, Waldhorn wrote an important paper, using the phrase "crippled programs syndrome" to describe an interrelated set of reasons for federal program inadequacy. This paper served as an overarching framework for a number of papers written by Stanford academics in various fields.

"Crippled Programs Syndrome" Applied to Federal Jobs Programs

Professor Joe Sneed applied the "crippled programs syndrome" idea to the employment field. He identified these deficiencies (source: untitled draft in author's possession):

Inadequate resources, including funding and authority.

Conflicting goals.

Bureaucratic rigidity combined with centralized decision making in remote Washington, DC, offices.

Bureaucratic rivalry among competing agencies of government made a mockery of planning as agencies focused on protecting their turf.

Pseudo participation by sub-units of a bureaucracy that lacked authority within their own organizations.

Pseudo citizen participation in which presumed beneficiaries of programs weren't apprised of all the alternatives available to them, and weren't given resources to be real partners in planning.

Sneed then made these observations about the changes in the Jobs and Employment Committee: "Employers successfully demanded of the committee that [it] work with established and community-based agencies to provide them with training subsidies. In agreeing to this, the committee backed away from its initial protest strategy and has moved closer to community control and collaborative planning strategies. The result has been to somewhat undermine mass participation in committee activities by diminishing the committee's ability to reward participation alone with jobs. The long-run effects of this remain to be seen." It did not take too long for these effects to become apparent.

Waldhorn's seminal paper argued that the sources of program inadequacies were to be found in vague or contradictory legislative mandates, guidelines that failed to unscramble these legislative problems, inadequate funding, lack of coordination and/or competition among programs with similar goals, and incompetent administration. On closer examination, one sees that conflicting goals are sometimes built into the programs. Thus urban renewal claimed to improve and increase the stock of affordable housing while at the same time increasing a city's tax base. The latter required commercial or industrial development or high-priced housing; the former did little for city revenues. Which of these conflicting goals would prevail was largely a matter of which had the constituency with the greatest power. The bottom line: the programs could not realize some or all of their proclaimed goals. Anyone who became involved in the administration of programs suffering from the crippled programs syndrome soon became infected by the syndrome! MCO was no exception.

Model Cities:

The Debate Continues

Rich Sorro was one of the MCO's most thoughtful and militant leaders. He was one of the principal leaders of the populist democrat caucus. Unlike most core leaders, he brought labor organizing and left political experience to his role in MCO. He was the chair of the Jobs and Employment Committee whose skillful negotiations and militant nonviolent direct action obtained many jobs for the people of the Mission. I interviewed him in 1996, almost thirty years after MCO's formation. His experience, and reflections on it, are worth deep consideration. Ironically, he was the victim of the very processes he described when we spoke. When I sat down with him, he was executive director of the Mission Hiring Hall, the Model Cities transformation of the Jobs and Employment Committee and its point system. [Bracketed portions are my comments.]

The Rich Sorro Interview

"How did the old Jobs Committee work?"

"In the old MCO, we had the point system. People with the most points had the first shot at a new job that came in. If they didn't want it, they could pass. They knew there'd be another. People would pass on great jobs at Foremost-McKesson because they knew they could get a job at Safeway or at PG&E. I see people now who are retiring from jobs they got because they were in the committee. They've been there twenty-five years, and they're retiring out. People like those people who are young now will never find a job like that, a job from which they can retire with a pension. They don't exist for the people we see now, the people who come in to apply for jobs through the Mission Hiring Hall.

"The Jobs Committee made employers s—t in their pants. We could negotiate and even dictate the terms under which people were hired. We'd then refer the employer to existing agencies in the community and tell him that these agencies could provide him with whatever he needed if he didn't have the training inside his own company. That was his responsibility, not ours. We had the ability to make the interview process null and void. If we referred people, the employer would have to hire them. And they were good people. [As the Jobs and Employment Committee developed a track record, employers who once fought it came to look at it differently. Many of them remarked on the quality of the people sent by MCO. We knew we were sending good people, because the people who went to the jobs had 'earned' them by participating in the activities of the committee. They were motivated to work.]

"Company interviews now screen out our people. Here's an example of how we worked. We got people placed at Safeway. Safeway didn't have any bilingual people working in their stores in the neighborhood before we went to them. Our people would get screened out in an interview because English wasn't their first language, or because they didn't speak college-type English. Everything that was grounds for rejection applied to our people. With our old system, Safeway had to take our people. We integrated the Safeway workforce. We went after banks and knocked them over—one a week. Same with other companies. Sometimes we'd make a mistake and pick on someone too big. But most of the time, community action [pickets, boycotts, sit-ins] worked to get us to the negotiating table if employers wouldn't negotiate with us at first.

"We didn't have professional 'job developers' in the Employment Committee. The people, their negotiating committees, and their action were the job developers.

"We also supported our people once they were on the job. There was a situation where the employer wanted to fire someone because it turned out he had a police record. He had straightened out, and he wasn't doing anything wrong on the job, but it showed up after he'd been hired that he had a police record. The union wouldn't handle it, so we went down and met with the manager. We asked if the employee had been doing anything wrong; when we found out he hadn't, we said, 'We want you to keep him.' It got to be a heated argument in which the manager ended up admitting that he himself had a police record. So we really pushed him. We said to him, 'What if you'd been fired every place you went because you had a record?' They kept the person working there.

"If you were the chairman of one of our negotiating committees [for each targeted company, the Jobs Committee would establish a negotiating committee; I trained the negotiating committees], you commanded the same level of respect as the company's CEO because there was an equality of power. I'll never forget the experience of being chairman of the Employment Committee. You went into a negotiation with a crowd of people behind you. Some of these were people who'd never been out of the Mission. The employer would think we were being unreasonable, but what was unreasonable to him was reasonable to us. These companies were doing business in our neighborhood or in San Francisco and no one from our neighborhood was working there. So it was reasonable that some of our people should be there.

"We had a sense of power. The last thing an employer wanted was for us to do a community action. They'd call the police when we were going to come see them for a meeting—there would be some plainclothes cops around. We weren't going to do anything violent, but there was just a fear about us. We went to see Kodak, and they called Pacific Bell about us. We had a friend inside Pacific Bell who told us about it. Pac Bell said, 'You should meet with them.' Kodak had just been in a big battle with an organization like us in Rochester. They asked Pac Bell if we were like that organization, and Pac Bell said, 'We think so.' They flew a couple of executives out here to meet with us because they didn't want a battle like the one in Rochester. They didn't even have many jobs in San Francisco. They offered us an economic development package. They'd help us set up a company, and buy products that we'd produce. Unfortunately, we weren't set up enough in the MCO to take them up on that. We had an Economic Development Committee, but it wasn't developed enough for us to have a system to refer Kodak to that committee and get something going.

"We got things offered to us that you'd never get in any other circumstance. It gave members who had low self-esteem a big boost. People saw they could make changes. They'd never been in a CEO's office before. They'd never done anything like what we were doing. We were always in control of ourselves, but we weren't there to make friends. We wanted to make a deal. There's always time to kiss and make up, but if we had to fight we would. We grew because we kicked ass downtown. Regular neighborhood folks really got off on that stuff. The threat of community action is what got us what we needed. [After a number of negotiation sessions with the phone company, MCO reached an agreement for a substantial number of jobs. As the negotiating committee left Pacific Bell's downtown building, I turned to the chair and said to him, "Wasn't that great?" I was referring to the number of jobs we'd won. "Yes," he said, "that vice president called me 'Mr. Lopez.'"]

"I went into the Employment Committee with many years of frustration behind me. It was a place where people could vent that frustration, people like me who were fed up with the way we were being treated. You could vent and then move in a positive way. It gave direction to your anger. There was humor, militancy, and craziness. Some situations were really tense. But we never lost our humor. We had an action with Hibernia Bank, the Irish bank in town. No people of color working there. We weren't sure whether we were going to go in there with shamrocks painted brown or tortillas painted green, but we knew we were going to do something humorous. We decided on the tortillas and stood in line to deposit them in the bank. We got jobs there.

"The spirit we created was really contagious. People who got jobs through the committee would come back to the committee to give something back to the community. People on the street knew about the committee. You knew that this committee was doing something for the people. I learned things in the MCO that I'd never have learned anyplace else. And they worked in other places too. In South of Market, the POC [Pilipino Organizing Committee] used some of these tactics and they worked there too.

"The MCO was people of all races and nationalities who lived in the Mission. One employer told us that he had an affirmative action hiring plan, and that he couldn't deal with us because of this plan. We told him, 'We're people of all races and colors and we don't care about your program.' That style worked. The time was right. Actually, the time is right now. The time is always right."

"What Happened Later?"

"The Mission Coalition fell apart over Model Cities. People were fighting for titles, positions on boards of directors and administrative jobs in the funded agencies. When MCO got started, it drove Model Cities. The MCO convention at USF showed that Model Cities was driving MCO, not the other way around.

"The rank and file from the Employment Committee didn't care about any of that stuff, but the leadership got caught up in it. You had a whole pack of neighborhood people carrying briefcases around. This was the fundamental cause of the weakening, and later breakup, of the MCO. People got divided up into different agencies that were getting Model Cities money. And it wasn't all that much money to begin with.

"A secondary cause of the collapse of MCO was Latino nationalism. In the heyday of MCO, the racial thing didn't exist. We recognized the importance of Latino culture, that Spanish was the second language of the community, and that you had to have bilingual meetings. But we also knew there were other people in the neighborhood: Filipinos, Samoans, Anglos, Native Americans, some Blacks. MCO lost its sense of inclusiveness. The nationalists disrupted one of the meetings I was chairing and asked why it wasn't being conducted in Spanish. They knew I didn't speak Spanish. It was just a nationalist thing. The nationalism didn't come from the rank and file, either. It was mostly from the middle class. MCO lost the ability to fight that kind of thing off. In the earlier days we had the feeling that we're here to help people—whatever their race.

"For a while, the Hiring Hall maintained the point system. But the feds came in and told us that we couldn't require that a person go to meetings to apply for a job through the Hiring Hall. We then told people that they could apply, but that if they wanted to work for the job they should get active in the committee. But by this time things were falling apart anyway."

"What's it like now?"

"Now there's lots of competition for jobs. We refer people and they go to a competitive interview. We send four or five people to apply for one entry-level job. It's awful. It divides us. In the old Mission Coalition, it wasn't competitive, because there wasn't a screening process. The point system screened people. The employers took people as we sent them, and they got good people. That's the core difference between then and now. Jobs are so competitive now. San Francisco people who live in the Mission or Hunters Point or South of Market or the Fillmore can't get these jobs.

"Now we advocate for resident hiring, go through the legislative process, but we can't raise hell. The leverage is gone. With all the jobs programs in place, the situation is worse, as far as the quality of jobs Mission residents can get. Jobs are either low-pay or requirements are too high for our people to qualify. Some of the jobs require two years of community college or some other kind of degree. When you analyze the jobs, they don't really require this kind of training, but the employer can put what he wants in the job description. There was a job at one of the local museums that required an art degree. When you analyzed the job, it wasn't much more than being a janitor. There was another job at a medical center which they called a 'laboratory technician' job and required two years of college education. When you analyzed that job, it wasn't much more than a filing job. In the old days, when we went in for entry-level jobs, it didn't matter what the job description said."

What If There'd Been No Model Cities?

Forty years later, veterans of MCO still discuss the Model Cities battles, "community control" versus "institutional change," and whether or not the Model Cities program was, on balance, a plus or minus for the community. Two contradictory things are simultaneously true about Model Cities. First, the funds created, sustained, and expanded important programs that benefited the community. Second, the funds were, in part, the source of the decline and fall of people power in the Mission, and without that power the people are unable to defend and advance their values and interests. It is too speculative to ask what might have happened had there been no Model Cities at all, or had the institutional change approach been taken. There is no question that the Model Cities program brought substantial benefits to the neighborhood and its residents. Almost two thousand units of affordable housing have been built or rehabilitated by the Mission Housing Development Corporation. The Mission Hiring Hall developed a sophisticated training, job development, and job placement program. A child-care program created hundreds of slots for children of working parents. Education programs were sponsored by Model Cities. Also, many former MCO leaders rose to responsible positions administering these programs. At the same time, most knowledgeable observers agree that it was Model Cities that tore the MCO apart.

What might have happened without Model Cities? Could the MCO have come into being without the threat and promise of Model Cities? Maybe. People in denominational leadership positions, like Reverends Bill Grace and Dave Knotts, and Jim Guinan, Grace's counterpart in the Episcopal diocese, were willing to fund such an effort. Mission District and Latino community leaders, some with roots in the Alinsky/Fred Ross Community Service Organization days, might have legitimized and given initial leadership to it.

Might the MCO have won more concrete benefits for its community and developed more leadership in the community had the mayor, the Board of Supervisors, or HUD excluded the Mission as a target area for the program? Perhaps. A sophisticated jobs campaign, using the point system to build more and more power behind it, could have negotiated with employers. A similarly sophisticated affordable housing campaign might have continued to organize tenant associations, supported rent control, and negotiated with banks, savings and loan companies, insurers, the city's public housing authority, and others to rehabilitate and build new affordable housing units and to preserve existing neighborhood housing. Militant direct action might have stalled gentrification by sustaining "an atmosphere inhospitable to investment" until the development that would result from that investment would benefit everyone. The San Francisco Unified School District already operated children's centers for preschoolers who needed child care before, during, and/or after school. A different MCO could have fought to expand this child-care budget and create administrative, teacher, and teacher-aide jobs in it for Mission people, rather than create the Model Cities–funded Mission Child Care Consortium. Perhaps even more child-care slots might have been created in this way. An MCO unfettered by Model Cities might have joined with the Bay Area's religious leaders and supported the development of parallel organizing efforts in other neighborhoods and, with such organizations in place, been a catalyst in the creation of a citywide and even regional federation.

In one sense, the speculation is idle. But in another it is not. If we cannot imagine alternatives, they will not be pursued.

MCO in Light of Current

Community Organizing

Practice and Theory

The first draft of this book was written shortly after I left the MCO. It then sat for many years until a writing grant let me revisit it. It then sat again until people in the Mission District began asking me about it because word got out that I was writing about MCO. I began to relook at the prospect of publishing it. In between, I started work on another book that included much of the more theoretical material that's now here. Many people had asked me over the years to tell the story of MCO. Books had been written that talked about it as the most powerful San Francisco grassroots organization of its time. I thought the lessons learned were important to share, and that the story itself was a dramatic one. In the rewrite, I tried to remain within the framework of what was considered "best practice" community organizing in those days. There are things we did poorly, barely did, or didn't do at all that, had they been done or done differently, might have led to a different MCO outcome.

I've had more than thirty-five additional years of experience in the field now. And there's no beating 20/20 hindsight. Further, the field has developed significantly. When I worked for Alinsky in 1967 and 1968, there were "Alinsky projects" in Chicago, Buffalo, Rochester, and Kansas City. Tom Gaudette, one of Alinsky's most talented early organizers, was working independently of Alinsky and consulted with another small group of organizations, mostly in the Midwest. PICO (Pacific Institute for Community Organizing), now one of the national organizing networks, developed from that work. At the end of the 1960s, Alinsky's training institute opened in Chicago. In 1972 Alinsky died and Ed Chambers took over direction of the Industrial Areas Foundation. He and a talented group of organizers took community organizing in new directions that are beyond the scope of this book. Others branched off into new directions, so that there is now an alphabet soup of training centers, networks of organizers, and local community organizations around the country. Barack Obama worked with the Gamaliel network. DART, based in Miami, is yet another. There are regional networks, like the InterValley Project in New England, as well. ACORN is more rooted in the Fred Ross/Cesar Chavez approach. National

Training and Information Center and Midwest Academy are yet other strands that grew from Alinsky's pioneering work. With the benefit of what has been learned in this cumulative experience—if we knew then what we know now—these additional observations can be made on what might have been done differently:

Pay greater attention to the base we had in the churches. Each church in the Mission had its own particular internal dynamics, strengths, and institutional difficulties. Leadership training on matters having to do with the "body life" of the church could have strengthened those churches that were in MCO, deepened their commitment to the federation, and increased the numbers of MCO participants among their members. Ongoing biblical reflection and Christian education, continually connecting faith with action in the world, could have deepened the meaning of that faith and strengthened people's commitment to MCO. Both the Protestant social gospel and the Catholic social encyclicals provide rich sources for such reflection.

This point is clearly a case of 20/20 hindsight. Community organizing as a field had not yet begun to plumb the depths of possibility open to leadership that took either religious faith or secular democratic values seriously and translated that seriousness into organizational development. Victor Frankl's *Man's Search for Meaning* is a good place for organizers and leaders to gain an understanding of this appetite of the soul that gains no nourishment from consumerism. By transforming consumer members of faith communities into "co-creators," we could have accomplished far more than we did in the Mission. We didn't know how to do it, and, more importantly, we didn't think about doing it. Nor was it yet quite so apparent that the country desperately needed this kind of leadership. Parenthetically, equivalents to what this kind of values-based approach does in churches can be done in unions. Start with the preface to almost any union's constitution, where you'll invariably find an homage to democracy and the dignity of the human person. Then ask the question, "What does this mean in our practice?" and a whole series of questions will follow.

Some years later, I had a very intriguing experience. I led a two-day organizing workshop in rural Nebraska in the mid-1980s. There were forty-five people there, about a third of them United Methodists. There were two to five of just about everyone else: Lutherans of different strands, Episcopalians, UCC, Presbyterians (PCUSA), Catholics, and Disciples of Christ. Near the conclusion of the workshop, I asked them to form small groups of their own denominations and come back to the group as a whole with a reflection on the meaning of what they'd been exposed to in the workshop thus far. I told them to draw either from biblical material or from their denomination's or faith's teachings and doctrine.

The groups went off, spent about thirty minutes together, and came back with their reports. One told of their crisis hotline (it was during the farm crisis), another of food pantries, yet another of clothes closets, and still another of their counseling.

When the groups finished their reports, a Methodist district superintendent shot his hand up. I recognized him; he asked, "Mike, did we do this assignment right?" I told him, "No. What did you think the assignment was?" He repeated it as I had intended it. I asked the group how many of them had his understanding of the assignment. About a third of the hands went up. I asked, "What happened?"

The answers were interesting and very important:

Some were afraid that something presented from their own particular perspective would be divisive. "Oh," I said, "you mean you want a pablum Christianity that doesn't celebrate unity in diversity?"

Some admitted to being biblically illiterate; they hadn't thought deeply about the relationship of their social action/social welfare concerns and their faith, other than to think of the church as an institutional base for doing good works. "What's the difference between you and a social worker?" I asked.

Some were embarrassed to talk about faith—kind of an implicit "it isn't done in polite society" attitude. "What are you doing in the church?" I asked.

At the end of an intense discussion I said, "Now I understand why the religious conservatives are beating you. They make demands on their people. I take your faith more seriously than you do." (They all knew I was a non-religious Jew.) You could have heard a pin drop. In the years of my continuing work in rural Nebraska, this story was retold more than any other.

Challenge pastors to view themselves as organizers. Most pastors include counseling, caring for members, operating social service programs, preaching from the pulpit, adjudicating internal conflicts, formal teaching, and administering the nuts and bolts of the church in their job descriptions. The emphasis will vary from person to person, but these elements remain. Some organizers now challenge pastors to see their central role as guiding people to live by core faith values, using a community organization as a key vehicle for the expression of those values. But the organizing process itself is used within the church to deepen it as a community—"community" here defined as "a group of people sharing a common faith who support and challenge each other to act powerfully, both individually and collectively, to affirm, defend, and advance their values and interests." The church (mosque, temple, or synagogue) and the community organization become alternative centers for creating a culture that challenges consumerism, rugged individualism, and invidious status distinction based on income or other characteristics.

Create real local membership units among the unaffiliated people who participated in MCO's activities. The Jobs and Employment Committee and the Housing Committee provided clear opportunities to build membership units in MCO—tenant associations and employee clubs at workplaces. Membership in a member organization was a formal requirement to participate in MCO's jobs campaigns, and tenant associations were created for participation in the Housing Committee. MCO staff assisted the unemployed and underemployed, and tenants, to develop groups that took on the minimum characteristics of a member organization. But we didn't help these groups develop a more sustained identity, let alone become "communities" in the sense I use the term above for church development; nor did we sufficiently work with the committees' leaders so that they would see the importance of MCO internal politics to the activity they so loved—direct action for jobs and tenant rights. A much stronger base for the populist democratic approach could have been created through both of these committees.

Make greater use of formal educational tools to deepen understanding of the world in which we worked. A common view on the left is that most people are brainwashed, suffer from "false consciousness," or are apathetic. At best, this is a very partial, and not very helpful, view. I think people have a commonsense understanding about how wealth and power interact, that those with the former have much more of the latter, and that "you can't fight city hall." Labor or community organizing afford everyday people the opportunity to challenge the status quo. In the course of action, teachable moments arise when people can specifically learn how power works. And they like learning that. We could have more effectively used these teachable moments. I remember collecting a number of corporations' annual reports and bringing them to a Jobs and Employment Committee meeting. Members were fascinated to read about these corporations and find interlocking directorships among them. In the course of action research, they also identified big-money people who were donors to local politicians. We did this research to identify possible targets for direct action.

Celebrate our heroes and create a story that could become part of public and parochial school curricula. Wearing the simple brown and yellow "MCO" button became a source of pride for people at the core of the organization. When the jobs and tenant organizing campaigns were at their peak, if you were wearing an MCO button on 24th Street, or at a parents' night at a local school, or at a social after Sunday services, you might be asked, sometimes by someone you didn't even know, how the such-and-such campaign was going. Local heroes were being created. Their work was celebrated within the organization, but more could have been done there and also in relation to the formal education of San Francisco's young people. Why couldn't public and parochial schools have a supplementary text that told the stories of mothers and fathers, sisters and brothers, grandparents and neighbors who were making history in their community? Why couldn't leaders of MCO be speakers at civics classes—paid what it would cost them to take time off from their regular job, and given a speaker's fee, too?

Use one-day and weekend retreats to bring diverse groups together to share their family, church, union, neighborhood, nationality, and community stories. Such gatherings could be used to further challenge the "isms" that lead us to see "The Other" as a less than fully human person. This happened informally within the MCO, and the organizing setting forged relationships that broke down stereotypes. But formal workshop techniques make it possible to speed up and deepen these opportunities.

Develop mutual aid activities to supplement negotiations with decision makers in business, major nonprofits, and government. Credit clubs, buying clubs, babysitting pools, tutorial clubs for after-school homework, and support groups are among the relatively simply organizational devices that could have solved real problems for people in the Mission. These might have become cooperatives and credit unions, or they might have remained more informal. In either case, they could have solved real-world problems and enhanced solidarity. Cooperatives have a rich tradition in Spain and Latin America, so a number of MCO's members were familiar with them. There was also a small agency in the Mission whose purpose was to foster the idea of cooperatives. Our organizing staff made a halfhearted attempt to support the idea and soon abandoned it when the difficulties of starting co-ops became clear. We could have been more patient.

Develop an organizer training program within the MCO. Last, but perhaps most important, I wish we had spent far more time training organizers. It could have started within member churches. We might have had a six-to-twelve-month program in which a trainee would keep his or her regular job and receive a small stipend to pay for child care or other costs. The only promise to the trainee would be that she or he would gain skills that could be used at home, at work, in church, and elsewhere in life. Those who showed an aptitude for organizing might then have been invited to take a next step. We might have persuaded our most committed pastors to think of having a part- or full-time "internal organizer." In Catholic parishes, for example, this might have been one of the women religious (nuns) who were already working in the parish but largely engaged in casework or other kinds of activities.

Today organizing is more professionalized. Radical organizers of the 1930s called themselves "professional organizers," but they had no separate organization of organizers, and they were paid a pittance. Today a number of "organizing networks" exist. In one way or another, they claim to professionalize organizing. There are positive and not-so-positive dimensions to what they're doing.

The positives include careful screening; extensive apprenticeship-based training; ongoing support for people in the field; close supervision and mutual accountability for results; efforts to recruit women and racial and ethnic minorities into what once was a white man's business; recognition that burnout/occupational stress is a danger in this field; economic security for practitioners; and continuing education for those doing work in the field. Each of the networks has these characteristics in varying degrees.

On the other side, too many strutting peacocks think being an organizer is akin to playing king of the mountain (manifested, for example, in sharply competitive comparisons of turnout at demonstrations or big meetings, with less attention to less quantifiable but perhaps more important leadership development questions). I see organizers speaking for communities that can and should speak for themselves. Pay and benefits are questionably large and there are other perhaps all-too-human follies. Network sectarianism says, "My approach is best and I'm not going to work with people in another network" and bad-mouths the work of others. A young organizer told me an amusing story in this regard. She applied to each of three different organizing networks. In each interview she asked, "What makes you different from the other networks?" From each she got the same answer: "We take leadership development seriously."

I think the equivalent of an old craft guild or a religious order is needed for organizing. In addition to pride in craft, it needs to make the humility of St. Francis a core value among practitioners. While providing perhaps lifelong security with a good pension plan for those who do the work for some specified number of years, it should not pay people far more than what is earned in the communities where they work. In some of the old CIO industrial unions, top elected officers were paid no more than what the highest-paid category of workers received under the union's collective bargaining contract.

Other possibilities. There are additional things we might have done in the Mission about whose merit I'm less confident—the use of formal conflict resolution methods, for instance, or formal classes on subjects that might have been of interest to members. The point of all of this is that community organizing as a field is maturing. Not all the mistakes of the past need be repeated.

▮ Some Things We Did Right

There are some things we did in the Mission that were good. Among the things we did right were these:

MCO sought to organize everyone and everything that existed within its turf. Churches and unions, merchants' associations, nationality organizations, political groups of all stripes (though political parties themselves were not allowed membership), organizations of the young and old, newly formed tenant unions and block clubs, and others were all brought under the MCO umbrella. Organizing new groups meant that unrepresented or underrepresented people gained a voice in MCO. Too many organizations today are content with being federations of religious institutions, perhaps adding a few of the most interested unions. This has serious limitations. First, there will be little challenge to engage in more militant tactics, even if the situation calls for them. Church people tend to be too polite to use them, despite Martin Luther King's eloquent defense of nonviolent direct action. Second, there won't be a critical mass of people experiencing a common problem the way that, for example, the tenants of a badly managed, high-rent, poorly maintained building experience their landlord.

MCO's tactical repertoire included carefully conducted negotiations, legislative testimony, boycotts, disruptive direct action, marches, rent strikes, careful electoral participation, public shaming, media use, and more. Careful research supported proposals made to institutional decision makers.

MCO's ability to remain broadly based while engaging in very militant direct action was a function of the truly multi-issue character of the organization. Middle-class merchants and homeowners were as committed to MCO as low-income tenants and unemployed youth and adults. That's because the organization delivered for all of them, and because of the relationships that were forged among these diverse people as a result of their common membership in MCO.

MCO's emphasis on leadership development identified hundreds of leaders and potential leaders and trained most of them—starting with the basics or enhancing skills they already had, and adding new ones. This training paid off within the MCO action program. But it had benefits elsewhere as well; many leaders told MCO organizers how they applied the lessons they learned in MCO action to the rest of their lives, ranging from how they raised their children to how they dealt with coworkers and a boss.

Some of these positive elements of MCO's experience were abandoned or minimized by subsequent generations of organizers. Recently some of the earlier practice is returning to the field.

▓ Avoiding Problems of the Past

External forces, combined with internal problems, were too great for MCO's initial vision to prevail. The desire to maintain a strong, independent organization was there; building a mass democratic involvement of the membership to keep the organization theirs was not. But it may be that nothing could have made any difference, that the confusion of radicals over community control, the desire of minorities to have their chance at running programs, the absence of any strong allies in labor or other significant sectors of American life might have left no alternatives. This is my view, one borne out by the fate of all the mass organizations of minority communities of this period.

For a community or mass organization, the difficulties are immense. The tendencies toward becoming an agency, toward absorption in one of the political parties, toward comfort and cooptation, toward internal factionalization and away from struggle around issues are powerful. Four things are necessary, I think, if these tendencies are to be avoided.

First, the vision of leadership and membership must be developed. This vision must combine careful attention to local issues and organization building with a sense of participation in something bigger, something that will be part of turning the country around, of taking power back from the "fat cats" and returning it to the people, of judging public policy through the lens of economic and social justice, and of participation by people in its determination.

Second, there must emerge in the local organization-building and issue struggles a sense of power that comes from victories won in struggle. This is what will involve large numbers of people and encourage them to take part. So-called apathy will be overcome when people find themselves in situations where they can do something. With this sense of power there will be excitement, meaning, and fun. These are the glue of a successful people-power organization.

Third, democratic membership control must exist in these organizations. As the people build them, so can they control them. Forms for effective participation must be elaborated and nurtured. Democratic membership control is the final guarantee of the integrity of the organization.

Fourth, these organizations must be funded through activities of their members and the people who will benefit from their action. No foundation, government agency, church, or other charitable body is going to long fund such an organization without distorting its character. Self-financing is a difficult lesson to learn. It is just beginning to be mastered by people's organizations around the country.

Who Pays for

People Power?

The question of who pays is a major one. One of the Mission Coalition Organization's major early strengths was that it was "leadership-intensive": a very small professional staff supported an amazing amount of voluntary effort. In MCO's first year, its expenses were about $25,000. (This figure doesn't include MACABI's loaned staff or Ben Martinez's assigned work with MCO). At its three-year peak, the organization's annual expenses were roughly $40,000 (about $240,000 in 2009 dollars). I thought MCO could raise this core budget by a combination of dues and member-based fund-raising activities. This did not happen.

External and Member-Based Fund-Raising

Even though Alinsky was not in San Francisco, his agitation within the churches benefited MCO. The United Church of Christ, United Presbyterian, American Baptist, and Episcopal denominations gave MCO a total of about $24,000 for the first year. Later, Catholic funding came as well. In those days, both Catholic and mainline Protestant churches had mid-level judicatory as well as national offices to support this kind of community organizing.

An additional $12,000 per year from The San Francisco Foundation rounded out the budget. A handful of other foundations also supported organizing, and MCO received small grants from them over the next couple of years. Community-based fund-raising activities brought the first post-convention year budget to about $40,000. Earlier contributions from Laborers' Local 261 and the United Presbyterian Church gave the organization its financial start.

Contrary to some claims, external funding does not necessarily impose conditions on what an organization does. Rather, an organization imposes conditions on itself when it applies for the funds. In the case of MCO's initial funding, this did not happen. All the initial funders wanted was a broadly based community organization that could represent the community. For the Laborers' Union, this representation would be in dealings with the mayor. For the churches, it meant an Alinsky-tradition community organization. The San Francisco Foundation simply supported a broadly based community organization.

MCO never mastered membership-based funding for its core budget, and I didn't give that kind of fund-raising the priority it deserved. It was probably the biggest weakness of my work. Yet such funds are the essence of independence. The dues that MCO's member organizations paid were too low, and payment wasn't strictly enforced. According to the MCO constitution, if your dues weren't paid, your delegation wouldn't be seated at the convention. That simply didn't happen. We could have defined the ten weeks before a convention as a fund-raising period for all the member groups so they could be paid up in their dues.

MCO grassroots fund-raisers never made more than $3,000 ($18,000 in 2009 dollars) for a single effort. This wasn't bad, but it wasn't enough, either. We did several fund-raisers, but the organization as a whole didn't give them the high priority it gave the Model Cities campaign—they were simply an activity of the fund-raising committee. I think it would have been possible to substantially increase dues for member organizations and do two fund-raisers a year that would each raise twice to three times what we raised with those we did. This could have funded a core budget that was independent of external sources.

Because we had member Presbyterian, Catholic, Lutheran, Methodist, United Church of Christ, and Episcopal churches, we still could have tapped Catholic dioceses and Protestant regional and national denominational bodies. That would have let MCO grow. If an additional organizer could bring in new member groups, and if the new member groups carried their share of the fund-raising load, the new organizer would soon have developed a constituency that paid her salary and overheads. We didn't do that.

Looking back on the fund-raising MCO did with foundations, I am struck by how badly it was done. I cultivated the relationship with John May, then executive director of SFF; I wrote the funding proposal; I worked the proposal through the foundation's process.

Here's what I think I should have done. I should have told John May, "The kind of organization I want to build has to be owned by its leadership; they have to take responsibility for raising its budget; to the extent they need supplemental support from you, they're going to need to come talk with you and convince you of why they need it. You now know me well enough to have confidence in what I'm hoping to accomplish in the Mission. The next people you're going to hear from about MCO are its leaders. I hope you enjoy meeting them, and I hope they're convincing when they come to you."

I should have shown a proposal-writing committee some sample proposals, reviewed some foundation guidelines with them, told them who I thought were the likely funders and how to do the research to find others, walked them through writing some proposals, critiqued first drafts, and role-played the program officer they were going to meet. In the beginning, I would attend the meeting as a silent participant, so I could do an evaluation with the committee afterward. There were plenty of people within the organization who could have written proposals.

The whole relationship between the foundation, the leaders, and me would have been better had I done this. The foundation would have met with the people whose interests the organization was supposed to serve, rather than someone who wanted to get paid to work with those people. MCO's staff would have been dependent on the work of the leaders, instead of on my work. Our organizing staff could have treated foundations as we treated other decision makers: training leaders in how to approach them and hold them accountable.

About fifteen years later, I did most of these things working with several groups that wanted to initiate organizing projects. In most cases, I never even met the funding sources. The local leadership bodies presented proposals to the foundations and church bodies and told them that I was providing them with technical assistance (I was their consultant). By that time, a lot of these funding sources knew who I was. But not all of them. The local fund-raising committee had to present funders with the reasons why they wanted to contract with "the San Francisco-based ORGANIZE! Training Center" for community organizing training and consultation. They also had to make the case for hiring an Alinsky-tradition organizer. They did just fine.

The relationship between outside money and internally generated funding is a complicated one. I am not suggesting that the former can't be properly used. I do believe that it can't be used for the core budget of a people-power organization without undermining the organization. And I believe that it has to be negotiated, not gained in what is now essentially a supplicant process. Nowhere do I know of organizing groups that ask to meet with leaders of foundations who support them to jointly develop proper guidelines for community organizing. And even farther beyond what seems to be thinkable is the idea that foundations claiming an interest in poverty, social and economic justice, empowerment, and related ideas who don't support organizing should be approached to do so, and held accountable if they don't.

Is Core Budget Self-Funding Possible?

It wasn't wildly impossible for MCO to fund its core budget. Today there are institution-based and faith-based community organizations (unions, religious congregations, and other groups) that have dues ranging from a minimum of five hundred dollars per year to a maximum of ten thousand. Maybe some dues are even higher now. There are "individual membership" organizations with dues of ten dollars a month. These are good starting places to build a core budget from the bottom up.

These same organizations engage in raffles (with donated prizes), ad book or corporate campaigns, and other membership-based activities that raise fifty thousand dollars or more each. One or two such events a year can bring in big dollars. And an interesting thing I learned in MCO was that some of the people willing to engage in fund-raising activities would not engage in the action of the committees; had it not been for the fund-raising activity, the only time I would have seen them was the annual convention. They didn't like meetings, and they were nervous about direct action. But participating in the fund-raising gave them a way to be part of the organization.

Together, dues and one or two good fund-raisers can raise a core budget that provides for a lead organizer, a second organizer, and some office support staff. And there will be a great deal of pride associated with the accomplishment. I wish I'd done better at it.

Don't Throw the Baby Out with the Bathwater

Some who have made a critical analysis of the proliferation of "community-based nonprofits" and properly described a growing "nonprofit-foundation industrial complex" want to totally abandon foundation funding. They point to foundations' structural unaccountability: boards of directors are typically self-perpetuating (internal nominating committees name successors), they are not disciplined by the market in the way a for-profit enterprise ultimately is (unless government bails out the failure—a very different subject matter). Like other nonprofit organizations with internally nominated boards of directors, they are only distantly accountable to the legislation that enables their existence.

I don't think it's possible to expand organizing without foundations playing a role in the process. So how could foundations that want to support people power, and organizers who want to build people power, relate to each other? Here I'll only address the question for an already established organization, not one seeking to get off the ground or one that is just in the mind of an organizer.

In the first place, volunteer fund-raising committees should deal with foundations. If organizers want to do background briefings for program officers at foundations, fine. But part of "owning" and "growing" an organization should be the responsibility to fund it. Leaders can take on that role. There is an abundance of training workshops now that organizations can send volunteer members to in order to learn to write proposals. A member of the community organization's staff can also do this kind of training. Nor will it be difficult for these members to learn to adjust a core proposal to the specific requirements of the small number of foundations that will fund organizing. Nor will it be difficult for leaders to follow up after the submission of a proposal. If a group wants to meet with a program officer, and it has difficulty getting the meeting, it can start generating phone calls into the person's office to show that the community supports the idea of the meeting. These need not be hostile; they need only say, "I'm a member of X organization, and I'd like you to meet with our organization so we can tell you our story." Program officers who have such meetings have afterward told me how thankful they were for the opportunity to hear from real community leaders and learn firsthand what their organization was doing. But this requires that there be a real organization to begin with!

Foundations should have standards by which to measure whether an organization is internally democratic, representative of the constituency for whom it claims to speak, and engaging significant numbers of people in action on matters of concern to them. And these should be negotiable. None of these are too difficult to measure. But the measures are for different outcomes than in more "program-oriented" funding guidelines that might look at how many new people receive a specific service. To help an organization grow, a foundation might offer a one-to-one (or higher) match for dollars raised from dues or fund-raising activities—like raffles, ad books, or the Frank Hunt donut sales earlier described. (The genius of Hunt's idea was that it separated the sheep from the goats with no effort on his part: if your organization was real, you could sell a lot of donuts—and earn for your organization a lot of money. If it wasn't, you wouldn't.) When an organization has succeeded in raising its core budget internally, the foundation might offer a three-year grant for an organizer whose job would be to expand membership—with the understanding that after three years, the new membership base would generate sufficient funds to support an organizer position and its overheads.

And for foundations there's this benefit as well: when volunteer leaders and members raise the organization's funds, it's because they are invested in it and want its staff to work for them. Their fund-raising is a testimonial to the fact that the organization not only benefits them, but means something to them. I would think a foundation staff person would far more enjoy hearing from the direct beneficiaries of an organizing effort than from an organizer whose salary is on the table.

▨ "Contract Out" Organizing

While the community-based nonprofits can be an obstacle to organizing, they can also enable it. In the MCO story we saw how a few agencies—namely OBECA/Arriba Juntos, MACABI, and Centro Social Obrero—were instrumental in launching the organizing effort. Today, with the proliferation of these agencies in most low- to moderate-income communities, particularly communities of color, a dozen of them could get together and each chip in three to ten thousand dollars, depending on their budget size, to launch an organizing project. Better-paid executive directors could contribute from their salaries. They could even line-item the expenditure in training and consulting services.

Such agencies could contract with an experienced organizer or organizing network. This was done in San Francisco's Tenderloin by a housing management group that had been hiring its own "organizer." The problem was that the organizer worked for the landlord. Even though it was a very tenant-oriented, nonprofit landlord, two persistent problems arose. When there were conflictual issues, the tenants really didn't fully trust the organizer. And the landlord hired the organizer to "educate" the tenants on what was possible. Organizers in these situations told me they were "in the middle" between the tenants and the landlord. That's not a good place for an organizer to be. The organizer should be on the side of the tenants. Let the tenants discover financial or policy constraints in the course of negotiating with a landlord. Then let them propose to the landlord that together they go to the sources of the constraints and negotiate with them. These might include HUD officials, local politicians and regulators, lenders, insurers, or others. (It is clearly true that many nonprofit landlords are severely constrained by budget, guideline, and legislative policy limitations.)

An organizing group with which I was consulting at the time convinced the landlord that if the constraints were real, the tenants would understand that—but they had to discover it for themselves, in negotiations with the landlord. I had seen this kind of thing happen in MCO with private landlords who couldn't get home improvement loans from local financial institutions. I had no doubt that it would work in relation to HUD guidelines as well. Once they had discovered the very real constraints imposed on the landlord externally, the tenants would join in the search for additional funds or in an effort to change the guidelines. Indeed, that's exactly what happened, but it took some imagination from the community-based nonprofit landlord's executive director and her board of directors, plus her commitment to grassroots leadership, to get her management group to sign a contract with an independent organizing group.

▨ Cesar Chavez on Money

No one better expressed the importance of bottom-up funding than the United Farm Workers' initial organizer and leader Cesar Chavez. In an oft-cited 1966 interview, he addressed the important topic of members funding the union in its early days. What he said then is no less true today for people-power democratic organizations.

We started with [the principle that] no matter how poor the people, they had a responsibility to help the union. If they had two dollars for food, they had to give one dollar to the union. Otherwise, they would never get out of the trap of poverty. They would never have a union, because they couldn't afford to sacrifice a little bit more on top of their misery. The statement "They're so poor they can't afford to contribute to the group" is a great cop-out. You don't organize people by being afraid of them. You never have. You never will. You can be afraid of them in a variety of ways. But one of the main ways is to patronize them. You know the attitude: Blacks or browns or farmworkers are so poor that they can't afford to [pay for] their own group…

So we began the drive to get workers to pay dues so we [the organizers] could live, so we could just survive…At a farmworkers' convention, we told them we had nothing to give them except the dream that it might happen. But we couldn't continue unless they were willing to make a sacrifice. At that meeting everyone wanted to pay $5 or $8 a month. We balked and said, "No, no. Just $3.50. That's all we need."

At the new union's convention, of 280 people present, 212 signed up and paid $3.50 (about $24 in 2009 dollars) in monthly dues. Talking about a farmworker who used his grocery money to pay his dues, Chavez said, "With the kind of faith this farmworker had, why couldn't we have a union?"

Politics and Vision

During the final period of preparing this manuscript, Barack Obama won the presidency. His call for "change we can believe in" inspired tens of thousands of people to become involved again in politics, viewing it as a vehicle for social change, and led to a high voter turnout among groups that typically had low turnouts in the past. What concrete shape will this vision take? What is the relationship between what Obama articulated and his equal emphasis on the idea that change comes from below? His charisma epitomizes one idea of leadership. His emphasis on change coming from below articulates another.

The Role of Leadership

A new school of American historians, exemplified by Howard Zinn in his *People's History of the United States*, challenges the view that it was great heroes who created and developed the best of our country's traditions. They point to struggles "from below" and identify unsung local heroes and heroines. This history from below is a necessary correction to earlier historical narratives that focused on big-name figures.

In the discussion of major visionaries that follows—Alinsky, Chavez, Lewis, King, Malcolm, and Kennedy—I do not intend to suggest that they existed separate from the history that was being created from below. They were created by the millions of people who took some part in action, the hundreds of thousands who became more substantially involved, the tens of thousands who made social movement and organizational activity a part of their lives, and the thousands who became local leaders and organizers. At the same time, these visionaries gave expression, direction, and hope to organizing and related activities, strengthening and unifying them and making them more powerful. Zinn's corrective on traditional history is an important one. Its danger is to dismiss the role of leadership.

Beginning with the Back of the Yards Neighborhood Council in Chicago's stockyards neighborhood, Saul Alinsky developed and spread the idea of powerful community organizations that brought under one umbrella all the varied interests of a working-class or poor urban neighborhood: homeowners, tenants, workers, the unemployed, seniors, youth, parents, children, small business owners, and others. Alinsky viewed the local institutions and organizations of these neighborhoods as assets to be tapped and brought into a common united voice. When people lacked a voice, the professional organizing staff would develop new groups, such as tenant associations or block clubs. Powerful organizations created by Alinsky's small professional staff were able to make significant improvements for their members and the broader constituency. The organizations' small staffs relied on the talents and energies of local leaders, some existing and some newly developed. Alinsky built from below but used his own national reputation, and the authority of national religious leaders whom he influenced, to strengthen what he was building. Similarly, Student Nonviolent Coordinating Committee organizers in the Deep South were identified with Martin Luther King Jr. or with the sit-ins that were on TV news, even though what they were doing was developing local community organizations around the right to vote, and around the local issues that could be resolved if Blacks were voters.

Today, no major metropolitan area is without broadly based community organizing efforts, often affiliated with one or more of the national organizing networks. Whatever their form, these organizations seek to provide an effective voice for the powerless. They are guided by the justice and democratic values, teachings, and traditions of the religious faiths of their members, or the secular, small-d democratic origins of the U.S. Declaration of Independence and Bill of Rights.

The massive organization of large numbers of people who have been excluded from participation in, and receipt of the benefits of, society is not only possible, it has occurred in American history. Visionary leaders have expressed, focused, and inspired organizing that took place at the base. The leaders and the base are yin and yang to each other, not either-or.

If we look at the great steps forward for the marginalized, excluded, discriminated against, and exploited in the U.S. in the last seventy-five years, it is impossible not to observe that they were led by men and women of vision whose overall objectives went beyond building one particular organization or winning one specific victory. For example, John L. Lewis's United Mine Workers of America poured money into the organization of industrial workers in rubber, steel, auto, and other industries. The miners and their leaders understood that their own interests required the organization of workers like themselves in other industries. But a larger sense of justice and solidarity animated them as well. CIO political action in the 1930s included the bread and butter of immediate situations but also included broad issues of social justice and war and peace. How the CIO might have developed had World War II not interceded, breaking Lewis from the rest of the CIO and giving corporations the opportunity to reassert their preeminence in America's political life, none of us can ever tell. We do know that Lewis ran his union with an iron hand; in this he had the support of the miners, but everyone who examined the decline of the United Mine Workers and the subsequent struggle of the Miners for Democracy knows the price later paid for Lewis's leadership.

Martin Luther King Jr. and the Southern Christian Leadership Conference and the Student Nonviolent Coordinating Committee made clear on numerous occasions that they were interested in changing an unjust system, not simply integrating Blacks into "the system" as it existed. King placed himself in the middle of the struggle to organize workers in the South and spoke out against the war in Vietnam. There can be little doubt that he considered himself a man of the left and placed himself in a radical tradition in his attacks on racism, poverty, and militarism in the United States.

Malcolm X, in his last years before being assassinated, developed a broad vision far beyond his initial separatist nationalism. Shortly before his assassination, he was making overtures to Martin Luther King Jr. for some kind of relationship. Among street youth and adults who were not connected with Black churches, Malcolm was the hero, not King. But Malcolm understood that he and King spoke to and for different constituencies within the Black community, and that they had to find a way to work together. In the documentary film *The Democratic Promise: Saul Alinsky and His Legacy*, Rev. Franklin Florence, leader of the Alinsky-formed FIGHT organization in Rochester, New York, says he asked Malcolm about Alinsky before supporting the Rochester effort. "Malcolm," he reports, "said Alinsky was the best organizer in the country."

In the 1960s, Cesar Chavez and the United Farm Workers (UFW) combined the tough organizational abilities of Lewis, so desperately lacking in King, with a promise for a democratic union and a vision of a democratic society. Now they were no longer "forgotten workers," but workers who became the object of raids by the powerful Teamsters Union. At least for a while in UFW-organized areas, locally elected committees monitored the contracts and developed leaders among the farmworkers to run their own union. Their vision was of an organization whose members controlled it because they had struggled to build it. Unfortunately, Chavez also had some of the Lewis tendencies…but that is another story.

Finally, during this period Senator Robert Kennedy began his journey toward a politics that championed the causes of those who were marginalized by mainstream American politics and the country's economy. Perhaps this journey began with his brother's assassination. His 1968 campaign was filled with appearances across the country in solidarity with local struggles—in Appalachian hollers, Latino barrios, and Black ghettos. Had Kodak not settled its long battle with FIGHT in Rochester,

Kennedy would have convened Senate antimonopoly hearings on the company. In 1969 Kennedy's widow, Ethel Kennedy, visited MCO and toured the Mission, deeply impressing members and leaders with her integrity and compassion for the people there. The Robert F. Kennedy Memorial Foundation placed one of its first interns at MCO.

Whither the Country?

In the mid-1960s, the stirring of large numbers of people of a variety of backgrounds was expressed in the rise of such impressive leaders as those just mentioned. These leaders were at least talking with one another. Even more important, they might have met with one another to see whether some kind of united action against social and economic injustice could be created. Had there been a Robert F. Kennedy Jr. presidency, they might have coalesced, as the CIO did within the New Deal coalition of the 1930s. The hope that this could happen—mostly in the period from 1964 to 1968—was dashed by assassinations and the crumbling of social movements.

Beginning in 1964 with the run of Alabama's segregationist governor George Wallace to be the Democratic Party's candidate for president, we saw the power of the backlash against the civil rights movement. Richard Nixon's election in 1968 capitalized on that backlash, as well as dissatisfaction among Americans with the prosecution of the war in Vietnam. There followed in the 1970s a period of great unrest among the American people, unrest that included among its sources inflation, failure to address racism and poverty, and Watergate. By the 1980s, the earlier movements for social and economic justice were relatively quiet, but another group of people, particularly white working- and middle-class people in cities and suburbs across the country, was in motion, voicing concerns and making demands. The growing conservative movement captured the new energy. The labor movement continued to decline. Religious conservatism replaced the reform impulses supported by both Catholics and mainline Protestants in the 1960s. Indeed, what was once mainline Protestantism became "old-line Protestantism" as Evangelical, Pentecostal, and Holiness churches grew, and elements of these movements began to appear in most of the mainline Protestant churches as well. Only recently have these theologically conservative traditions begun to reconnect with the Biblical bases for action in behalf of social and economic justice.

How will this new set of voices organize in the context of the Obama administration? How will they seek to make power more accountable? Who will they see as allies and who as enemies? Will some of them continue to express their concerns in antigovernment, "free market," and individual morality issues and fear of The Other, or will they focus on corporate superprofits, the greed of CEOs and other executive officers, and government irresponsibility and lack of accountability? At this writing, a majority of Americans believe we were lied to about the reasons for war in Iraq and want the country to withdraw its troops. Survey findings indicate majority support for reforms such as national health insurance to cover all people; government support for low-income people; fair trade versus so-called free trade; and tax reform under which everyone pays a fair share. Given the chance, workers in the private sector say they would support a union if they weren't afraid of getting fired or seeing their employer move. The majority of Americans say they favor equal rights for racial and ethnic minorities, women, and gays.

The economic crisis that erupted with the sudden slump in the stock market and crash of historic financial and insurance institutions is taking place as I write. What it will mean is impossible now to tell. What can be said is that major changes will take place. Who their beneficiaries will be, what new policies will be adopted, and what new alliances will take shape in the body politic are now open questions. If President Obama and his congressional allies are unable to contain and reverse the economic downturn, there is the danger of a new right-wing revival.

The struggle over these questions will be taken up by the new leaders and organizers of our time. They too will be people of vision, likely to be declared unreasonable by their peers—as the leaders of the CIO and the civil rights movement were before them. Yet in my view it is the very struggle over these questions that has been the source of every great movement for progress in the country. One can begin with the American Revolution and trace our history through Jeffersonians, Jacksonians, abolitionists, Knights of Labor, populists, suffragists, Wobblies, the CIO, the movements for civil rights, women's rights, and gay rights, and on and on—and the answer is the same. Entrenched power, privilege and prerogatives, wealth and status only crumbled when they were challenged by a democratic vision. This vision became part of the consciousness of large numbers of people who themselves became part of a visionary effort as they took the first risk of marching on a picket line, seeking to register to vote, or engaging in a sit-in or a sit-down. The first defiance of established authority in the name of democratic rights, social and economic justice, respect, and recognition is heroic for each individual who risks it. The capacity for this heroism exists in most people; it is the job of the new organizers of our time to inspire it and build on it.

■ The State of American Politics

The present concentration of wealth in America makes a mockery of any meaningful definition of democracy. Concentration of wealth translates into concentration of power. You simply cannot have vast power in the hands of a very small number of people and relative powerlessness among the vast majority and still have something that can seriously be called a democracy. The power to buy politicians and political parties, to move jobs from one place to another without the restraint of collective bargaining, regulation, and other countervailing forces, to redline and destroy neighborhoods—all these and more are available to corporate institutions that are largely unaccountable to anything or anyone except a quarterly bottom line and a mythical "free market." At best, we can say that democratic forms remain—and they are important because they offer us the opportunity to organize—but the substance has to be reclaimed. And though it is too far beyond the purview of this book for any elaborate discussion, I will say that we cannot solve the problem of concentrated power and at the same time be a world empire.

The social problems that the country needs to face, similar to the problems that exercised people in the Mission District to organize themselves into MCO, remain to be seriously addressed. That will require large numbers of people to negotiate, lobby, strike, boycott, vote, demonstrate, disrupt, shame, and otherwise make it known to political and economic decision makers that business-as-usual will not continue unless issues of economic and social justice are addressed. It takes massive people power to create economic and social justice. And it takes organized power to enforce victories once they are won.

My final round of editing this book allowed me to add this update to my thinking as we enter the fourth month of the Obama administration. There is a danger in the Internet age that people will think clicking a key on their computer will be sufficient to create the change from below that is needed. To move the kinds of changes through the American political system that are required to undo the damage of the last thirty years will require far more pressure from below than that. As of this writing, I don't see that kind of demand being expressed.

An even greater danger is that people will think, "President Obama will take care of things." That is a problem of charismatic leadership—people defer to it. Or, alternatively, there is now an expectation that because we elected a president who promised to change Washington, it's up to him to do it. As sociologist S. M. Miller puts it, there's a demand from the left for a transformational president without a transformational electorate. It won't happen.

▓ Build People Power

Large numbers of people can be organized around a lowest significant common denominator. They have been throughout the history of the U.S. They are now being organized throughout the world. But community control is not a strategy that will contribute to such organization. In the two years of its initial growth, particularly in its housing and jobs campaigns, MCO demonstrated how this people power can be built. MCO did not seek to "control" or "administer" anything in either of these areas of action. But people power was able to wrest significant concessions from owners because it could affect their bottom lines of profit. Later, rent control legislation accomplished on a broader basis what these early organizing efforts accomplished building by building. But legislation did not build people power, because this was not the central objective of the campaign to pass it.

Community control, either in its radical or liberal understanding, inevitably absorbs the time, talent, and other resources of local people in the administration of activities characterized by the crippled programs syndrome. At the very most, nonreplicable tiny islands of success exist in a sea of despair. We now have almost half a century of history of the community control project. Upon examination, it fails the test; it doesn't work. Whether viewed as simply administering existing programs or as creating new ones, the effect of community control is to co-opt social movements and community organizations in a way that leaves them powerless to expand and deepen their bases of participation, extend support to newly organizing allies, and make proposals for change that fundamentally address powerlessness, inequality, and other injustices of our times.

The central characteristic of a people-power organization is that its ever-increasing numbers act as agents of their own emancipation. MCO demonstrated that character, even in decline: increasing numbers of people came to each of its first five conventions. With greater numbers of people comes greater people power. With greater people power comes the possibility of institutional changes that reach deeply into the sources of resistance to democracy and to social and economic justice. In our mind's eye, we need to picture a national, indeed international, federation of people's organizations capable of mobilizing tens of millions of people to act on an international agenda: to end exploitation by major transnational corporations and other international institutions, and to foster respect among nations, and negotiation—not empire building in the name of "democracy"—to settle differences. There is no shortcut to building such people power. It begins locally, uses small victories to demonstrate the efficacy of collective action, shifts people from passivity to participation, and with greater numbers moves on to bigger victories. It engages people in relationships with one another that break down stereotypes of The Other, and it builds from there. Thirty-five years after the beginning of MCO's decline, community organizing in the United States, while far from realizing its full potential, shows some of these possibilities.

In our mind's eye we can imagine national and international federations of people-power organizations that can effectively act at every level of government and corporate power. In the forums of these federations we can also imagine deliberations on how concentrated government and corporate power can be redesigned so that the tendencies of these entities to exploit and otherwise take advantage of people are mitigated. We can imagine debates about ownership: cooperatives, worker ownership, breaking up concentration of ownership, and public ownership. But the outcome of these debates would be policies that could be translated into effective action with real-world results on the ground.

By the 1990s, I was doing workshops that included people from all over the world. In these workshops, we could begin to imagine that people-power organizations might align themselves with one another to challenge the most entrenched self-interests in the most powerful institutions. The same workshops that I'd begun doing with local leaders after I left the Mission brought the same conclusions from followers of liberation theology and conservative Catholics, social gospel and mainstream Protestants, and theologically conservative Evangelicals and Pentecostals. Role-playing, taking people step-by-step through the experience of dealing with self-interested systems that didn't care about "poor people," made it possible to break through resistance to people-power organizing rooted in the values of democracy, justice, equality, and community.

Indeed, there are glimpses of this possibility in a community organization that changed policies of international financial institutions like the West German Development Bank and the World Bank, both of which agreed to withhold loans to Philippine President Ferdinand Marcos. Marcos sought these loans for a Manila port expansion program that would eliminate some of the Tondo Foreshore lands in Manila Bay. From Marcos's point of view, the squatters living there were disposable people. He didn't count on the Zone One Tondo Organization (ZOTO). In many ways, ZOTO was a Philippine equivalent of the MCO. It was organized by Herb White, an American organizer and ordained clergyman whose work was sponsored by an ecumenical agency called the Asian Committee for People's Organizations and funded by the World Council of Churches. Those same glimpses of possibilities are in his work with his wife, Jessica Fernandez, in Bombay (now Mumbai), India, and the continuing work there led by their former trainee Rabial Mallick. Similarly, new possibilities can be found in the accomplishments of the Office of Urban Advance, a very small unit in the well-known international relief organization World Vision. There Robert C. Linthicum, an evangelical Presbyterian who learned organizing in Chicago from a protégé of Saul Alinsky, showed how Indian untouchables (Dalits) could organize and move the Madras (now Chennai) government to do things they and the government never thought would be done. This community organizing tradition, modified and contextualized for fundamentally different social, economic, political, and cultural settings, is now taking root in Africa, Latin America, and Asia.

▨ What, Then, Was MCO?

To appreciate MCO's complexity and significance, you have to look at it from multiple perspectives, including at least these:

Politically, it was a partisan nonpartisan center-left alliance, populist and progressive, with pluralist and, particularly in its education and culture committees, nationalist support; at the same time, in its appreciation for local traditions, small business, and neighborhood preservation, it had a conservative streak as well.

Socially, it encompassed the entire range of racial and ethnic identities in the Mission, all age groups, men and women.

Culturally, it was Latino but carefully offered symbolic and real expression to every group that was in it.

Economically, it was low-to-middle income in its constituency and issue focus, though its Planning and Community Maintenance Committees gave expression to what is more often found in upper-middle-class, city planning–oriented organizations. It included welfare recipients; low-income, unskilled, nonunion workers and well-paid, skilled, union workers; civil servants, building trades, and service-sector workers; small businesspeople and professionals; tenants, homeowners, and small landlords.

Religiously, it was Catholic, mainline Protestant, and, surprising for the times, Evangelical and Pentecostal. The latter were mostly monolingual Spanish-speaking churches whose members had immigration, affordable housing, and employment issues. In many of the churches, families were often deeply conflicted as children raised in the U.S. fought their tradition-bound parents.

Organizationally, MCO moved from a loose-knit confederation to a federation that both respected the identity of its member organizations and developed an agenda of its own. MCO's committees were the principal vehicles for action on issues that came into the organization from the member groups.

Strategically, it sought to unite the broadest base possible around a lowest significant common denominator program that targeted government and business as the institutions whose structures, policies, and practices had to change if justice was to be achieved.

Tactically, it ranged from moderate to militant. It always started with efforts at good-faith negotiation. When it couldn't get a meeting with someone, or when a meeting was going nowhere, MCO was ready to escalate and make creative use of a wide arsenal of nonviolent action tactics.

But no matter how much complexity MCO encompassed, its most basic idea was a simple one: in large numbers of people, united by vision and purpose, operating through a democratic organization, there's power for good.

Whither the Mission

During the mid-1990s dot-com boom based in the San Francisco Bay Area, the Inner Mission was threatened with annihilation by gentrification, as it had been before by urban renewal. In the absence of people power to "create an atmosphere inhospitable to investment," rapid change took place in the neighborhood.

When the boom went bust, the process dramatically slowed…but it did not stop. Sporadic direct action sought to inhibit the changes. By the mid-2000s, the city's governing body was favorable to affordable housing and neighborhood preservation, but that sympathy didn't prevent the continuing slide toward gentrification. What, then, for people power?

■ The 1970s to Early 2000s

I was out of the Mission by mid-1971, though very much in touch with what was going on through the eyes of what had been the majority caucus of the Mission Coalition Organization but now was split into two competing factions. The breakup of the old majority caucus was very personal and painful for me. Organizers are like artists; the organizations they help create are like canvases on which artists paint. When the canvas is destroyed, the artist loses a part of herself. So an organizer cannot help but feel strongly about something into which she has poured so much time, energy, talent, and ego. Supporters of the institutional change approach ended up as the losers in the struggles within MCO. Yet I cannot fully share the anger they have toward those who defeated them. They contributed to their own defeat. All of them were victims of the Model Cities process.

John Anderson, the mayor's first liaison with the Mission for Model Cities planning and as good a civil servant as one could find, once said to me, "The reason I'm looking forward to MCO getting Model Cities is that I want you to see the kinds of problems we have, when you become part of the Establishment." His statement serves to summarize the Mission's history. It is also a warning. Even the best people in the Establishment are trapped by its limitations. As our working relationship with city hall developed, we found a strong ally in our one-time adversary Michael McCone. He worked hard to get public agencies to cooperate with MCO and was sometimes as frustrated as we were by their resistance to change.

As long as basic decisions are defined within the framework of what corporate power and bureaucratic intransigence will allow, social programs in the United States will be inadequate. Broadly based independent organization is indispensable to the development of an effective challenge, in city halls, state houses, the Congress, and the White House, to the power held by large corporations in the U.S. today. Whether this power is broken up or nationalized, consumer controlled or worker controlled, decentralized or centralized, or some combination of these is all beside the point now. An intermediary strategy to challenge corporate prerogatives and power and government lack of accountability is what has to be built. Forums for discussion within an organizing movement can address program, policy, strategy, and tactics. But the people-power organized framework, rooted in values and a vision of democracy and justice, capable of challenging these prerogatives and unaccountability, has to be created.

Urban renewal as a federal bulldozer program was defeated in the Mission. BART was completed, and land transactions rapidly took place. No organization existed to maintain the uncertain climate—one of direct action in the form of rent strikes, sit-ins, and other manifestations of people power—that inhibits speculation. To make things more difficult, no one large, speculative interest was developing the Mission—thus no clear target like the San Francisco Redevelopment Agency existed. Rather, a series of small developers, realtors, investors, and financial institutions were making deals. The Latino middle class in the Mission was sufficiently developed to open a savings and loan association. Anglo and Latino realtors were busy as private transactions gentrified the Mission. It was a Latino franchise holder who got the opportunity to operate a McDonald's at the busy BART corner at 24th and Mission. It was Frank Hunt, MCO's ally in the Mission Merchants Association, who bought properties on several of the BART corners. Development in the Mission now is helter-skelter, some positive for the neighborhood's residents and institutions, more negative.

The issue-oriented people were in disarray when MCO collapsed. Only some who had been in the Planning and Housing Committees managed to continue in action; their vehicle was the Mission Planning Council, but it was far smaller than MCO. The lessons of people power receded into the past, even as they were cited to justify then-current positions. And then the dot-com boom threatened to totally transform the Mission into high-tech office space and gentrified housing.

The boom went bust, but even without it, the slow, steady process of gentrification, in housing and small business, moved forward. During the past thirty-plus years, as the Mission Housing Development Corporation (MHDC) built about two thousand affordable housing units, a significant multiple of that number was lost to private development of one kind or another.

A new generation of activists is struggling to deal with the economic forces, particularly gentrification, at work in the Mission. While their particulars are unique to the present situation, they share too many characteristics of the old Mission Council on Redevelopment, MCO's predecessor. Like MCOR, they are largely single-issue in their approach. There is no real grassroots organization at the base of what the activists do. Occasional mobilizations turn out a couple of hundred people, but the idea of a presence in the Mission that could bring more than a thousand people to an annual meeting to determine the community's future is now only a dim, sometimes fond, sometimes hostile, memory.

Indeed, another echo from the past sounded in 2004 and 2005, during a bitter clash over the role of the MHDC. This story is almost a book in itself. Like the period following MCO's initial Model Cities victory, this contemporary tale has elements of both tragedy and farce. Finally, the MHDC board fired its executive director. Most of the staff left in protest. Both the board leadership and the replacement executive director had been leaders in the MCO—and in the group that turned it into a mass action organization! Were they now sellouts, as radicals, militants, and activists in the Mission claim? I don't think so. But the fired executive director and the staff who left raised a fundamentally sound point: gentrification is slowly driving low- and moderate-income people, the businesses that cater to them, and the institutions and organizations in which they participate out of the Inner Mission. With economic recovery, these pressures will resume. Someone has to build the capacity for powerful action against gentrification, or the Mission District and the whole of San Francisco will in the not-too-distant future suffer the fate of other gentrified neighborhoods. Low- and moderate-income people, the businesses and services they patronize, and the religious and social institutions that give meaning and pleasure to their lives will suffer large-scale displacement. That has already happened to San Francisco's African-American community.

▨ The Current State of Affairs: 2009

Today, the Inner Mission is rapidly gentrifying. Condos replace rentals. Run-down Victorians are purchased and restored by affluent professionals who want to live in the heart of the city. Some low-income residents are lucky enough to be able to move into attractive subsidized housing, but they are a numerical minority. Some low-rent housing is preserved through rent control legislation and by landlords who care about their tenants. San Francisco is the most expensive city for housing in the continental U.S.

Old, inexpensive, neighborhood-patronized restaurants are replaced by chic, expensive ones that offer valet parking to tourists and customers from all over the Bay Area. Old bars and taverns are replaced by hip clubs, art galleries, or boutiques. Commercial property owners aren't subject to rent control. A longtime owner may have a relationship with and loyalty to a longtime tenant. But when he sells, the new owner will have a huge mortgage and a different idea of how to make money on what he bought. A storefront in the heart of the Mission recently had its rent increased from $2,500 to $5,000 a month.

Churches are losing their members. Other local institutions are shrinking. The new affluent residents aren't neighborhood-bound. Their cosmopolitan tastes and interests take them all over the city.

But the Mission is still contested terrain. Battles are waged; most of them are lost. The kind of power that MCO represented no longer exists in the Mission.

Is gentrification inevitable? Are market forces going to do to the Mission what urban renewal couldn't? No doubt the tendencies are in that direction. On the other hand, a San Francisco Planning Department document proposes zoning and other land-use ideas that would preserve many of the unskilled, blue-collar jobs that remain in the district. Plans for mixed-use commercial or industrial space combined with affordable housing are on the drawing boards. The economy's downturn may dramatically slow what the market is doing. The terrain of the Mission, as noted in my preface, remains contested. Only an MCO counterpart, modified for today's conditions, is lacking.

Perhaps a group of Mission leaders will play a role analogous to that played by that early handful of church and Latino community leaders who had the vision to start what became the Mission Coalition Organization. No doubt the specific organizational form, strategy, and tactics will be different. We live in different times. As I write these words, the country is sinking into recession. But the underlying principles of people power remain.

On October 4, 2008, there was a celebration of the fortieth anniversary of the founding convention of the MCO. I read excerpts from this book to the assembled group and added, "Now I want to make a challenge to some of the people who are here. What I'm about to read isn't in the book yet because I'm hoping that I can write a different ending. But here's what it might say:

> I am disappointed that not one of the agencies created by Model Cities is taking the lead to do what MACABI, OBECA/Arriba Juntos, and Centro

Social Obrero did in 1968. These three agencies took the lead, along with the churches, in sponsoring the development of MCO. They recognized that they weren't people-power organizations, but that they could play a role in facilitating the development of people power. People like Alex Zermeno, Adan Juarez, Lee Soto, and Herman Gallegos remembered their Community Service Organization experience and applied it to the development of MCO. Others, like Abel Gonzalez, recognized that there was a need for a broad alliance in the Mission. Staff members at MACABI like Joan Bordman, Elba Tuttle, and John McReynolds put their talent to work building MCO. Where are the agency boards, directors, and staff today who are doing the equivalent?

I cannot tell you now whether the challenge has been accepted. I am working with some of these agencies to do for this time in history what MCO did in its time. It is too soon to know what they will do.

We now have a new national climate, with the election of Barack Obama as president. Obama, with the strategic assistance of Marshall Ganz—an old SNCC and farmworkers' union organizer—developed very sophisticated mobilizing approaches to build a new kind of electoral machine. It was central to his election. But as he has noted many times, "Change comes from below."

Obama will be responsive to the kind of agenda that was developed in MCO. It is the responsibility of people on the ground to put that agenda front and center before the new administration, before Congress, and before countless municipalities, counties, special districts, school boards, state governments, corporations, and major nonprofit organizations. That will require something different from the electoral mobilization organization that played such a large role in Obama's campaign. And Obama understands this. Asked during the primary whether Martin Luther King would support him or Clinton, he responded, "He wouldn't support either of us. He'd be out in the streets building an independent social justice movement."

What Obama does with the electoral organization that was put together for his campaign is separate from what people who want a small-d democratic agenda in the country must do. Obama's agenda is a presidential one. Community organizing's agenda should be to push the president. There will be plenty of people pushing him from Wall Street, the auto industry, and other elite circles. If there is not a counter-vailing push, organized independently of Obama, hopefully with his blessing, we will be disappointed in him as a president—and will have ourselves to blame.

Whatever is built now, it will have to be bold. The times demand that. There are lessons in the MCO experience. MCO's core values at the height of its people-power period were democracy, equality, diversity, fairness, security, neighborliness, and justice for all. Not a bad agenda for the twenty-first century.

■ A Postscript

Though my outlook on the outcome of the MCO may seem grimly deterministic, another, more positive kind of determination came into play here: the determination of people with a passion for social justice. Determined community and religious leaders had the vision to "sponsor" a process that led to the Mission Coalition. They hired me to build people power, not to be a program administrator, advocate, or service provider. They knew the risks, and they took them. Organizers built the MCO, just as determined leadership led it and continued to build it, and determined members acted in behalf of their community. They could not work outside the framework of their period, and this is the tragedy of their story. But within it they succeeded as few communities have. They took control of their destiny and, for a brief period, they made history in San Francisco. Their history came to be known by community organizers and leaders elsewhere in the country.

When I was in the civil rights movement in the Deep South we sang "Freedom Is a Constant Struggle." I think that is how it always was and how it always will be. After all, it is not a new idea that the price of liberty is eternal vigilance.

Teaching

Political Theory

As my own work as an organizer continued, I sought to systematize a way to introduce people to aspects of political and sociological theory—i.e., how do citizens, potential citizens, residents of a place, workers, unemployed people, welfare recipients, and pastors and other leaders answer the question, "How do I understand the world in which I am living?" As part of a four-day workshop on organizing, I developed a three-hour, highly interactive segment in which I primarily ask questions. The sequence of the questions is connected with what workshop participants are doing in their community (or labor) organizations, and it builds on scenarios and role-playing that come earlier in the workshop. I wasn't doing this yet in MCO days, but this segment of the lengthier workshop would have fit well with what people were doing and learning in MCO. And reviewing it here will help answer the questions "How was MCO able to unite a broad constituency behind its action program?" "How did people who were tactical moderates and political conservatives become 'militants,' 'progressives,' and radicals?" and "How did conservatives who remained such decide it was better to work within an organization like MCO than not be part of it?" As a reminder: I use the word "radical" to mean getting at the root of things. At the root of the things we dealt with in MCO was powerlessness combined with the capacity, which exists in everyday people and their institutions, for powerful action.

The overall framework for these questions is "How do we move people from inaction to engagement?" Almost everyone in MCO, from conservatives to radicals, agreed this was a key question the organization faced. In ongoing discussions, the values to guide MCO action had been identified—those of the major religious traditions of the world and the secular, small-d democratic tradition.

The first step in the theory part of my four-day workshop is to ask, "What are the problems you want to address in your organization?" All kinds of things are said in response, ranging from "overcrowding at Marshall Elementary School" or "a $50 per month rent increase in my building" to "people in my church don't earn enough at their jobs to make ends meet," "people in my neighborhood are unemployed," or even more general responses, like "unemployment," "poor quality education," "affordable housing." Some people will identify things like "racism," "sexism," "discrimination," and "prejudice." Others will say things like "rent control," "community control of schools," and "job training and motivation programs." These are all written on a chalkboard or easel pad. I then draw lines around the lists so they are in four groupings:

Group 1	Group 2	Group 3	Group 4
$50 rent increase in my building	Unemployment	Racism	Rent control
	Quality education	Sexism	Community control
	Affordable housing	Classism	
Overcrowding at Marshall School		Prejudice	

I then ask, "What do the items in each column share in common, and what distinguishes them from the other three columns?" This discussion takes a while, perhaps ten to twenty minutes. I want it to. I then add the following headings or categories to the columns and ask the group if they are acceptable:

Group 1	Group 2	Group 3	Group 4
"Problems"	"Topics"	"Analyses"	"Solutions" or "Proposed Solutions"

Often these words have already been used by people in the workshop. After some discussion, there has been agreement on these categories and the brief definitions or explanations I propose for each:

A problem is specific; it is something people experience.

A topic is general.

Analyses seek to explain why things are as they are.

Solutions or proposed solutions seek to diminish or eliminate problems.

"If you want to get people who feel powerless to a meeting, where do you start?" There is agreement that you have to start with their problems, or, in organizing terms, "start with where people are, not where you'd like them to be."

"Why do people have these problems?" This is a question that also leads to lots of responses: "the power structure," "racism" (or any of the other isms), "unemployed people are lazy" (or lack motivation, or are untrained), "politicians don't care" (or are owned by the people who pay for their campaigns), "the school district is incompetent," "teachers are inadequate," "the people downtown are screwups," "some people just don't care," "it's always been this way and always will be this way," "landlords just want to make a buck," and the list continues. I list these responses, grouping them again, on my working space.

Group 1	Group 2	Group 3
The power structure	*Unemployed are:*	It's always been this
Racism	Untrained	way and always will
Other isms	Unmotivated	
Incompetent	Lazy	
	Screwups	
	Students are:	
	Unmotivated	
	Lazy	
	Parents don't care	

I ask people to give me words to categorize the groups. I write what they say on the workspace. I then ask if the following categories (some of which they may already have come up with) include everything they've said:

Group 1	Group 2	Group 3
Fault of "the system"	Fault of the person	In the nature of things
		Ordained by God

Whenever I do this, people agree that these problems exist or persist either because they are the "fault of the person" with the problems, or the "fault of 'the system'" that has the authority and resources to solve the problems, or a combination of the two. Minor examples might be that tenants don't take care of their apartments, or the landlord ignores problems of maintenance and repairs, or a combination of the two.

Sometimes people say the problems are inevitable. I say that if anyone thinks all these problems can't be solved, that they are in the nature of things or ordained by God, then that person is in the wrong workshop. That always brings a laugh.

I then ask, "Can we agree that by 'the system' we mean a combination of values, institutions that embody or put into practice these values, and decision makers who occupy key positions in these institutions?"

Again, my experience has been that workshop participants agree that to the extent a problem is the fault of the people experiencing it, then they have to change;

and to the extent it is the fault of the system, then the system has to change. Ways to change the people include training, counseling, motivation, education, or even psychotherapy.

I ask, "Is there anyone who thinks that all the problems on our list are the fault of the people experiencing them?" No one does. I then say, "We're now going to look at that portion of a problem that results from something the system is or isn't doing, and I ask, "Why don't the decision makers fix the problems?" Again, after discussion and categorizing of ideas, there is agreement that if the system isn't solving a problem, it could be because:

It doesn't know about it

It is incompetent, or

It has different interests

After the question "If the system doesn't know, what do you do?" there is agreement that the strategy to change the system would be to educate or inform it. After the question "If the system is incompetent, what do you do?" there is agreement that the strategy to change the system would be to train its personnel, restructure or reorganize it, or replace it if it is hopelessly incompetent. And finally, after "If the system has different interests what do you do?" there is agreement that the strategy for change is to change its interests or create an alternative system.

We agree that at least in some instances, and to some extent, problems exist because something we can call "the system" or "the power structure" has an interest in keeping things the way they are, in preserving the status quo. That interest could have to do with money, status, power, or some combination of all of these.

Conservatives, centrists, liberals, progressives, and radicals who participate in these workshops agreed to the conclusions drawn from this step-by-step approach to understanding the world. The conservatives generally think "the fault of the people" is the reason for problems. The radicals think it's "the fault of the system."

If conservatives and centrists agree that something is the fault of the system, they emphasize that this is because the system doesn't know about the problem; other centrists and liberals acknowledge that possibility but emphasize the incompetence of the system; some liberals and the radicals acknowledge what has already been said but emphasize different self-interests of the system. Some of them think you can change the interests of the system; others think you have to change the system as a whole or create an alternative system—which in this context means new or parallel institutions, such as alternative schools or cooperatives. This sometimes becomes the subject of heated debates that I let continue for a while before taking the workshop participants to a next step.

Role-playing is an extraordinarily powerful teaching tool, one that I used often in the MCO and one that I use in teaching this particular material. The workshop participants agree to use a specific problem to illustrate what we are discussing. Often we use the example of a landlord who has raised the rent in his building 25 percent with no changes in his costs—maintenance, repair, or other. We stipulate that he has good tenants, because we are illustrating changing the system, not changing the people. I then tell the group that I am going to play the landlord and will give them time to prepare themselves to negotiate with me.

Two kinds of lessons are learned in this role-playing. One set of lessons has to do with how you organize yourselves to present something to a decision maker; that's not what I want to talk about here. Suffice it to say that after I divide and confuse the group with my responses to what they have to say, they will agree that they need spokespersons, a step-by-step process for presenting their case, caucusing (a time-out) to talk among themselves if they get confused or divided, a cutoff point at which they will end the negotiations if they aren't resolving anything, and a next step if agreement is reached or if action is required.

There are also theory lessons to be teased out of the role-playing. The radicals and liberals generally agree that it is logically possible that the landlord doesn't know the hardships being caused by a 25 percent increase in rent. And they know that while there may be no conservatives and centrists in the workshop, there are very likely to be conservatives and centrists in any tenant body, and that all the tenants have to be united if they are going to win with their landlord, so the radicals and liberals will go along with "the landlord doesn't know" as a beginning assumption. That means telling stories about the hardship such a rent increase would impose on otherwise good tenants. But those who are skeptical of this theory say, "If it turns out that after we tell the landlord the problems and he doesn't budge an inch, then you centrists and conservatives have to be willing to look at a different explanation for his behavior." The conservatives and centrists have to agree.

I then play the role of an affluent landlord who simply wants to maximize the profit he can get from his building, saying things like, "I'm sure you can find cheaper housing if you move out of San Francisco," or "You don't have to live here if you don't want to. I know there are people who would pay the additional 25 percent for these apartments." At some point it becomes evident to everyone in the room that I am not going to budge. I am increasing the rent not because I don't know the problem that will cause for my good tenants, but because I have a different interest—maximizing the immediate income I can generate from my building. The group acquires a different understanding of why the landlord is acting this way and saying these things. And a strategy follows.

The catalyst for education in this situation, as it was in the real-life experience of MCO's Housing Committee, is what landlords say and do. In the MCO, it became apparent to all that most of the landlords encountered in the Housing Committee wanted to make as much money in the short term as they could from their buildings, no matter what the consequences for their tenants. In fact, for the most part they didn't care what the consequences for their tenants were—if the tenants couldn't pay, they could move; other tenants would quickly replace them. Landlords who cared preferred stable, good tenants to short-term profit maximization; other landlords had actual relationships with their tenants that were important to them. We didn't see them. This newly acquired knowledge changed how the conservatives thought about landlord-tenant relations, and it opened their minds to thinking differently about why the world is the way it is and what has to be done to change it so that it will be more just.

Similarly, in the cases where landlords weren't making repairs because they couldn't get home improvement loans, radicals learned that you couldn't paint all landlords with the same brush. In these cases, a landlord became an ally in a visit to a lending institution that might be redlining the neighborhood.

There is another facet of the learning. To the extent that people don't want to organize themselves to develop the people power to address their circumstances, then—just to that extent—conservatives are right: if people are unwilling to organize to bring about change when a real possibility for such organizing presents itself, then it becomes the fault of the people that they are in the circumstances they find themselves in. But there is now an important change in the "fault of the people" idea. It is now the job of leaders and organizers to challenge people to act on their values and interests.

Workshop participants now conclude that building people power is essential to change systems that are unaccountable to values of fairness, justice, and democracy. They further conclude that the role of leaders is to shift people from nonparticipation to participation in an ongoing effort.

And it is my conclusion that most people do want to participate when they are presented with a believable plan of action, one that offers the possibility of concrete accomplishments.

Member Organizations of the MCO/Miembros de la Organización de la MCO*

These are the member organizations of the Mission Coalition Organization in 1970. Each of these groups was entitled to representation at the annual convention; almost all of them were there. Each was also entitled to representation at the monthly Delegates Council meeting. The 1971 list grew even longer.

■ Churches and Church-Related Organizations

All Nations Church of God (Church of God/Pentecostal)

Ayuda Social Católica Salvadoreña (Catholic)

Bethany Methodist Church (United Methodist)

Catholic Council for the Spanish Speaking

Círculo Latino de San Juan (Catholic)

El Buen Pastor Church (Presbyterian)

First Samoan Congregational Church (United Church of Christ)

Full Gospel Revival Temple (Pentecostal)

Grace Senior Center (Lutheran)

Grupo Latino de San Pablo (Catholic)

La Iglesia de Dios (Church of God)

Lebanon Presbyterian Church

Lily of the Valley Church (Pentecostal)

Men of St. Paul's (Catholic)

Mission United Presbyterian Church

---

*Compiled from 1970 "ad book"

New Testament Church of God

Olivet Presbyterian Church

St. Charles School (Catholic)

St. James Sociedad Católica Guadalupana

St. John's Episcopal Church

St. John the Evangelist Parish Council (Catholic)

St. John's Lutheran Church

St. Joseph's Guadalupe Society (Catholic)

St. Kevin's Catholic Church

St. Kevin's Teen Club

St. Peter's Parish Council (Catholic)

St. Teresa's Parish Council (Catholic)

Second Spanish Baptist Church (Southern Baptist)

Nationality, Civic, Political, and Cultural Organizations

American G.I. Forum (Latino veterans)

Casa Hispana de Bellas Artes

Comite Civico Cultural Cubano

Centro Colombiano de San Francisco, Inc.

Filipino Community of San Francisco

Filipino American Mission Organization

Grupo Bolivariano

Latin American Student Organization

LULAC (League of United Latin American Citizens)

MAPA (Mexican-American Political Association)

Organización Latino Americana

PAST

Philippine American Cultural Foundation

▩ Unions, Professional, Business, and Worker Organizations

AFT Local 61—MCO Alliance Committee (American Federation of Teachers)

Centro Social Obrero (Latino caucus in Laborers' Union)

Delano Support Committee (Farmworkers' boycott committee)

ILWU Local 10 (International Longshore and Warehouse Union)

Junta Hispana de Real Estate Brokers

Mission Family Center Workers

Mission Head Start Teachers

Mission Merchants Association

New Careers

Painters Local 4

Unity Latin and American Laborers

▩ Block Clubs, Tenant and Homeowner Associations, Neighborhood Groups

Agrupación de la Zona

Buena Vista Block Club

Capp Street Association

East Mission Action Council

East + West of Castro Improvement Club

Greater Mission Citizens Council

Holly Courts Tenants Union

Humane Society for Tenants

Junipero Serra Improvement Association

Latin American Mission Homeowners Improvement Association

Mission Home Owners

Northern Utah District Residents Association

Potrero Hill Residents and Homeowners Council

Twenty-fourth Street Tenants Association

Twenty-fifth + Folsom Tenants Union

United Neighborhood Organization

Upper Noe Valley Concerned Citizens

Unión de Inquilinos de la Bryant y 22nd

Upper Valley Street Block Club

Community Agencies (Social Service, Advocacy, Others)

Horizons Unlimited

La Raza Legal Defense

MACABI (Mission Area Community Action Board, Inc.)

Mission Neighborhood Health Center—Model Cities Committee

Mission Rebels

OBECA/Arriba Juntos (Organization for Business, Education and Community Advancement)

RAP (Real Alternatives Program)

Parent, Student, School, Educational Organizations

Asociación Educacional Hispano Americana

Bryant School Area Community Organization

Marshall School–Community Organization

Mission Area Parents

Mission Parent Policy Advisory Committee (Head Start)

Mission English Language Center

Montes' House to House English Program

Women's, Youth, Senior, Athletic, Consumer, Welfare, Other Associations

Bernal Heights Ladies Club

Consumer Action Council

COBRA

Deportivo Moctezuma

East Mission United Neighborhood Youth Organization

Friends of HELP

Gran Fraternidad Universal, Fundación del Dr. de la Ferriere

LAICA

Latin American Baseball League

Mission Area Youth Organization

Mission Strike Support Committee

Mission Welfare Rights Organization

MANY

OPMLA

State College—Mission Club

Teen-Agents for Action

1970 Elected and

Appointed Steering

Committee of the MCO*

Among the ethnic groups and countries represented by either appointed or elected leaders on the MCO Steering Committee were Mexican-American, Puerto Rican, Italian-American, Mexican, African-American, Nicaraguan, Filipino-American, Salvadoran, Irish-American, Anglo, Native American, Colombian, Peruvian, Guatemalan, and Bolivian. In the following year, the constitution and bylaws were amended to add Italian-American, Irish-American, and Pacific Islands vice presidents.

Executive Officers

President/Presidente: Ben Martinez

1st Executive Vice President/1ro Vice Presidente Ejecutivo:
Elba Tuttle

2nd Executive Vice President/2do Vice Presidente Ejecutivo:
Joe Del Carlo

3rd Executive Vice President/3ro Vice Presidente Ejecutivo:
Vito Saccheri

4th Executive Vice President/4to Vice Presidente Ejecutivo:
Abel Gonzalez

5th Executive Vice President/5to Vice Presidente Ejecutivo:
Rev. O. F. Brown

6th Executive Vice President/6to Vice Presidente Ejecutivo:
Ena Aguirre Spackman

7th Executive Vice President/7mo Vice Presidente Ejecutivo:
Raul Moreno

*Compiled from 1970 "ad book"

Other Officers

Recording Secretary/Secretario de Archivo:
Virginia Sheldon

Corresponding Secretary/Secretario de Correspondencia:
Linda Marquez

Treasurer/Tesorero:
Jose B. Miranda

Nationality Vice Presidents

Mexican Vice President/Vice Presidente Mexicano:
Manuel Marin

Nicaraguan Vice President/Vice Presidente Nicaraguense:
Guillermo Vivas

Salvadoran Vice President/Vice Presidente Salvadoreño:
Marina Amaya

Mexican-American Vice President/Vice Presidente Mexicano-Americano:
Reyes Martinez

Central American Vice President/Vice Presidente Centro Americano:
Miguel Ortiz

South American Vice President/Vice Presidente Sur Americano:
Rosario Anaya

Afro-American Vice President/Vice Presidente Afro-Americano:
Elmira L. Neal

Anglo-American Vice President/Vice Presidente Anglo-Americano:
Sherman Welch

Filipino-American Vice President/Vice Presidente Filipino-Americano:
Joe Topacio

Interest Group Vice Presidents

Business Vice President/Vice Presidente Negocios:
Juan Escobar

National Vice President/Vice Presidente Nacional:
Angie Alarcon

Youth Vice President/Vice Presidente Jóvenes:
David Farias

Senior Citizens Vice President/Vice Presidente Ancianos:
Salvador Ornelas

Block Clubs Vice President/Vice Presidente Clubes:
Larry Del Carlo

Committees

Housing Committee Chairman/Director de Comite de Vivienda:
Flor de Maria Crane

Planning Committee Chairman/Director de Comite de Planeamiento:
Jack Bourne

Youth Committee Chairman/Director de Comite de Juventud:
Ventura Martinez

Police Committee Chairman/Director de Comite Policíaco:
Joe Topacio

Employment Committee Chairman/Director de Comite de Empleo:
Larry Del Carlo

Health Committee Chairman/Director de Comite de Salubridad:
Isabel Orozco

Community Maintenance Chair/Mantenimiento de la Comunidad:
Ophelia Balderrama

Consumer Committee Chairman/Director de Comite de Consumo:
Mina Martorella

Recreation Committee Cochairs/Directores de Comite de Recreación:
Roberto Lomeli and Rev. Hank Scherer

Draft Committee Chairman/Director de Comite de Reclutamiento:
Fr. Jim Hagan

Finance Committee Chairman/Director de Comite de Finanzas:
Joe Del Carlo

Cultural Committee/Director de Comite de Cultura:
Amilcar Lobos

The People

Who Made MCO

Looking for a better life, they or their forebears came to the U.S. from Argentina, Bolivia, Chile, Colombia, Costa Rica, Cuba, El Salvador, England, Germany, Guatemala, Honduras, Ireland, Italy, Mexico, Nicaragua, Peru, Philippines, Poland, Puerto Rico, Russia, Samoa, and Spain, or they were Native Americans, who were here before the rest arrived, or Africans who came against their will.

Unfortunately, my field notes didn't include many names that, at the time, easily rolled off my tongue. Now, as I conclude this book some thirty-eight years after the events took place, I am unable to recognize all those who should be remembered by history as the people who made MCO what it was in the days I was its community organizer. But here are some of the people who have not already been mentioned in the text:

Rev. O. F. Brown, Rev. Luis Gordiany, Fr. Bill Justice, Rev. Enola Maxwell, Fr. Gene McAuliffe, Fr. Jack McCarthy, Rev. Joe Meza, Fr. Jim O'Malley, Fr. Rev. Jerry Pence, Fr. Peter Sammon, Rev. Hank Scherer, Rev. Charles Schindler, Rev. Elmer Schmidt, Rev. Jim Zimmerman; Angie Alarcon, Ricardo Alba, Rita Alviar, Rosario Anaya, Chuck Ayala, Ophelia Balderrama, Earl Blanchard, Jose Chappa, Maruja Cid, Sal Cordova, Cora Cruz, Henry Cruz, Ron Cruz, Juanita Del Carlo, Jim Donton, Juan Escobar, Enrique Espinoza, Dave Farias, Avelino Figueroa, Dan Frerking, Greta Glukowski, Anne Gregorich, Jess Hernandez, Ernesto Iglesias, Alberto Lemus, Chris Limbocker, Amilcar Lobos, Kathy Loos, Rich Loos, Frank Lopez, Rafael Lopez, Roberto Lopez, Segundo Lopez, Alice Martinez, Reyes Martinez, Ventura Martinez, Mina Martorella, Jose Miranda, Dan Moulton, Joan Moulton, Elmira Neal, Salvador Ornelas, Ron Ortiz, Juan Pifarre, Ernestina Pinott, Miguel Quiroz, John Ramirez, Ray Rivera, Gene Royale, Santiago Ruiz, Fele Sala, Butch Salazar, Virginia Sheldon, Alex Soria, Ena Aguirre Spackman, Salamo Sua, Jesse Tello, Joe Torres, Joaquin Valencia, Octavio Vega, Guillermo Vilas, Jose Wheelock…and many more.

And nonmembers who, with their research, legal, planning, and other skills, were supporters of what the people of the Mission were doing: Harry Brill, Jerry Mandel, Sharon Martinas, James McAlister, Armando Menocal, Peter Richardson, Judith (Dunlap) Sandoval.

▨ Index

HEYDAY INSTITUTE

Since its founding in 1974, **Heyday Books** has occupied a unique niche in the publishing world, specializing in books that foster an understanding of the history, literature, art, environment, social issues, and culture of California and the West. We are a 501(c)(3) nonprofit organization based in Berkeley, California, serving a wide range of people and audiences.

We are grateful for the generous funding we've received for our publications and programs during the past year from foundations and more than three hundred and fifty individual donors. Major supporters include:

Anonymous; Audubon California; Judith and Phillip Auth; Barona Band of Mission Indians; B.C.W. Trust III; S. D. Bechtel, Jr. Foundation; Barbara and Fred Berensmeier; Berkeley Civic Arts Program; Joan Berman; Book Club of California; Peter and Mimi Buckley; Lewis and Sheana Butler; Butler Koshland Fund; California State Automobile Association; California State Coastal Conservancy; California State Library; Joanne Campbell; Candelaria Fund; John and Nancy Cassidy Family Foundation, through Silicon Valley Community Foundation; Malcolm Cravens Foundation; Creative Work Fund; Columbia Foundation; The Community Action Fund; Community Futures Collective; Compton Foundation, Inc.; Lawrence Crooks; Laura Cunningham; Donald & Janice Elliott, in honor of David Elliott, through Silicon Valley Community Foundation; Federated Indians of Graton Rancheria; Fleishhacker Foundation; Wallace Alexander Gerbode Foundation; Richard & Rhoda Goldman Fund; Ben Graber, in honor of Sandy Graber; Evelyn & Walter Haas, Jr. Fund; Walter & Elise Haas Fund; Charlene C. Harvey; Cheryl Hinton; Leanne Hinton and Gary Scott; James Irvine Foundation; Mehdi Kashef; Marty and Pamela Krasney; LEF Foundation; Michael McCone; National Endowment for the Arts; National Park Service; Pease Family Fund, in honor of Bruce Kelley; Philanthropic Ventures Foundation; Resources Legacy Fund; Alan Rosenus; San Francisco Foundation; Seaver Institute; Skirball Foundation; Deborah Sanchez; William Saroyan Foundation; Contee and Maggie Seely; Sandy Cold Shapero; Stanford University; Ruth E. Sutter; Jim